What the re

"If you are i
touch your h
and courage a
buy, or borrow a copy of this book and read it. You'll never regret it."

— Stanley Orris, *Grand Forks B.C. Gazette*

"An extraordinary family . . . a strange, mixed-up family, but one possessed of courage, enterprise, determination, wit and vision.

— *Windsor Star*

"George Murray was a Scotsman, refined and educated, and a visionary. . . . He married a raw, but volatile and voluble Kansas farm girl, Margaret Lally, whose Grade 3 education taught her very little about syntax. They led a life which included violent quarrels, bankruptcy, poverty, monumental successes, travel, adventure, and hard work."

— *Calgary Herald*

Presenting Goodread Biographies

The Goodread Biographies imprint was established in 1983 to reprint the best of Canadian biography, autobiography, diaries, memoirs and letters in paperback format.

Books in the series are chosen from the hardcover lists of all of Canada's many publishing houses. By selecting a wide range of interesting books that have been well received in the bookstores and well reviewed in the press, we aim to give readers inexpensive and easy access to titles they missed in hardcover. A new selection of books is added to our series twice yearly, every spring and fall.

You'll probably find other books in the Goodread Biographies series that you'll enjoy. Check the back pages of this book for details on all titles in the series. You'll find our books on the paperback shelves of your local bookstore. If you have difficulty obtaining any of our titles, get in touch with us and we'll give you the name of a bookstore near you which stocks our complete list.

The Newspapering Murrays

Georgina Keddell

Goodread Biographies

For my father
George Matheson Murray
1889-1961

Published in hardcover in 1967 by McClelland and Stewart Ltd. First published in paperback in 1984 by Goodread Biographies Canadian Lives series publisher: James Lorimer

Canadian Cataloguing in Publication Data

Keddell, Georgina, 1913-
Ma Murray and the newspapering Murrays

(Canadian lives)
Reprint. Originally published: The newspapering Murrays. Toronto: McClelland and Stewart, 1967.
ISBN 0-88780-130-7

1. Murray, George, 1889-1961. 2. Murray, Margaret L. (Margaret Lally), 1888-1982. I. Title. II. Title: The newspapering Murrays. III. Series.

PN4913.M8K4 1984 070'.92'2 C84-098945-8

Goodread Biographies is the paperback imprint of
Formac Publishing Company Limited
333-1657 Barrington Street
Halifax, Nova Scotia
B3J 2A1

Printed and bound in Canada

Contents

I have squandered the splendid years that the Lord God gave to my youth
In attempting impossible things, deeming them alone worth the toil.
Was it folly or grace? Not men shall judge me, but God.
I have squandered the splendid years:
Lord, if I had the years I would squander them over again,
Aye, fling them from me!
For this I have heard in my heart, that a man shall scatter, not hoard.
Shall do the deed of today nor take thought of tomorrow's teen,
Shall not bargain or huxter with God.

— Padraic Pearse's "The Fool"

Acknowledgements

I wish to acknowledge help from several sources in writing this book. First, my parents. Darling egotists that they were, they have kept every file of every publication they ever put out from the South Vancouver *Chinook* in 1913 to the present. Every fireman in every small town in which we ever lived was forewarned about it. "Raise this window thus and there they are," instructed my father. "Let the rest burn."

From these files which freshened my memory, I have gathered the material here presented. My father died in 1961, and my mother is far more interested in the future than in the past. Without the files and the co-operation of the *Alaska Highway News*, my brother, Daniel, who is its publisher, and the Bridge River-Lillooet *News*, the book just couldn't have been done. Margaret Murray is today quite capable of adding new and wonderful chapters to this story and does so at odd moments when conversation sparkles with old friends who drop by to visit her in Lillooet. On cue, however, she just doesn't perform..

Then there was that household jewel, Molly Meyer. "All right, you lot, outside and play," she used to order. "Your mother can't hear herself think!" Mrs. Meyer was a very special person in our household. And there was Dorothy Forster, our Fort St. John librarian. "Tell me when it gets dull," I said to her, handing over the first hundred sheets. If a village librarian doesn't know what people like at the beginning of a book, who does? When she handed it back, Dory reported that she fell asleep at the part outside the *Chinook* office at Thirtieth and Main Street. "You better fix *that*," she advised. And I did.

A little further along and my farm-wife friend was philosophical but helpful. Vera Loucks was then putting a book of her own through the publishing offices. "I'll type those Lillooet chapters so they look new to you and you can see better what's wrong with them." she said from the depths of her experience.

However, it was much later that I began to realize what more experienced writers already know: that a biography of one's own parents is usually next door to impossible. The writer has trouble detaching herself. Kitty Moar of Edmonton had taken some chapters to her University of Alberta workshop for consideration. The answer had come back that the material was wonderful but who was the story about? If it was a team story, why was I so self-conscious in writing about my father?

It was then I called on Mother's Holy Ghost. "Look," she used to say to me when I was first learning to report for the paper, "all you have to do is relax and ask. I never yet saw the accident, meeting, riot or gold strike that the Holy Ghost couldn't handle if you asked Him. It's like you take a crowbar to open up your skull and the light pours in. Don't look at me like that. How do you figure I fill up these editorial pages when your father is away at Victoria?"

Thirty years later, I am convinced the divine inspiration not only got me over the rough spots of emotional involvement with the story, but threw in a minor miracle as well. How else does one explain the young New York journalist who came to Fort St. John in the summer of 1963 looking for material on my mother. "Take this," I said, shoving six pounds of manuscript at him, "and save us *all* time."

To this capable craftsman, Lawrence Elliott of Babylon, New York, I owe a very great deal. His firm but sensitive blue pencil led me through the final redraft. Would that other novice authors were as lucky!

G.M.K.

Prologue

On October 3, 1958, at one-thirty in the afternoon, destiny kept its forty-six-year-old date with the Peace River. The Pacific Great Eastern Railway, over the breaks in the north bank of the mighty old river, came ringing in from the west in a triple header, three sections, converging behind three engines on the end of track. A huge crowd of people in a semi-circle on the prairie, stood waiting to welcome it. Civilization, reaching across the rugged vastness of British Columbia, had finally caught up with these twentieth century frontiersmen in the town called Fort St. John.

"If they ask me," said Margaret Murray to her husband, "I am going to get up on that platform. Here they come now. Do I look all right? What will I say?"

For almost fifty years she had been asking him these same questions, seeking the assurance she needed where her form three Kansas education left off. And he was always there — across the kitchen, across the desk, across the make-up table or across the miles by long distance telephone — to guide, watch, inspire or instruct. For these were the "newspapering Murrays." George had made a success of a second career, politics. Margaret, in making a career of her husband, had stumbled into one for herself and it was threatening to outshine them all. She was here to cover the arrival of the railroad for her newspaper, the *Alaska Highway News.* He was here to observe the fulfillment of a dream, half a century old.

"Think of the years we've worked and waited. That they would humiliate us like this. Mother of God, that they could forget," Margaret's eyes brightened with tears.

"My dear girl," said her husband, quietly, "when God Almighty made time, he made lots of it. What is fifty years? Don't dwell on it. Don't even mention it."

"Dearest," she said, turning to him, "you say it. You get up there . . ."

How many countless times had he indeed been "up there." From 1912 to this day, he had stumped in hundreds of speeches for the extension of the Pacific Great Eastern Railroad into the valley of the last great undeveloped river system on the continent, the Peace. And in between the speeches, he had written countless editorials in a dozen newspapers and periodicals in Vancouver — and actually established weeklies in Lillooet and Fort St. John — to finish the job. "When we found out in Lillooet that we weren't getting anywhere pushing, your father decided to move north and pull the thing in," Margaret years earlier had written their son and daughter, overseas during World War II.

Dan and Georgina were here somewhere today, with *their* children, to share this moment with their parents. And now George looked down at his small granddaughter Margie. "No," he said to his wife. "This is Margie's and my day together. And we're not spoiling it with any more speeches than we have to."

Slowly, quietly, with bells ringing, the three orange diesels met at the end of track. "Hell, where's the smoke stacks?" asked a Rose Prairie farmer who hadn't been out of the country in years. "Don't they have whistles any more? No belching? No snorting? This ain't trains, this is street cars."

But it was trains, and Number One, with the entire British Columbia Cabinet draped over the tender and smiling broadly, led the way. In the ten private cars behind, presidents of railroads, leaders of finance and industry sat and watched the slowly passing wheatland which covered the last few miles of the seven hundred and ninety mile run from the coast.

Baltimore and Ohio, Cotton Belt, New York Central, Wabash, Ohio & Chesapeake, Milwaukee, Santa Fe, Union Pacific — if you were old enough, part of the show was observing these nostalgic names on the cars so far from their home yards.

"Grandpa," said six-year-old Margaret, suddenly tightening his hand in excitement. "Look, a black man."

Almost immediately, coloured porters in white jackets were out beside their step stools and the three trains were disgorging people all over the horizon. The section on the right carried paying passengers. From behind the engine on the left came cameras and trench coats and young men with their hat-brims turned up — the press. This was the most exciting day in the past thirty years of North American railroading history.

Down off the tender stepped the Premier and his entourage, and the Highland Pipe Band paced off "The Barren Rocks of Aden."

"The PGE today," Jim Nesbitt had written in a syndicated column that morning, "is fulfilling the dreams of scores of promising politicians and countless thousands of people as it chugs into the Peace River Country. By one of the queer quirks of fate it has fallen the lot of W.A.C. Bennett to be Premier on this tremendous occasion in the life of B.C. He is convinced that if he had not come along the PGE would never have crossed the Rocky Mountains . . . Well, he could be right, but someday, someone was bound to come along and send the PGE into the Peace . . ."

Ignored, George sat on a pile of ties, thinking. Nothing is right and nothing is wrong, he mused to himself, but timing makes it so. Here we are, with this glorious opportunity unfolding. It is our due at last, and we are too old. Here is the achievement of a lifetime of anguish. Were we invited? No. No one remembers . . .

It was hard to tell about the cheering. Speeches were going on. A smattering of hand clapping, and nearby a whistle or two, met his ears before being snatched by the wind and borne away.

"Grandpa, I'm hungry," said little bright-eyes running up.

"Hush, dearie, we'll soon be going home . . ." Again he was far away.

He stepped back into the heavy timber that covered the path leading to the new grade on the north shore of Burrard Inlet. He had the mother of this little girl by the hand, and they had just walked over about a thousand miles of wooden plank sidewalk. "Hush, dearie," the words echoed down the years. "Some day, we'll have dinner in a big train that will come out of that forest. Mashed potatoes, sausages, silver, ice in the glasses . . . you'll sit and look out on this water, and over there towards Victoria . . . and as a special treat, I'll let YOU *leave the tip . . ."*

The heavy blows of a sledgehammer and a mob of people indicated that the golden spike was being driven. "Like that, Margie, see." He reached over with his stick and tapped the iron holding a tie. "That means that the railroad is finished."

"Grandma made everyone laugh, didn't she?" asked the child, "Is her leg cured today?"

"Ach, your grandmother is in the fairies. Haven't I told you that before? She can pretend hard enough so that it doesn't hurt any more. You must always be very proud of your grandmother . . ."

> *He was breathing heavily from the exertion of running up the sidehill.*
>
> *"Margaret, dear heart . . ." He scarcely looked at the lean-to room, throwing his hat on the packing box dresser. "They say you aren't badly hurt. What happened?"*
>
> *"I was coming down that mountain too fast. Caught in the gravel and rolled. I got acid on my legs. The good little people were with me. I was hurrying to make the gas car home for your meeting tonight . . ."*

"Run, Margie, and find Grandma, and tell her we're waiting here for her. And I will visit with Mr. Holland." He turned to greet an old friend.

Later that afternoon, as a hundred barons of moose-meat sizzled in a hundred Fort St. John ovens, fifteen hundred potatoes bubbled indoors and out, and washtubs of salad and an acre of pies were readied by the ladies of the town for a giant free meal for all comers, the veil was slipped from the Mackenzie monument on the Alaska Highway by Premier Bennett. George, carefully dressed, without the cane, and apparently in his old form, made his last public appearance. His speech was not reported.

The reporter who covered the monument ceremony said simply, "I couldn't report it. I'm sorry. I don't see how you could . . ."

Farewells are sometimes so poignant that reporting them requires a dimension not found in any lines of type.

Mother Starts Protesting

Margaret Teresa Lally, that most Canadian of females, had been born — persuading, arguing, and selling — on the third of August, 1888, at Windy Ridge, Kansas. She was the seventh of nine children of Irish peasant immigrants, Patrick and Margaret Lally. From her first wail of protest as the neighbour woman grabbed her by her slippery little heels, she has kept things lively for her family and anyone else within earshot. Her father called her "trouble-the-house."

"Is that you, Mag? In the name of God, where have you been? Does it take two hours to get seven cows home half a mile? You young imp of Satan, what is it this time? Answer!"

"Where have I been?" came the breathless reply. "I'll tell you where I've been. That gawdammed roany got caught in the barbed wire down at McAtee's corner. That's where I been. She'd a' ripped her teat clean off if I hadn't seen her in time."

"God forgive you such language!"

At school, grades went by the reader — first, second, third. Margaret never got to fourth. At thirteen, she left school, following a row with the teacher over who was to clean the stove. "It's not fair, I've done my turn," said she, and heaved a can of dried corn all over the front of the room.

There was lots to occupy her while the family decided what next to do with Mag. Life on a Kansas farm was milking cows, shooking corn, hoeing potatoes, salting pork, and picking apples. It was enduring cyclones and living a couple of winters in a root cellar with mostly turnips to eat. It was scrubbing floors. It was helping the neighbours through sickness and laying out their dead. "Look, Ma, Mrs. O'Brien's poor old fingers aren't crooked any more. Why?" Or it was the scary heavy breathing of the family cow which browsed under the window where the corpse lay, surrounded by ice and candles.

It was fighting the McCoy kids and saying the rosary and kicking the hired man in the stomach when he snuck up on you in the tall corn with lust in his eye. It was staying at Irish Creek while you made your First Communion. "The most important thing of all, children, is to remember God and to be always in the state of grace by being on shaking-hands terms with the Holy Ghost."

And now it was her mother tenderly kissing her good-bye beside the waiting democrat as she left for her first job, beseeching the "Blessed Mother to spread her beautiful blue mantle around you, my darling girl, and protect and keep you." And Margaret — a lump of a girl, bespectacled, awkward, unused to the new shoes, her best calico only emphasizing her big bosom — when she climbed into the democrat and drove down the road, a strange and lonely quiet settled over the old farm house and everyone wept for days. For they were Irish and tears came easily to them because their emotions were so violently joy or sorrow.

At seventeen, having spent four years in the kitchens of Western Kansas as a hired girl, Margaret Lally decided to resume her education. After all, her little sister Bess was already through teacher's college. Margaret had by now learned to control her temper, to do her cussing under her breath, and to adopt a philosophical attitude toward what she considered unjust.

She sewed herself a wardrobe, packed her meagre belongings, and took the train to Freemont, Nebraska, there to enroll in one of those typically American institutions which teach three years in one. She paid her tuition out of the school dishpan and graduated *cum laude* as typist, bookkeeper, filing clerk, shorthand writer, and business administrator. The fine points of grammar completely eluded her. In her newspapering career in later years, the construction and length of her sentences, her dangling participles, and atrocious technique generally were the despair of typesetters and the joy of her readers. She has always been sublime in her ignorance, and no doubt the vivid, poignant, and sometimes lurid qualities in her writing would have been ruined by formal education.

She got a job at the Shipley Saddlery Company in Kansas City, famous for western saddles. For a year the shirt-waisted bookkeepers had been tucking notes in with invoices that accompanied the orders from Alberta. It had been Margaret's idea, of course.

"Who's M.T.L.?" sang out the office boy one day as he distributed the morning mail.

"That's me," answered Margaret from the depths of her ledger.

"What have I told you about the verb 'to be,' Miss Lally?" The office manager's voice was thin and irritable.

"Sorry ma'am, but that's my letter, anyway."

Katy, the girl on the next ledger, and Margaret were friends and exchanged confidences. Katy looked up. "He never answered, Peg!" she whispered.

"Well, he did so. And look, he sent a snapshot."

The Shipley girls worked up quite a correspondence that winter with their Alberta customers, and collected a sizeable album of walrus moustaches, watch chains, buffalo coats, plug hats, and stetsons on a series of Canadian cattlemen and cowboys. They seemed all to be great broad-shouldered men, standing, sitting, leaning, and either smiling or frowning for the edification of the writers of the pert little notes.

"There were six of us girls working in the shipping department of the Saddlery Company," Margaret has recalled since, "and five of us married Canadian men."

In any case, by spring, Margaret left for Canada. And her younger sister, the school teacher Bess, went with her.

The Pullman Heads West

And here were the Lally sisters, Bess and Margaret, bound for Canada, facing each other on the faded red plush of the Northern Pacific passenger coach, pointing west. They were good-looking girls. Both had brown curly hair, deep set blue eyes, and even white teeth set in wide mouths. Margaret had the fashionable hour-glass figure of the day without the need to sew ruffles on her corset cover. But Bess, who was tall and very slim, had some sewing to do on hers. Both had ankles which were said to be well-turned.

The girls stayed on the train to Seattle and got part-time typing jobs on the day of their arrival. But the winter was grim with sickness. First Margaret and then Bess were laid low with rheumatism and pneumonia. Their shabby bed-sitting room smelt of dampness and oil of wintergreen. They made novenas for a return to health and at the same time wrote glowing letters home about how well they were doing. One night, Margaret climbed the rooming house steps for the last time. She had made up her mind at Benediction. The everlasting rain was surely going to rot the roots of such prairie flowers as the Lally sisters. They would go north to Vancouver.

"Thanks be to God, the rent is paid. I got $15.00 cash. You have medicine money, and I'll send for you in two weeks," said Margaret. "Don't start cryin' or I'll start, too, and I need all my wits to catch that Canadian Steamship in forty minutes. Don't it sound great? Canadian Steamships."

"*Doesn't* it sound great, Peg! For heaven's sakes."

But the door had banged and Margaret was on her way.

Three days later the landlady brought up to Bess an envelope with a Canadian pink three-cent stamp, heavily cancelled in black, and addressed in her sister's flourishing hand. Everything was peachy. She had a job making beds at a new and *decent* hotel which paid for her room. Tomorrow she'd see about whistling up a couple of more-fitten jobs for them. In the meantime, there was the sun on the snow-capped mountains as the boat docked, the lighthouse in the harbour, and the nice old codger on the deck who'd told her about Stanley Park.

Seven-thirty A.M., and not a soul in sight. She was so busy thinking about the Irish troubles as she stood and looked at Queen Victoria that she almost got run down by a big motor-car full of men singing and waving their hats. They must have been going twenty miles an hour and such a smell and smoke followed them! It was really no wonder they almost ran her down. The traffic seemed queerest of all. Everything ran on the wrong side of the street. Real foreign. The newspapers looked funny too, and people talked different.— "Doncha know." All the policemen wore big droopy mustaches and rolled their *r*'s. Ladies dressed like men to ride horses in the park. The biggest hotel in town served tea on the porches under hanging baskets of geraniums.

"It's real ding-dong up here," she finished her letter, "but somehow I like it and I think you will. You can't help it. It's sorta romantic. People talk softer and they treat you nice. I can't get over the birds singing, fit to burst their throats. It makes you want to know what's behind those lovely mountains, and what's on the other side of that ocean. Oh, and the trees! They're just like the men — big — they reach almost to heaven. Be a good girl and remember, even if I *am* in redcoat territory, I'm less than two hundred miles from you. So don't be lonesome . . ."

The job Margaret got was selling subscriptions for the brand new *B.C. Federationist,* the province's first labour newspaper, launched just about the time she got off the Seattle boat.

"Oh, then you know something about the labour movement?" their personnel man had asked her. Some of the joy went out of the smile but the *avant-garde* of subscription saleswomen in Western Canada didn't move a muscle. "Some," she answered, and picked up the kit.

It was quite a responsibility to be given the authority of the Labour Federation in Vancouver to represent them. The first rumblings of next year's construction and real estate crash could be clearly heard, and besides, women just didn't do these things in 1912.

"Why should I?" asked the doctor of eye, ear, nose, and throat, in the first office on the top floor of the Vancouver Block. "Why should I want — what is it? — the *B.C. Federationist*?"

Such a blunt question threw a girl off balance. But Margaret rallied. "Doctor, you look like a man of great understanding, and I'm sure among your patients will be many who are very interested in the labour movement right now, and they would be bound to appreciate . . ." (It got better as it progressed.) "And it's just $1.50 for two years!"

After blanketing the waiting room tables with the *Federationist* in the two top floors of what was surely the biggest office building in Vancouver, Margaret was in funds again, and those Alberta cowboys seemed a little nearer.

There were also odd typing jobs in the Pender Street real-estate offices. One day the Underwood Agency called her about a job in the country.

"Where in the country?" asked Margaret.

"Well, South Vancouver, really. But quite a ways out, maybe ten miles by streetcar. It's permanent, and they only want to pay $12.00 a week. But they may pay more if you see them yourself."

"Who?"

"The Greater Vancouver Publishers is the firm name. A very agreeable young man. They need a bookkeeper."

"I'll go," said Margaret.

"Oh, and Miss Lally. I forgot to say his name. It's Murray. He puts out a weekly paper. George M. Murray."

A Cub Reporter Named Murray

George Murray was brought up on oatmeal porridge and maple-syrup breakfasts on a hundred-acre farm near Woodstock, Ontario. He was Canadian as the Maple Leaf, Highland Scots on both sides, and the second of eight children of Margaret Abigail "Piper" and Daniel Gilchrist "Smoker" Murray. The nicknames indicated different Sutherlandshire clans with the same name who came to Canada following the infamous Scottish clearances. One great-grandfather had lost his eyes while serving as a pipe-major in the Battle of Waterloo, and had been rewarded by the gift of a quarter-section of land in the Brock District of Upper Canada. The voyage over the ocean in unheated ships took many weeks, and children and adults alike died on the way.

". . . Aye, faither, it's no' the ocean this day I canna see the shores, but the officer says they straitch for miles in a fine, wide valley. Mony wi' our names have settled here, forbye. Wolfe's men, d'ye see. It's the St. Lawrence . . . a bonny sicht, faither . . ."

George was dreamy and liked school and read books and the *Youth's Companion* from cover to cover each month. Often, when his mother looked for him, he was over the nearest hillcock, weaving into the cloud pattern high above some of Tennyson's "Locksley Hall." He had fair curly hair and large brown eyes and tolerated a velvet suit for Sunday church.

"And George will chust read books for a livin'," snorted his farmer-uncles when the children's future would be discussed. "Get your noggin out of that, George, and tell us what you're doin' with your life."

"I will make great speeches, and I will write stories for the newspaper," said George. At eleven, he followed the funeral cortege of a Cabinet minister around Oxford County all one solid day, in order to get a better look at the Prime Minister, Sir Wilfrid Laurier, who was among the mourners. On his arrival home, he was rewarded with a thrashing in the driving barn, following which he carved GEORGE MURRAY, M.P. in letters a foot high on the barn door.

Life in Zorra was sowing and harvesting and exhibiting at the Embro fair. It was giggling into your hymnal, as your maiden aunts raised their strident voices in praise every Sunday at Chalmers Presbyterian; and on weekdays, it was staying out of the way while your mother scrubbed, starched, churned and sewed, and your father took every spare moment from his farm work to endlessly curry the driving team. It was the singing, dancing, and fiddling of the Piper Murrays as against the dour, proud, and handsome Smokers, who sat with their pipes as austere as the stone they fashioned into houses and fences. It was reading the Toronto *Globe*, arguing against the liberals and, at sixteen, reporting the Sunday morning sermons, Saturday night meetings, and after-school obituaries for the Woodstock *Sentinel Review*. Everyone knew where to find him after classes each day — at the newspaper office.

He took to wearing the family tartan shawl on his cold weekend walks into town. The old Scotsmen, in the square early with the market wagon drivers, discussed it. "Don Smoker's Geordie is a fair exhibeetion in that danged plaidie, mon. It looks chust foolish."

"Fiddle the plaidie. He's a grand fist on him for quietin' his tormentors, dirt on them. And he's fine at the writin' and all."

And he *was* good at writing. He was gifted with a total-recall memory so that happenings, names, events, dates, initials, and other details, once learned, were never forgotten. On the other hand, he had great difficulty always recognizing the frail fabric of his dream and keeping on top of it. He loved reverently, intensely, and from a distance. Highland men are very good at this, but their women have little patience with it and believe in keeping the dream in its place. His mother knew all about dreams. Her handsome husband was another of the same. It was she who saved up the egg money for the day coach to Ottawa and Geordie's first job in the big city. It was no dream but a short supply of reporters in Canada in 1908 that landed young Murray a job. The day after he graduated from high school, he sent out twelve franked wires to twelve eastern newspapers and got two replies. One was from the Ottawa *Journal.*

Once on his own, a fierce pride in accomplishment took over young Murray. It was as if the old Gaelic admonition, *Cuimhnich air no daoine o'n d'thainig thu*, "Remember the men from whom you were sprung," became a guiding force that motivated his life. He was proud of the great-grandfather who brought his sons to Canada and proud of the Jacobite tradition which surrounded him. He was proud that his people had fought with Bruce at Bannockburn and raised the standard for Prince Charlie. And he felt that he would be the one of all the Murrays with the vision, the understanding, and the courage to hold high the torch for old blind Alexander, to repay with his own success his numberless ancestors who stained the heather of Scotland defending succeeding generations of their blood and their seed unborn.

And so the young chieftain was really riding into the west. And Ottawa was merely a pause where he might pick up reinforcements. His thick Highland wrist which, he was sure, would one day wield dexterously the claymore for freedom and justice, settled temporarily over the keys of a typewriter at the Ottawa *Journal.* By day he covered police court. After hours he immersed himself in the bubble and boil of the little capital on the Ottawa River which, just then, bulged with financiers, railway magnates, foreign investors, and businessmen intent on vigorusly advancing the twentieth century in Canada. It was an era in which even school children took sides in politics, and George was so much a Liberal that Toryism sickened him. In an era of hero-worshippers, he unashamedly worshipped. The sophistication which earmarked later generations of young newsmen was preceded by enthusiasm, a certain spirituality, and an insatiable curiosity. He and his friends fought out the issues of the day nightly at Bowles Lunch.

"And does Sir Wilfrid's footman hand you into the carriage?" The laughter around the table was hearty. But George did ride to work with the Prime Minister. They shared the same Elgin streetcar.

"And as sure as you live, he *does* talk to me when I ask him. He either says, 'Sit down, young man,' or he waves me on for 'Another time, young man.'"

From Sir Wilfrid's own lips came the Prime Minister's recipe for a young man's success. It started out with the requirement of at once joining the political party of his choice, to add his youth and strength to stable government. But George himself soon found another truth to be self-evident: that decay in government sets in on the followers, not the leaders. The maggot was in the apple with the Laurier government, and in order not to compromise his principles or become tainted in a job that required objective handling, he pushed on.

This was how it happened:

The white-tiled interior of Bowles Lunch was almost empty, and all the noise was coming from one table. It was past midnight.

"Toffs", said the char with the bucket and brush.

"No, newspaper fellers," said her companion of the mop and pail. "Come here near every night or so. All they do is drink coffee and talk."

"You Gorman, you Kendall . . . you take your Asquiths and your Roosevelts. The greatest head of state today is Sir Wilfred . . . right here in Canada." The coffee mug arced through the air for emphasis.

"Okay Murray. State your case for that damned Frenchman, and make it good," said McTavish. "You haven't been here six months. What do you know about Laurier's thoughts on anything?"

Suddenly a dark overcoat was rattling the Sparks Street door.

"Hey, that's Larkin," said someone. "Let him in, somebody."

"Not bloody likely," said Bucket and Brush.

"Orders is orders," said Mop and Pail. So the quartet gathered their hats and trooped to the door. The heights of thought, expression and resolve as regularly propounded by the Journal's young reporters at Bowles, had been reached and passed for that night.

"You, Murray. You're the one I'm looking for." Jimmy Larkin would be all of twenty-one years of age. A blue-eyed Ottawa Irishman who presided at the Journal's news desk.

"Where in hell did you get that Boy Scout yarn, Murray? Not from Baden-Powell, that's certain."

"No, from a friend of his. Fellow named Campbell whose father was secretary to the Marquis of Lorne in the old days. Campbell was just passing through. I met him at the Russell Hotel."

"Well, I don't know anything about the Marquis of Lorne's secretary or Campbell or anyone else. But the old man doesn't believe it. He wants to see you first thing in the morning. You're a good man, Murray, and I just hope you know what you're talking about in that story . . . otherwise, the chop for you."

"But I tell you, the thing is true . . ."

"Don't tell me. Tell Muir, and make it good. Goodnight."

There were thirt-eight worn creaking wooden steps to the Journal's editorial room . . . thirty-eight steps to the chopping block . . . a tug on the waistcoat, an easing of the hard collar with the index finger, a smoothing of the hair, and a fingering of the four-in-hand, and Murray set course through the desks and wastebaskets for the ME's office.

"Murray here sir. You wanted to see me?"

"Ah yes, Murray. Sit down, my boy." This executioner was very civil. "About that Baden-Powell story, Murray, and the Boys' Movement . . ."

"Yes sir. What about it?"

"It's the best damned story that's come across my desk in a year. I congratulate you."

"Well, thank you, sir . . . that is, I thought . . . well, I was given to understand you were very upset about it."

"Yes, well, that's changed. It seems that Mr. Ross, our publisher, had dinner with the Governor General last night, and this morning he sent me a note on it. Baden-Powell is very anxious to get it started in Canada. Naturally I was very gratified to be able to say that we already had an excellent story standing on it. PD is very pleased, I might say."

"Well, I'm glad that's over," said Murray.

"Over? Why, it isn't over, it's just starting. Mr. Ross wants you to sit on this Boy Scout movement until it is organized. He'd like a story a day, he says."

"A story a day? Why, my source has sailed for England. That's all I know about the thing. All I have to work on is a pamphlet or two and what I remember reading out of magazines and papers."

"Your problem, Murray. Keep it coming. That's all."

Several sleepless nights, and dozens of library reference books later, it became obvious to Mr. Murray that something would soon have to give on the Boy Scout movement. He hoped it wouldn't be his job! The newspaper was besieged with phone calls from parents and ministers. Small boys around Ottawa were tying knots, starting fires and waving flag messages all over town and district from instructions carried in the Journal. The Governor General, Earl Gray, was calling P.D. Ross every other morning and saying, "What ho, old man, and is there anything new on this boys' movement? Excellent idea. Excellent, old chap . . ." And the Managing Editor, Mr. Muir, had caught the spirit of the thing and was making his daily good deed a call for more copy on the subject.

"By George, Larkin, if only someone would blow up the Rideau Canal, or burn down Hull again, it would take their minds off this cursed Scouts movement and give me a little peace," said Murray.

"What you need is to catch the spirit of scouting, Murray. You know, like never give up on patrol . . . what's that, point six or seven?" Larkin's eyes were laughing.

The moment of decision had arrived. George slammed on a hat, threw on his overcoat, and went home. That evening, he stopped by the 43rd Armouries, where he had made friends of some of the junior officers.

"Gentlemen," said George, after greetings were exchanged, "the Evening Journal is very interested in getting the Boy Scout Movement launched here in Ottawa. And I want to ask some of you to act on a temporary committee."

The young militiamen were somewhat startled with this suggestion, but Murray passed around his precious pamphlets and said that it was Baden-Powell's wish to get the movement under way in Canada at once.

"And I move that you, Lieutenant Tucker, be acting temporary provisional chairman."

"I'm willing," said Tucker, "but what do we do now?"

"Well, I move that we name Lieutenant Pinard secretary pro tem," Murray was becoming very bold indeed. "Then," he said, "we'll all meet again and add to our numbers, and draw up an agenda. And now I move that we adjourn."

It worked. The Boy Scouts movement in Canada was on its way. Mr. Ross's friend in Rideau Hall was named Chief Scout. Mr. Muir had his story, but by the time it was in type, young Murray was on the train for the west.

It took a great Winnipeg editor to straighten him out on his professional loyalties. For Garnet Clay Porter was one of the greats of his day on this continent. He was an American — in fact, a first cousin of O. Henry — and equipped professionally and emotionally to work over the starry-eyed young cubs who came out of the east and nourish and enrich their promise. By the time George Murray got to Regina, he was capable of press gallery assignment for the McGinnis *Standard* and other senior duties which allowed more time to continue his love affair with the Canadian prairies, whose sunny robes swirled out in shimmering splendour, now pale, now golden, changing tints in the searing, ripening winds. By the time he got to Edmonton, he had caught on to beefing up a dull week by making news happen!

In the early days of this century, the bigness of the West matched the bigness of men's plans. The downy-cheeked CPR clerk, with whom he played shuffleboard for sasparillas, could and did wind up president of the CPR. The kid's name was Coleman. The fellow reporter, who wangled him a berth on the *Bulletin* at Edmonton, could and did make it big in advertising. His name was MacLaren. There were dozens more but nobility, courage, and quality marked them all.

There were setbacks and disappointments, but it was always westward. At Edmonton, it wasn't the skate race at dawn in red underwear down the Saskatchewan River that terminated George's association with the *Bulletin*. It was the

Robbie Burns Night dinner at which he and MacLaren celebrated the promotion that accomplished *that.* George, always the laird after a few drinks, ploughed into a lippy waiter with his claymore fist and spent the rest of the night in jail and the rest of the year in deep remorse.

But the depression, painful though it was, no doubt produced the macabre touches with which he embellished a murder trial for McGillicuddy's paper in Calgary, and brought him a fabulous offer from *Collier's Weekly.* And the night the offer arrived, as he walked in the quiet darkness beyond the edge of town to his lodgings, like a pibroch sounding in the foothills the moaning whistle of a train echoed across the prairie, George tore up the letter. This Murray, this chieftain, would go clear across the Dominion, and some day he would return and mark his path with a string of newspapers.

Vancouver in 1910 was one of the most exciting cities in the Dominion. It was exactly twenty-four years old, the first town council having been elected in 1886. It was building faster than any city in Canada, and its promoters were a cosmopolitan lot. Vancouver fairly sparkled in the brilliance of its social circle, having drawn to it aristocrats from the four corners of the earth.

The hottest thing in real estate in 1911 was the borough of South Vancouver which was being built up furiously. As a separate municipality, it gave every indication of eagerly supporting a newspaper of its own. Young Murray ranged over the city, made many contacts, and became well-informed on the plans and the backing for the promotion of this particular district. Besides, his uncle had heavy investments on the southern slope of the municipality.

"My God bless me," said Ken Murray, "the only thing you're good for is dreaming, and maybe writing. Politics, you say, you want to get into politics . . ." Words failed the older Murray at this point, and instead of swearing, he went into a mirthless little laugh which actually seemed to hurt him. He loved the boy who by now was part of the household. But if he were only a man of the everyday business world, you could handle him, cope with him, understand and help him.

"How much?" said his uncle, reaching for his cheque book.

"I don't want your money," said George, stiffly. "I just want your support. I just want to be able to say that I'm your nephew. I want to have your opinion — if possible your favourable opinion — and your moral support."

"You're a young fool,.. said the uncle. "I'll see,"

George turned to leave the office.

"Hauld on. Hauld on. You're not in a hurry are you? A man named Prowse has a building at Thirtieth and Main that might be just what you're looking for. And if you're having any legal work done, go to Mackenzie Matheson. He's a cousin of your mother."

By May of 1912, the Vancouver *Chinook* was on its way.

Vancouver in 1912

When Margaret Lally got to the end of the Main Street carline at Twenty-fifth Avenue, after an hour's ride from downtown Davie and Granville, she saw that the girl at Underwood's had been dead right when she said it was in the country. For on either side of the board sidewalks, which stretched up toward the office of the Greater Vancouver Publishers five blocks away, were upturned raw stumps, their roots still moist and brown. Fiddlehead bracken and fireweed grew in profusion.

"The Underwood people sent me about a job for a bookkeeper. I would like to see Mr. Murray, please," said Margaret, as the office door closed behind her. The place smelled of new wood and varnish

"Young lady to see you, George," called out the pleasant-looking young man at the counter.

"Send her in," said a voice behind the glass partition,

and Herb Stein waved Margaret into the office marked "Publisher."

"Good morning Miss, ah . . . won't you sit down? I'll be with you in a moment." He turned from his typewriter only fleetingly.

"Lally," supplied the visitor. "Margaret Lally." She plucked off her gloves, adjusted her hat, and wondered for the first time if it really was as becoming as she thought. But then this employer was not only young and handsome, he was obviously very busy. The sunlight, winking on his cufflinks, drew her eyes to his hands. Generous, well-groomed hands. And from his glistening watch-chain, her glance moved to his face. These Canadian guys got better and better. Just wait till I tell Bess about this one, she mused, making mental notes of the dark hair, brown eyes, and well-shaped brows.

"Well, Miss Lally, we have a publishing business here, as you are aware, and instead of selling saddles or town lots, we sell white space. We require someone to keep our books, and to help in the office with the telephone, and perhaps even to make calls on our accounts when that becomes necessary."

"Do you have many accounts?"

"You'll get an idea by looking through the advertisements. Have you seen the paper?" He picked an edition from the desk, shook the folds open, and held it for her to see. Any formality evaporated. "By George, great, eh?" There was no mistaking the pride in his voice.

"Well, I guess," said Margaret who wasn't sure what was great about such a small paper. "It must take a lot of money. Establishing a paper, I mean."

"Oh, a *lot*. And a lot of ability, if it's done well. But it takes faith, too. And it takes hope that your plans will work out and you can accomplish some good for your community."

"Faith and hope, huh? And charity?" She was smiling back, but her wisecrack had misfired.

"Yes. Yes. The greatest of all." He suddenly stopped and looked at her. "You know, Mis . . . ah . . ."

"Lally."

"Miss Lally, I think you'd like the newspaper business. We are barely established, but you can see the development out here in South Vancouver. Do you like Vancouver? One of the most beautiful cities in the world. Have you seen the harbour? This province is rich enough to make it the greatest port on this side of the Pacific. The potential of this province is beyond the dreams of Midas. Only now is it being opened up, and our paper is dedicated to this proposition . . ."

"But Mr. Murray, I'm an American y'know. I don't know much about what's behind those mountains. About all we got in Kansas is lots of hot wind and, y'know, tall corn."

When Margaret emerged a half-hour later, she was the *Chinook's* first bookkeeper, at a salary of fifteen dollars a week. The paper was two editions old, and she had the last one tucked under her arm.

George Murray had gone to Mr. Mackenzie Matheson in the spring of 1912, as suggested by his uncle, and had had this lawyer draw up a company in which Murray sold shares in the newspaper to Vancouver's real-estate promoters for one hundred dollars each. There were plenty of takers, and when he had a little money gathered together, George acquired the Sunset Printing's old Campbell flat-bed press, which had once printed salmon-can wrappers. Composing tables, type cases, casting box, job presses, and a hundred and one items of printing equipment were moved into the back shop. But the *piece de resistance* was the linotype — seven thousand dollars, F.O.B. San Francisco, the latest word in linotypes, with every conceivable attachment. Seven employees, with John Jackson as foreman, followed the contraption into the shop to produce twelve pages of the *Chinook* every Thursday, and turn out letterheads, envelopes, statements and other printing forms, as well as dodgers, business cards, and real-estate promotion literature.

South Vancouver in those days was a number of things. It was the McGeer family, owners of the dairy, twelve in number, of which Vancouver's famous Mayor, British Columbia's legislator, and Canada's Senator — Gerald Gratton McGeer — would be the most famous son in years to follow. It was General Wolfe School, with a mustard-coloured wood siding and big outside staircases; Mr. Slater, the butcher, who sold minced meat at ten cents a pound; and Waldon Brothers' Grocery (Jim, Hotha, 'Arry, and Wullie was the way Margaret, to whom an English accent was something new, recalled them!). It was real-estate firms like McKim, Hamilton, and Hopkins, with Mr. Hopkins playing his violin at 5.30 P.M. if business had been good that day. It was the Municipal Hall, where councilmen engaged ratepayers in fisticuffs regularly, the Bursill Institute, with its founder's bathtub never filled with anything but books. It was a melting pot of Canadians new and old, who had been infected with the enthusiasm and restlessness of the times, and who were anxious to see that the twentieth century did indeed belong to Canada. History would show that 1912 closed an era of terrific progress and development all over the west, but in South Vancouver no one was yet aware that it had all come to an end, and that the boom was over.

Inside a year, Twenty-fifth and Main would be a morgue. Neither the publisher of the *Chinook* nor his uncle who backed him could yet know the results of the 1911 Reciprocity Election at Ottawa, when the Conservative Borden government toppled Laurier's Liberals and drove American capital from Canada. Result: Vancouver was reduced to soup kitchens almost overnight.

The first indication that the pinch was on in South Vancouver appeared as citizens began taking a close look at their tax notices and at the municipal bookkeeping. Graft charges were levelled at the chairman of the school board, at the Councilmen, at corporation executives, and at government generally.

People were clamouring for development of the North Arm of the Fraser River as a harbour. They wanted B.C. Electric to extend carlines, and they wanted sewer and water facilities. South Vancouver, in six months dating from October of 1911, had erected 1,110 buildings, at a total of $1,300,000, and this at a time when a five- or six-room house was worth $1,500. Out at Collingwood, an entire subdivision was sold in ten days. At Joyce and Wellington Roads, lots were worth $750 — $50 down and $10 a month. "Only twenty minutes by streetcar from Main and Hastings," the ads said.

The South Vancouver *Chinook* arrived just in time to hold up a mirror to this confusing picture each week. There were strong editorials, letters to the editor, sensational reporting of municipal meetings — and great comings and goings to the new publishing house on Main Street.

"Quite a sheet you put out here,.. said Margaret to Bert Stein. Her eye wandered down the page to the heading marked "GOLD: AN EVERLASTING SOURCE OF TROUBLE." Then the subhead, "There are too many grafters around the Municipal Hall, charges Gold." Margaret read on:

> At a meeting of the Good Government League numbering several hundred and called for the purpose of condemning Reeve Gold, the spectre turned up at his own feast . . . the chairman refused to take Mr. Gold's hand, whereupon Gold swung into a great speech that drew the meeting to himself and brought forth terrific applause. "A Christian he calls himself," said Gold of the Chairman. "The fact that he will not shake my hand proves that he is a hypocrite. I am a Jew, and they say I am not as good as they are. Did not Jesus come to the world to lift up such as I am? Would not Jesus have shaken my hand?"

"Well," said Margaret. "This South Vancouver can't be as tame as it looks. Do you have many meetings like this to report?"

"Oh, our share," said Stein, smiling. "I think you'll enjoy working here,"

"See you Monday morning then,.. said the new girl, backing onto the wooden sidewalk out front and almost colliding with twelve feet of furnace pipe. The *Chinook* shared the long frame building with Peach's Plumbing.

"Between printers and plumbers, you've got to watch yourself around here, lady," said the teamster, lounging against a telephone pole. "You working in there?"

"I'm starting Monday," said Margaret, and headed down the planks. She spread the paper out and read it all the way downtown in the empty streetcar.

The South Vancouver *Chinook* looked the way all newspapers did fifty years ago. It was a little pale to the eye. Few pictures were used, owing to the expense of producing them. There were no sensational headlines either. The big problem was to include all the information the public demanded in each issue. But there was nothing pale about the treatment of the issues, and the standards of the *Chinook* were high.

"We do not accept liquor or tobacco advertising," said the paper's masthead. Righteous kind of bird, this Murray, Margaret mused.

"Since his Worship's edict forbidding smoking at the municipal hall, the true odour of the place falls on the nostrils of the ratepayer as he enters. This smell could not be damaged by the fumes of a thousand briar pipes." And sarcastic, too, she decided.

By the time Margaret had digested the paper, she could make a fair assessment of her new employer. He was lofty in his thinking, he didn't admire the government, he had a fight on with someone at the municipal hall, and he didn't care whether he got along with the banker or not. But he could sure sling the language! She decided that when Bess came up next week, she would start to night school and maybe learn to write like that.

Margaret was a complete success at her new job. She could collect accounts and keep customers happy. Her sense of humour, quick eager mind, and abiding curiosity made her a favourite with the staff. When she finished her office work, she read proofs or folded papers or wrapped up job work.

"Miss Lally," said Murray one day, "when you read those proofs for mistakes, try not to get too interested in the sense of the article. Try rather to detach yourself and read only words. Otherwise mistakes will slip by you."

"How can I, Mr. Murray, when it's all so interesting? What I can't get through my one cylinder is how you've had time to know all these people. Did you really know Mr. James J. Hill?"

"I met him several times in Winnipeg and Seattle. You remember now about those proofs."

"Yes, Mr. Murray. Say, Mr. Murray, how does a reporter know to ask the right questions? How could you ask questions of the president of a big railroad if you don't know anything about railroading?"

"You couldn't."

"Well, I mean . . . did you ever railroad?"

"No. I once carried a transit over Northern Ontario for the Canadian Northern Railroad and after three months walked three hundred miles back to Cochrane through black flies and bush. You might say I didn't distinguish myself."

"Well then?"

"Miss Lally, we have a wonderful institution in this — in your country too — called a public library. I recommend it heartily."

"Oh," came back a small answer, sized to fit the way she felt.

At quitting time the following Saturday noon, an order of one thousand brochures lay on the bindery table, for delivery that afternoon out to Collingwood. "Hey," said John Jackson, hanging up his apron and reaching for his suit coat, "isn't that a son-of-a-gun for you. Everybody gone and those damned things to package and wrap."

"What's your trouble, Jackson?" said George.

"I'm looking for someone to wrap up that Collingwood job. Margaret's a good kid. I thought she might do it, but I guess she's gone."

"Already?"

"Yep. To the public library to look up something about railroads."

"Is that a fact?" said Murray. "Railroads, eh? Tell you what, John, I'll come and do the Collingwood job myself."

"Bess, you know, it's really the dinkiest little newspaper you ever saw." Margaret was filling in her sister as the two of them walked up from the CPR wharf when Bess arrived from Seattle. "And, of course, those good lookers with the John B. Stetson hats are still riding the horizon out there around Calgary. But you'll like Vancouver. We get passes to the horse shows. There are two kinds of horses. Those in ospreys and diamonds and the four-footed ones out in the ring carrying the bowler hats and the ascot ties around. We get theatre passes, too. I got to hear Clara Butt the other night. Boy, can Clara sing."

Margaret worked early and late. She made friends with purchasing agents and was soon bringing in the job orders and staggering out to deliver them. If picking up district news meant sitting down under the correspondent's holly tree and sipping raspberry cider, then cider was Margaret's drink. If she was expected to handle the boss's urbane friend, Joseph Martin, King's Counsellor, with deference when he called at the office, she read up on the amazing career of Mr. Martin. Or she found out all about Highland Games in order to get the advertising for the annual kilt and bagpipe romp from Mr. Duff-Stuart at Central Park. Lum Fat the laundry man and Felix Penne, the newspaper's most eminent contributor, were all one to Margaret.

"Bessie." said Margaret, unpinning her hat and flopping into the rocking chair in their bed-sitting room on Sixth Avenue one night. "You haven't matured, you haven't aged, until you work for a weekly newspaper."

"Well, hang on a little longer, honey. We've got our fares almost saved up. Two more months and we'll move on to Calgary."

"You know, I haven't really thought much about Calgary lately. I wonder how that joker in the embroidered saddle is getting on."

"What you need more of, Sis," said Bess, "is diversion and amusement. You work too hard. We're going on a harbour cruise tonight. How about coming?"

"Not me, darlin'. I promised to go back tonight and help Mr. Murray with some typing."

An Answer to an Overdraft

Margaret wrote her first item while collecting real estate out in Collingwood. In the course of her hikes into the wilds of South Vancouver, she met and made friends with the clergymen and their wives who gave her their church news and other community announcements. She was hardly straightened out on the government and parties of Canada before she was reporting political meetings, and hustling around the municipality covering ratepayers' rallies, indignation meetings, "Asiatic Exclusion" committees, and the troubles of

Fire Chief Wand. Wand was seven feet tall, so if he stood on tiptoe he could look into any third-story window in South Vancouver without a ladder. He wore a cocked hat, and there was no doubt who the chief was. Besides being against fires, he was against Orientals.

Margaret chewed the end of her pencil off the night the ratepayers threw the Reeve of South Vancouver out into the stumps. But at the same time, she learned something about libel.

"Oh, now, Margaret, not out the window, surely?" Stein had said the next morning.

"God's truth. They took him by the seat of the pants and heaved him."

"You better check that with Murray. Reeve Rae might not like it."

"Boy, these Canadians sure take themselves serious," she wrote home to Kansas that week. "But anyways I like my job. For a little newspaper, it's sure exciting. My boss is a nice young man, a little vague and annoying maybe, but real handsome. He loves this country so much and talks so much about northern British Columbia that you forget what time it is and listen. The other afternoon we walked clear to Broadway — twenty-four long blocks — before I remembered to catch a streetcar."

As the *Chinook* caught on around Vancouver for being a completely outspoken publication, its circulation increased. And to bolster advertising revenue in a dwindling economy, special editions were laid on from time to time. In those days, travelling teams of advertising specialists made the rounds in the Pacific Northwest, and would undertake selling these editions on a commission basis. Several such teams visited the *Chinook*, and some of their methods and formulae rubbed off on the bookkeeper, who filed them away for future use, to be hauled out for review over the next fifty years, whenever times got a little threadbare.

Only rarely did Margaret Lally get through to her boss as a rather attractive young woman. He just wasn't looking.

"Bess," said Margaret one night after supper, "our clothes aren't doing anything for us. Mr. Murray's two aunts were in the office today. Talk about class. The dark one had on the prettiest cherry-red velvet hat with a grey suit and mink to the hem. The blonde one was in periwinkle blue, with a mink hat. Let's get out some magazines and see what little old Maggie can whistle up for us."

The next week the Lally girls emerged in a pair of grey flannel gowns, with cherry-red pan velvet yokes and buttons, and hats to match from Spencer's Millinery Department.

Even George Murray had to notice. "That's a very pretty dress you're wearing, Miss Lally," he observed as they were leaving the office.

"Well, thank you," said Margaret. "I made it myself, and one for my sister just like it."

That night, under the big green drop-light, which embraced the Murrays as they dined, George told his aunts and uncle that not only was she a wonderful bookkeeper, advertising saleswoman, receptionist, and proof reader, but she could also sew!

"I'm sure," observed Aunt Esther tartly, "that she isn't the only young woman who makes her own dresses."

"Hasn't she some funny name?" asked Aunt Marion, sweetly.

"Lally — Margaret Lally," said George. "Irish."

"Well, my God, bless me,.. said Uncle Ken, rising from the head of the table. "If she's all that good, you better marry her!"

"George isn't marrying anyone, are you, George?" purred Aunt Marion. "Anyway, I saw her the other day and she doesn't look like much to me!"

Margaret liked her job, her boss, and the people she worked with. But she had only meant to get her feet a little wet in Vancouver, and then to carry on to the real Canada of those wonderful broad prairies of Calgary. What she didn't yet know was that her heart was already committed.

George Murray was never really a bookkeeper's delight. Here was a young man who thought big, looked big, and spent big, a clever fellow and a splendid journalist. But how to keep track of him, harness him, keep him within a budget, and keep track of his movements, his expenses, his deals, and his plans? This was a big responsibility, even in 1912.

And Margaret decided to get out of it while the going was good. The magnificence of his plans took her breath away. His loyalty and generosity to friends and causes made her weep. The brilliance of his associates dazzled her. But his helplessness and dependence upon her troubled her.

The Christmas number of the *Chinook* in 1912 carried sixteen hundred dollars in business and was a knockout of an issue. Hal Hill had joined the staff, and he and Bert Stein, Margaret and George Murray, threw all their energy into selling, writing, and planning the issue. Two days before Christmas, Margaret spent the afternoon collecting bills. While travelling on the streetcar, along Broadway to Main, and home in time for supper, she made her decision. She would leave the *Chinook*. It was too much for her. She went straight to the room to talk it over with her sister.

The next day she told them at the *Chinook* that she was leaving. It was quiet around the office. Family men, perhaps, received a turkey, but otherwise bonuses or gifts were not distributed in offices at Christmas. And they were genuinely sorry to be losing her.

Late that afternoon, as she stuffed her papers into her desk drawer and covered her typewriter, Margaret said to the boss, "Anyway, it's been lots of fun working here. I've learned a lot, and you've been real nice to me. I'll get the bills out Monday, and you'll have plenty of money when this Christmas issue comes in. Besides, I want to see Calgary." She took the hat pin out of her large sombrero-style felt hat and put it in her mouth.

"Have you got a job?" asked Murray.

"I'm going with the Fullers. Charlie and Katey have a special edition all lined up with the . . . is it the *Calgarian?*"

"It's the *Albertan,* you must mean," said Murray.

"Well, whatever it is, I'm going to work on it. And so is Hal."

Murray raised his eyebrows.

"Hill, eh?" See much of him?"

"Oh no. Only around here. Got everything?" She snapped off the light, and the door clicked behind them. They were out on Main Street, all white and quiet in a fresh snow. They headed for Twenty-fifth and the streetcar.

"It's sure pretty looking down into those lights," ventured Margaret after a half block of silence.

"Reminds you of home, maybe?" said her companion.

"Kinda. By the way, I got you a little something for Christmas, Mr. Murray."

"You shouldn't have done that. I didn't get you anything," said Murray.

"Here," she said. "Merry Christmas!" and she shoved a tie into the big tweed overcoat pocket beside her. And then a large warm hand closed over the small black kid glove and held it all the way to the streetcar.

Margaret did go to Calgary as planned with the Fullers and Hal Hill, but they didn't leave until early in January. And she therefore had plenty of time to prepare her records and books for the new accountant. Margaret was relieved to see from the December statements that she was leaving the firm in a healthy financial condition. However, a letter from a firm called C. Gardner Johnson — "Scows, Tugboats, and Marine Transportation" — told a familiar story. The company was being forced into liquidation. They owed the *Chinook* hundreds of dollars. And the respected president of the firm, himself, wrote the letter. They would try, he said, to pay fifty cents on the dollar.

"Bring your notebook, please," said George, and as he dictated, he toyed with an elegant black gold-banded Waterman's fountain pen which carried his name in gold lettering along the side of the cap. It was a lovely pen, and Margaret had often admired how smoothly the gold nib slid over the paper almost by itself, so slim and smooth and well-balanced it seemed to be. She must save up and try and buy one, she thought.

"We have your letter of the twenty-eighth instant." Murray's dictation was easy to take, no er's or ah's. "And therefore, my dear Johnson, you may consider your bill with the Greater Vancouver Publishers paid in full. It has been a pleasure to do business —"

"But, Mr. Murray, my goodness," Margaret blurted out, "$385! If we even got half of it . . ."

"Don't argue. Gardner Johnson is my friend. And let me have it right away so he gets it in the morning."

"But Mr. Murray, three hundred dollars . . ."

"Please, Miss Lally. This is the last thing I'm asking you to do for me."

"Well," said Margaret grudgingly, "it's nothing to me, of course. I won't even be here. But the trouble with you is you have too many friends. Gardner Johnson is a rich man, for heaven's sakes. He would not write you like this if he didn't want to pay at least some of this account."

"Miss Lally," came the measured reply, "my uncle is a rich man too. Or he was until yesterday. A note he endorsed for a friend as a gesture of faith came back to him yesterday. Six months later. Seventy-five thousand dollars on demand. You have more money in your purse right now than my uncle has in the bank."

Margaret was stunned. "Do you really mean it? Are things really as bad as this? Oh, really, I'm terribly sorry. That would go real hard with him. How old is he? In his sixties, I suppose. What about his sisters? Of course, they're nurses, aren't they?" Margaret was talking fast now to cover up her mixed feelings concerning this amazing young man behind the desk.

She got up from her chair across from him and stood a moment. Murray kept toying with his pen, seeming not to hear or notice.

"I'll be right back with this letter," she said suddenly, and closed the door softly behind her as she went out into the main office.

"He's a swell guy," said Bert Stein, nodding toward the private office, "but money means nothing to him at all. I don't know what he's going to do after you're gone. Nobody else would care as much about the business as you seem to."

"Well, I can't do anything with him. And yet, you know, Bert, I admire the guy. I never knew anyone like him before. But if I stuck around here, he'd drive me crazy. Honest."

When Margaret returned with the typed letter a few moments later, George came out of his reverie and signed it. Then he got to his feet.

"Close the door," he said. She closed the door. "Miss Lally, I'm sorry you're going. I need you around here. But you say you must see Calgary. I want you to take this." He held out the fountain pen to her.

"Oh, I couldn't take your lovely fountain pen."

"I want you to have it. I want you to write to me with it."

"Why sure. That is, I — I can write with an ordinary pen. I might lose it. I don't even know how to fill it."

"I want to give it to you. I want you to remember me, and write. Will you promise to do that?"

"I promise," said Margaret, taking the pen.

"Good-bye, Margaret Lally." Those brown eyes of his

seemed to look right into her heart.

"Good-bye," said Margaret, and she rushed from the office to beat the tears she would rather die than let him see.

Marriage between Editions

When the crew that was ready to produce the special edition got to Calgary in January of 1913, they booked into the King Edward Hotel on Eighth Avenue. The first news they had was that the *Albertan* had changed its mind about the special edition.

But Charlie Fuller was a resourceful type. He had another project lined up for his crew within twenty-four hours. They were to go to work on the Calgary labour paper, the weekly *Labour Statesman*. Labour was big in Calgary at that time, as it was in Vancouver. The government was known as the Farmers' Government, and the United Farmers had an interest in the *Statesman*.

Margaret and Katey Fuller were sitting in the lobby, discussing the wardrobe they intended to purchase the next day and enjoying watching the early afternoon throng that came and went through the King Edward's wide double doors.

"Mrs Fuller?" The bellhop extended a silver tray with a call card on it. Katey took up the card and the blood drained out of her pretty face.

"Charlie's been taken to Holy Cross Hospital. Quick! My coat! Call us a cab! Margaret, it will be his heart."

Charlie Fuller had collapsed while talking with the editor of the *Labour Statesman*. The call had come from the newspaper office as they waited for an ambulance, so that by the time Katey and Margaret got to the hospital, Charlie was barely ahead of them. When she saw there was nothing she could do, Margaret left Katey with the sick man and returned to the hotel. Later that night, Katey tapped on the door as she went to her room. "Margaret, they say he will be well enough to talk by tomorrow afternoon. He wants to see you. I think he wants you to go to Vancouver for him. He's through, the doctor says. No work of any kind for at least three months."

Presently a uniform and cap whumped around the corner, and Mrs. Fuller was told that she and the young woman could have ten minutes with the patient. They found him propped with pillows, but weak from the agonizing seizure of the day before.

"Margaret," said Charlie, "I need money. I have lots of it out in Vancouver, if I could just collect it. Now you're a smart girl — smarter than Katey when it comes to collecting — and I want you to catch that westbound CPR tonight, if you can. Do you think you can?"

"Well, sure I can," said Margaret.

"Good girl," said Charlie. "Katey will get your ticket and give you enough to eat on. Monday, first thing, I want you to go to Bowser, Reid, and Wallbridge. They've got five hundred dollars for me. And I'm going to need it badly. The doctor says complete rest for months. With that five hundred, I could at least get back to Seattle."

It was agreed.

As Margaret and Katey walked down the platform beside the smoking Pullmans at the CPR station that night, Margaret was really happier than she had any right to be. She told herself it was because it was twenty below. The coast was going to look pretty good again.

"Well, Katey, we'll have that shopping trip when I get back. Is there anything I can do for you out at the coast?"

"Nothing. Just do your best for Charlie, and remember him in your prayers. The quicker I can get some money, the quicker I can get him out of here."

"All boa-a-a-ard!" called the porter. "Boa-a-a-ard!" The signal echoed all the way down the train. Margaret stood on the top steps. "See you in a week . . . 'bye!"

The engine was picking up speed. The station, cab rack, freight sheds slipped by. She went in and sat down in lower nine. Far ahead that old familiar steam whistle blew for a crossing, bringing back a jumbled pot-pourri of memories, but calling up even more vividly for a girl like Margaret the adventure that lay ahead. Clickety-clack, clickety-clack, two weeks notice, Mr. Shipley, Canada, click clickety-clack, Calgary, George Murray . . . "Oh, not your beautiful fountain pen . . . of course I'll write, of course I'll write, of course, I'll write . . ." click, clickety-clack.

George Murray was waiting for her.

"Margaret," he said, as he took both her hands. "Hal Hill wired me you were coming. It seems a year you've been gone."

"Well, for goodness sakes, I've only been gone a week."

"The *Chinook* is a morgue without you. And this time I'm keeping you right here."

"Oh, but I have to go back. Charlie Fuller is in Holy Cross Hospital awful sick. And I have to collect some money for him."

"Give me your baggage checks," said Murray.

"I haven't got any baggage. I tell you I'm going right back. I just came out to collect some money so that Katey can take Charlie back to Seattle."

They were now out on Cordova Street in the watery January sunshine.

"Have dinner with me tonight, Margaret, and let's talk this over," said George.

"Well, even if I do, I'm still going back to Calgary on Saturday."

"All right, then. Hotel Vancouver, six-thirty. I have some things to ask you." He shut the cab door, and presently the Lally sisters were reunited at the Dunsmuir Hotel.

"Look Peg," said Bess, "This fellow Murray. Are you fond of him?"

"Well, he *is* a nice guy, Bess. You have to admit that he is."

"Yes, but is there anything between you? Now tell me the truth."

"God's truth, how could there be? I've hardly said six words to the guy in all these months. He does the talking, and it's mostly about railroads, politics, and how he'd like to go to the Peace River corridor, wherever the hell that is. Besides, he's a Presbyterian, and his folks are pretty uppity. They'll have a rich girl all picked out for him. He should marry money, anyway, because he sure can spend it. But he has got class, don't you think?"

"Peg," said Bess, "I think you love the guy."

There was little question about it. Later, at the Hotel Vancouver, George Murray said, "You look wonderful, Margaret. I think that Calgary air did you good." He handed the menus to the waiter.

"Well, it was cold enough to do something."

"That's a becoming hat. I don't think I remember seeing it around the office."

"It's Bess's hat. Isn't that a knockout, that bird of paradise! She paid a whole week's salary — fifteen dollars — for this hat. If I could just keep the tail feathers out of that palm tree."

"Yes, well, this is a nice quiet spot. Perhaps we could have the table moved a little bit. Waiter! I want you to be comfortable, and remember tonight. You see, Margaret, I want you to stay here, in Vancouver, with me."

The table was moved away from the potted palm.

"Yes, but Mr. Murray, I explained about Mr. Fuller. I can't go back on my word, and him so sick and all."

"Nobody wants you to go back on your word." Their dinner was served.

"What an elegant-looking meal," said Margaret. "What did you say this was — steak *a la* something?"

"*A la briande*. That means with a special sauce."

"Well, now, that's funny. It looks like just steak to me — with mushrooms on the side. Did I ever tell you that I cooked for two years?"

"Is that a fact? It just proves that you're a wonderful girl. You can't know how I've missed you. You had to go away for me to realize how cheerful and light-hearted you were, and what an effect you had around the office."

"Oh, sure, sure."

"It's true, Margaret."

"Well, it's nice of you to tell me, Mr. Murray."

"Margaret, I'm really trying to tell you something else. I'm trying to tell you that I want you to marry me."

"Marry you? Me?" Margaret reached for a fast gulp of water. "Me a clerk and you the publisher. Me a Catholic and you . Glory be to God! What would my mother say? And what would your aunts say?"

"Well, your mother isn't marrying me, and you're not marrying my aunts, so why bring that up?"

"Oh yes, but it matters just the same. I only went to Grade III in school. Look at you! You got nice manners, and good taste — you want to be a senator for goodness sakes! Your folks are well off. Look at me! Bess says I ought to go to night school and brush up on my English. Besides, I couldn't be anything else but what I am. I couldn't be a Presbyterian. It would be like cutting off my hands."

"And I couldn't be a Catholic. It would be like dyeing my hair."

"Well, so what are you talking about?" The waiter glided up to the table. The food was being ignored.

"Everything all right, sir?"

"Excellent, thank you," said Mr. Murray.

"So come on, and eat your dinner. You'll never get out of here under three dollars, and that's too much to waste. And besides, I haven't even got to Maple Creek yet, or Okotoks. That's what I came to Canada for, to begin with."

"Yes, well, take your time." George Murray always knew when he was ahead.

The next day was Wednesday. Wednesday, February 5, 1913. George was up early and busy on the telephone. First he called the Bishop's Palace, and made an appointment for two o'clock to see Archbishop Timothy Casey. Then he called the *Chinook* and talked to Bert Stein.

"Bert," he said, "I want you to go home and get Gertrude and meet me at the Archbishop's Palace at two-thirty. I want you to take a cab and charge it to the firm, and it's important that both you and Gertrude be here on time. I'll explain when I see you."

It took six hours in a horse-drawn cab for the Steins to get from Collingwood to West Twenty-fifth Avenue, near Granville. The Palace was an official name only. It was a many-windowed, three-story frame building in a small lot, with high wooden steps leading to the front door and verandah. A housekeeper opened the door to their ring, and led them into a typical clerical parlour. They were forty-five minutes late.

"Well, if it isn't Miss Lally," said Bert Stein. "We thought you were in Calgary. You've met Mrs. Stein?"

Yes, they'd met. Yes, she thought she was in Calgary herself; funnily enough, she wasn't in Calgary, but in Vancouver. And it's rather warm in here, isn't it. Funny, to meet again here. Coincidence is an odd thing.

"As a matter of fact, we were meeting George Murray here at two-thirty. Now, isn't that . . . you're not with George? But, of course, ridiculous of me. But this is all very odd."

"Oh no, Bert Stein, it isn't ridiculous. I am here with George Murray. And he's in there with the Archbishop, arguing whether he's going to give us permission or not."

"Permission for what?"

"Permission to get married."

"Married to George? Look, kiddo, don't talk like that. That bird isn't getting married. I mean, he just isn't the — well — the marrying kind."

"Well, whatever kind he is, I'm marrying him, I guess. But it's Wednesday. Today is Ash Wednesday. I was on the train Sunday and I forgot everything about it. I told that to His Grace, but he didn't think much of it. 'Young lady, it's not a day for weddings, but a day for mourning,' he says."

"But George is a Protestant. Did he get permission for that, too?"

"Oh, I don't know that he'll get either one. The whole thing is crazy and hare-brained."

Suddenly the parlour door burst open. There stood a broadly grinning George with an envelope in his hand.

"We made it! And we have one hour and a half to get downtown to the Cathedral."

"Isn't it here?" asked Bert.

"I thought it was, but it isn't,.. said Murray. "You sell the firm here but pick up the contract downtown. I told His Lordship I hoped I'd never have to sell him advertising."

At the Holy Rosary Cathedral, under the three drop-shades of the electric light fixture in the rectory, Father Connelly married Margaret Lally and George Murray, while a cabbie stood outside watching the lights flick on, one by one, in the Dunsmuir Hotel across the street, and his four-footed "engine" refueled from a feedbag of oats. They were married just in time for supper, which had been arranged at the Elyseum Hotel down on Pender Street.

How many times on rainy afternoons did the Murray

children ask their mother about that wedding? What did she wear? Did she ride in a limousine? Did she have orange blossoms and white satin slippers? The answers were always so dull. She had been married in a suit, she said. But their father remembered.

A white jacketed and aproned waiter had glided in, bearing a silver bucket in the frosty depths of which rested a bottle of champagne.

"Oh," said Margaret, "not champagne! Oh George, we can't . . ."

"Piper Heidseck, Margaret, is for celebration," her husband said. "To a long and happy life together." In the distance, so that it sounded just exactly as it should, the Holy Rosary Cathedral suddenly struck up an arpeggio of bells.

Running Low on Cash

"Aunt Marion, Aunt Esther, I want you to meet Margaret, my wife," said George on that February day when he first brought her through the front door of his Uncle Ken's big house on Sixteenth Avenue. Margaret was looking her very best for this meeting with the family. Her smiles covered a heart bursting with the desire to please and be liked. The aunts were trained nurses in the Florence Nightingale tradition, and starched and professional in their treatment of George's wife. They didn't at first, approve of her. At this time both were in white and caring for patients in their own home.

"Well," said Aunt Esther, "for any favour..."

Those were her three words for alarm, disappointment,

or anything she wasn't expecting. And she wasn't expecting nephew George's wife at that moment, that's sure.

"Goodness, George, you might have phoned," said Aunt Marion. Both ladies thereupon threw their aprons over their heads and ran to the back of the house in tears.

Margaret stood on the centre medallion in the big blonde Turkish rug in the white drawing room and fished for a hankie to wipe her own tears. Uncle Ken suddenly appeared from nowhere, and stood in the open dining room doors.

"My God, bless me, man," he said to George, "couldn't you have phoned the girls that you were coming first?"

"Uncle Ken, this is Margaret," said his nephew, still trying to make things right.

"Well," said Uncle Ken, making a valiant effort, and extending his hand to Margaret. "It's a nice day."

In spite of the chilly reception, Margaret agreed to renting a flat in a building belonging to Uncle Ken, if it would help the family purse. And although relations improved, and the two Misses Murray made weekly sanitary inspections of the premises at Eighteenth and Main, they were no real comfort to poor Margaret, who was by now pregnant. They referred to non-nurses as "the laity," and generally carried on in a severely professional manner, even while visiting.

For seven of the nine months that Margaret carried her first-born, Uncle Ken patrolled the block with a hammer and banged away all day. The sharp blows echoed and re-echoed in the empty rooms, along empty halls and down empty stairways. The building was brand new and completely empty. The stores underneath had never been opened. Vancouver's financial collapse had come just about the time the last painter was taking down the scaffolding and removing the ladders.

The eight flats were the last word in middle-income dwellings of that day. Each was equipped with a "Canada Pride" wood and coal range, and the fuel lockers were in the back yard. Each had a bathroom with hardwood floors and full-length tubs, white porcelain inside, dark paint outside, sitting on four fancy cast-iron feet. Each kitchen had a "cold cupboard" with outside vents to keep vegetables cool, and a large sink with a porcelain splash panel through which nickel-plated faucets protruded, with a wooden drain board alongside. The floors were dark painted wood.

Margaret barely noticed. She was nauseated for the whole nine months and couldn't eat. There were no such things as calcium pills, orange juice, iron shots, or other aids. Finally when her time came, Margaret perspired and pulled on a bedsheet fastened to the iron rungs at the foot of the white-painted iron bed. A Victorian Order nurse attended, and the doctor was the choice of Aunts Marion and Esther. And for the first six months of her life, Georgina, the baby girl, was regularly rubbed in cocoa butter on the oven door, like a sick chick, in an effort to get nourishment through her skin as well as down her throat.

But presently everything returned to normal. The baby was gaining weight and able to sit up. As the infant picked up, so did the family relations. The love of the baby transcended the misgivings of the older members of the family for the newlyweds, and when any crisis arrived, this diplomat in diapers was hustled into a baby-bunting bag, a valise was packed, and an expedition dispatched to Sixteenth Avenue until the atmosphere warmed up. The child grew up to have the heart of a bondswoman, they said, to run a thousand miles from a fight, allow salesmen in the house, and buy all the wrong hats, usually from clerks who said, "On you it's marvelous." The child grew up to be me.

War came in August of 1914, and South Vancouver's collapse was complete. Times were very hard, and a dollar was a great deal of money. One morning, when George was leaving for the office, Margaret got his hat and went to the door with him. Leo, their huge black-and-white setter, returned to the fragrant kitchen to see what was left over from lunch. In the course of sniffing the premises out, he came to the crumpled bills — three pink two-dollar ones and one green one-dollar bill, all warm and deliciously smelling of fresh bread.

Margaret came fairly skipping into the kitchen to tidy the lunch things and get ready to go downtown. She spotted the dog. Leo's great tail was just disappearing around the hall doorway.

"Leo, what have you been up to?" said Margaret sharply. Then, fearing the worst, "Oh. Oh my God, not my money . . ."

She made a lunge for the dog just as the edge of the last bill disappeared down his big hungry pink throat. With Leo's head between her knees, she pried open his jaws, and did her best to get her hand down his throat.

The baby cried, and Leo howled.

She then picked the dog up by his hind legs to shake it out of him. But Leo was too long to shake. The baby cried louder, and Leo howled louder.

Make him throw it up . . . mustard and water . . . quick, the empty room across the hall! So she dragged the dog by the collar across the floor on his rump, out into the hall to the empty flat opposite, pushed him in, and closed the door. Warm water and mustard. Damn, empty kettle. She grabbed the howling baby, filled the kettle and ran to the phone.

"You're sure he's eaten it, are you sure?"

"Yes, dammit, of course I'm sure. Do you think I'd be crying like this if I weren't sure? What can I do?"

"Well, you can take him down and deposit him at the main branch of the Bank of Montreal." Big laughs from George and others in the background.

"Oh dearest, don't make jokes. I need that money so badly. Do you think mustard and warm water?"

"It wouldn't hurt to try. How about an enema? (More loud laughter.)

She banged down the phone, laid the baby in her crib, and proceeded to go to work on Leo. When mustard and water and burnt toast failed to produce any effect, she went out for the castor oil.

"I'll fix you, you miserable bitch, you robber, you hateful, horrible dog, you." And reached down the Epsom salts. Two hours, two drenchings, two laxatives later, Margaret was astride Leo again, this time with some paregoric to settle his nerves. They went around and around the morning-glory-papered room, Margaret all unaware that poor old Leo's internal economy had liquidated at last. In vain she went around examining the walls, looking for even an eyebrow of King George. But the bills were reduced to flecks of pink that wouldn't even cover the head of a pin.

And it cost seven dollars to repaper the room!

Margaret wheeled a pram through her first election campaign, distributing literature in South Vancouver for the Liberals.

In fact, the entire *Chinook* plant had been made available to the party without cost, and the lights at the newspaper office burnt late as the young publisher projected campaigns far into the night with his friends. Often George and Gerald McGeer, at that time a young law student, would walk home together to the Murray's Main Street flat and talk on the board sidewalk until Margaret would throw open the window and call down to them to either soften their voices or come upstairs.

The Canadian Banking Act was awful, said McGeer, at which point Margaret decided to put a stop to such talk on the street. It nailed people down (the young politicians were coming up the echoing staircase) and kept them down, he said, and besides the province needed to keep pace with progress . . . a paving program, Gerry, and new townsites (hat tossed on davenport), lower freight rates, George, to keep the grain moving, more elevators (coffee pot rattling), and open (table thump) that (thump) gawdammed Panama Canal (thump thump) or we perish! By now the baby was awake and everyone was good for another couple of hours.

Dawn streaked the sky over Kingsway before Gerald walked home to bed that night. Margaret was dead tired. But her husband had something on his mind. "Don't go to sleep . . . listen to me for a minute." He sat on the white counterpane beside her, and took her hand in his. "Margaret, you remember once I told you that, with God's help, you and I would do great things? And when we cash in, it will be in the thick of the battle where the big shells are exploding? Well, I feel tonight that over my head is hovering a good angel."

"Make your angel happy, then, for heaven's sake. Say your prayers and come to bed," said Margaret in a sleepy voice.

"Listen to what I'm going to tell you, Marg. It's the most important announcement I ever made. I'm going to run for the Provincial Legislature. I'm announcing myself tomorrow."

"Ummmmmmm," sighed Margaret, a second before the words got through to her. "You're what?" She sat straight up in bed and reached for her kimono.

"I'm the candidate for the Liberal nomination in Vancouver South as of tomorrow morning. George M. Murray,

M.L.A. Sound good?"

"It sounds perfectly crazy to me. What are you going to use for money?"

"I have backers."

"You better have. What about all those Liberal posters and blotters up at the office? I hope you have backers for them, too."

Now don't worry. That will be taken care of. We settled it all tonight. McGeer is speaking to my nomination, and it's next Monday night in the old Gaelic Church at Twenty-fifth. I wish I could buy you a new hat."

"I need shoes worse than a hat. New shoes might help my back. I hope I feel good enough to go to the meeting, let alone wearing a new hat!" Margaret was expecting their second child.

"By George, eh? You know, this is wonderful. This is my ambition. I've wanted to do this ever since I was ten years old. Did I ever tell you about cutting my name on the barn door at home?"

"You did."

"And about my streetcar visits with Sir Wilfrid Laurier?"

"Ah, my dear, you've told me everything, everything. I fell in love with your dreams as much as I fell in love with you. And I'll help you. And you'll win, and be a senator, or what is it, an M.L.A.?"

"Member of the Legislative Assembly. That's the provincial government."

"And you'll be the best damn M.L.A. that ever was. Only thing is, I won't be much good in the mornings for a while. It's broad daylight. Come on to bed, for heaven's sake!"

The nominating meeting was going to be splendid. Times were hard and issues lively. People were frustrated by the war. They felt taxed to death and on the Pacific Coast enjoyed no compensating payrolls to ease the burden. There were soup kitchens on Main Street in South Vancouver. With Murray's northern development platform — a north-south railroad to tap the rich resources of the interior — and McGeer's fiery oratory in support of his friend, the Liberals were bound to win in Vancouver South.

Well, they won all right, but Mr. Murray was not the candidate, and not the M.L.A. McGeer got so carried away with his introduction of the *Chinook's* publisher, that he wound around him the unfair banking act, the usuriously high railroad freight rates, and the abuses perpetrated by the reigning McBride government — and so inflamed the audience that suddenly the meeting turned into an emotional shambles. When McGeer paused for breath, someone nominated the speaker from the floor, and the stamping, applauding, perspiring listeners made it unanimous. To add insult to injury, McGeer walked off with George's hat — both had been hanging side-by-side in the cloakroom — and wore it home. And Margaret turned over her shoe money to pay for the hall.

"The boys," said Mrs. McGeer, mother of six of them, uttering the understatement of 1916, "are always getting things mixed up."

She took the Stetson off the hall rack the next morning and handed it to a dejected George while Gerald slept the sleep of a young man who had tasted the exhilaration of his first successful encounter with the public from a political platform.

For George there was double trouble. He soon found that nothing is deader than last election's posters and blotters, and nothing harder to collect than a political printer's bill. His uncle was pressing for money, so that besides running the *Chinook*, he had to free-lance for the dailies downtown to keep the barest necessities in the larder.

"George, supper is on the table." Margaret put down the newspaper she was glancing over. "You've got the imagination in the family, so you can pretend this rice is pheasant under glass. Actually, it's better for you," she said cheerfully. The menu that evening consisted of boiled rice and raisins, with brown sugar and milk, brown home-made bread, and blackberry jam, no butter. And tea.

"George, did you have to be so forthright in your report of that municipal meeting?" She was concerned about the report of a meeting in which Edward Gold, whom she had met in a story when she first joined the *Chinook,* was the subject of some colourful reporting in the paper she had just laid down.

"Well, I don't see how you could let a man get away with charges like he made. He called the councillors dirty Englishmen. He said they were hiding behind the flag. Or, as he qualified it, the oily rag." The country, of course, was deep into war.

"Well, eat your rice, dear. But somehow, it bothers me," said Margaret.

It bothered George, too, a few days later when he heard from Mr. Gold's lawyers.

About this time the love affair between the Pacific Great Eastern Railroad and the Murrays was blossoming and deepening. The line was then almost to Lillooet, inching along a precipitous rock face beside Seton Lake on one side in the vanguard of a corps of dynamiters, followed by sweating horses and labourers with their fresnos, crowbars, picks, and winches. Lillooet was about two hundred miles upcountry behind Margaret's beautiful mountains, and pushing through some of the most rugged country on the continent. The partners in the construction firm which built the railroad, Messrs. Foley, Welch, and Stewart, were good copy for a reporter. They were, besides, shrewd and far-seeing men of wealth who had come up the hard way. They were approachable and kindly.

One morning George was walking along Granville Street with Pat Welch, discussing with him the progress on the line. During the conversation, he mentioned the impending addition to his family. The two men stopped under the Birks clock, a landmark on Granville and Georgia Streets.

"You call me in the morning, Murray, and I'll have the exact mileage for you. In the meantime, here's a little something for that son and heir you expect," and with that Welch pressed a twenty-dollar gold piece into George's hand.

"Oh dear, how hard up we were," recalls Margaret. "I think we really were down to white navy beans in the pantry. Of course I made bread, but meat was out of the question. We lived on pots of soup, rice, porridge, and fruit I picked and canned myself.

"And what do you think your father did with the twenty-dollar gold piece? He went straight into Birks and bought a sterling silver pitcher and spoon for Georgina, and for the new baby a silken eiderdown for the crib and for me a pretty little amethyst rosary. And me, for God's sake, with my tongue hanging out a foot, for the taste of just a strip of bacon."

The night before their son was born, George cooled his

heels in the custody of the law. Reeve Edward Gold had charged the publisher of the *Chinook* with defamatory libel. As George awaited his old friend and lawyer, Joe Martin, Margaret fretted and fumed because she was afraid the baby she was expecting would be born with bars on its face. Eventually the case was dismissed with George being assessed the costs, which he had to borrow. And the new baby, far from suffering disfigurement, won every beautiful baby contest in Vancouver for the next few years, evidently having thrived on his thin pre-natal environment.

In a desperate bid to put his machinery to work in a dwindling economy, George Murray then joined his old lawyer friend, Martin, in a brief plunge into the downtown daily field. Machinery was moved from Thirty-third and Main Street to Homer and Pender Streets, where the Vancouver *Evening Journal* turned out to be the first of a series of dailies to be published at that address for the next forty years. George's idea in promoting the Vancouver *Evening Journal* was no doubt largely due to the need to keep bringing in groceries. But Mr. Martin was making a bid to form a government in Victoria, and fifty years ago the support of a newspaper was a basic requirement.

Martin, a King's Counsellor, was one of the colourful men of Western Canada. He had been a great and trusted friend of Prime Minister Laurier. In 1910, as Premier of British Columbia, Martin had made the decision that established the eight-hour day in Canada. He and Mackenzie King, then Federal Minister of Labour, worked out a scale for miners. Martin was fascinating to the young men around South Vancouver. He had served as a member of parliament both in England and Canada. McGeer was his law student. He was brilliant in law, a master orator, a connoisseur of women and wine, urbane, agnostic, and absolutely intense in his Liberalism. He was one of the great lawyers of his day, and one of the great politicians.

As a newspaper publisher, however, he left something to be desired. The Vancouver *Evening Journal* enjoyed a short but stormy passage and expired after several weeks from lack of advertising and capital.

Among the accounts Martin tried to line up for the new paper was a wholesale drug firm in Winnipeg, named Martin, Bole, and Wynn, of which his brother, Edwin

Martin, was president. Edwin was a prominent Methodist, and the Chamber of Commerce had just run him for Mayor of Winnipeg. Joe sent his brother this telegram: STARTING DAILY NEWSPAPER IN VANCOUVER STOP PLEASE ADVISE ALL ACCOUNTS PLACE ADVERTISING WITH US STOP AM BEING GIVEN UNFAIR TREATMENT BY LOCAL LIBERALS STOP REGARDS STOP JOE MARTIN.

A reply came back by return from Winnipeg. This was Saturday. By Monday morning insertion orders started to flood the Homer Street office of the *Journal.* "Please insert our two-inch single column cure for syphilis, gonorrhoea and premature pregnancy. See our Agent, Martin, Bole and Wynn, Winnipeg . . . Please insert quarter page, 'If pregnant write at once Bide a While Lying Inn Home, St. Louis' . . . Insert two column ten inches, 'Are you Impotent? Dr. Will Grant . . . Write Box 4312, South Bend, Indiana.'"

Not a line was bought by Woodward's, Hudson's Bay, or Spencer's.

Martin and Murray were running low on cash, and Joe suggested a joint-stock company and sale of shares. They discussed making a list of likely investors, and Martin led off with the name of his old poker-playing friend, Charlie Millar, owner of the BX stage line in Cariboo, then practising law in Toronto. Millar is the man who made the unusual will, leaving brewery stock to the Methodist Church, and a large sum for the great baby derby, which bestowed a small fortune to the Ontario wife who mothered the largest number of babies in the decade following Charlie's death.

George addressed a courteous letter to Mr. Millar and suggested he buy five thousand dollars worth of preferred shares in the Vancouver *Evening Journal.* There came back a reply immediately: AM WIRING MR. MARTIN $5,000 STOP DON'T SEND ANY SHARE CERTIFICATES STOP MAIL ME THE PAPER WHILE IT LASTS AS IT'S WORTH THIS TO ME TO SEE JOE PERFORM AS A NEWSPAPERMAN STOP CHARLES MILLAR.

Nor was the editor's lot all joy with the irascible and opinionated Martin in the publisher's office. A man named Winston Churchill was at that time rising to some prominence in the news, being First Sea Lord of Great Britain at the time of the failure of the Dardanelles campaign. When a news item concerning his discreditment was given front position, Martin at once phoned Murray: "Keep that damned Churchill out of our paper," he ordered. "He's an upstart and wholly unreliable."

The day the sheriff put the padlock on the premises on Homer Street was possibly the worst in a series of black days for the Murrays.

"I've failed you, Margaret. I've failed you and the babies. I've done all the wrong things. I, the big idea man, the publisher, the legislator, the orator, the boy wonder . . ."

"But George, my dearest, don't say that. You made an honest effort. I never could see myself three dailies in a town of this size. But then you had the backing, and all that machinery lying idle. A man can only do his best. Besides, you still have the *Chinook* . . ."

"Yes, but how long have I the *Chinook?* Four days a week not a hand turns, not a machine. I shouldn't be here in the first place. I should have stopped a bullet in France two years ago, but I did what I honestly thought was the honourable thing to do, to stay by my uncle and pay my debts."

"And it was the right thing to do. And something will turn up, you'll see."

The something that turned up had quite a twist to it. Margaret said flatly that it was a miracle, a direct answer to prayer. Uncle Ken said that it was an ill wind that didn't blow somebody some good. And the two aunts declared that they hoped the whole thing would be a lesson to George and that he'd get into some respectable line of business with the proceeds.

For George's pride and credit were saved by the very thing that ruined him. The crash in South Vancouver which wiped out so many people was the means of paying the mortgage and the creditors and disposing honourably of the little weekly newspaper. His reprieve was handed to him across the Municipal Clerk's desk, in the form of sheaf after sheaf of tax-sale lists. Thousands of names and descriptions of lots stretching from Twelfth Avenue to the Fraser River. The advertising bill amounted to seven thousand dollars. Seven thousand dollars! An unbelievable sum.

Despite the disapproval of the aunts, Margaret went back to the *Chinook* to look after the books. This time they even sent the crib over to Sixteenth Avenue to sweeten up the family humour. Georgina would be thoroughly spoiled during these interludes, re-dressed in madeira lawn and French kid slippers and hung in muffs and tiny kid gloves. She returned to her own home advising all and sundry who demanded obedience, "Hauld on, hauld on, my God bless me, can't I have any peace?" and appeared generally out of hand. So Margaret hired the First World War equivalent of a baby sitter, then known as a nurse-maid — Nellie. Those were sad days. The flower of Vancouver was lost in the war. Of George's intimate friends, he was the only one who stayed behind, and by the time the tax sale went through, and he felt he could honourably join up, it was too late.

Nothing but Prickles

One Friday in 1916, when things were at a very low ebb and George was wondering where his family's next meal was going to come from, he handed the familiar brown pay envelope to Gales Johnson, the pressman at the *Chinook*. Gales was a slight, quick-moving, nuggety little man, with the high cheek bones of his Icelandic ancestors.

"I hate to have to say this," said the publisher, "we'll have to cut you to two days a week, Gales. But we'll bring out a paper as long as we can."

"Well, good!" answered Johnson with enough cheer in his voice to surprise the boss. "I got me a homestead up Burrard Inlet, and maybe now I can get some work done on it."

"Where is it?" asked Murray.

"You take a boat to get to it. Fifty cents there and fifty back. It's about a mile and a half up from the wharf. Ten bucks to prove up on the land. Grow your own garden, a few chickens — that's the way to beat this kind of thing," he said.

"What kind of land?"

Gales laughed. "It wouldn't grow wheat, you bet. It's pretty heavy clearing, but it would grow a garden and you could run pigs — lots of that juicy bracken — and lumber! You can cut your own. Man, the size of the stumps you wouldn't believe!"

"Could I come out and see this place?"

"Why sure. Might even fix you up with a place of your own," went on Johnson. "That is, if you have the ten dollars to file."

"I certainly haven't got it today," A smile, then, "But I've got fifty cents."

"Nine tomorrow morning. Be at the dock," said Gales, and he was gone.

The next morning found George down at the foot of Dunlevy Street, amidst the pungent Vancouver waterfront mists and smells. The more he thought about it, the more attractive and solid a little piece of land sounded. A small group of passengers waited for the gangplank of *New Delta* to crash down on the oily timbers of the Howe Sound Navigation Company's wharf.

George was a little out of place in this mixed bag of company. The tweeds, shined brogues, and wide-brimmed Stetson gave him a city look, and he stood tall in a crowd of settlers with their pens of chickens, sacks of staples, goats on a string, and those endless rows of cardboard boxes and beat-up suitcases. George planned to look the land over, spend the night with his friend Gales, and return with a report Sunday evening.

Margaret, who had remained home with the children, was writing letters under the dining room drop light on the round oak table when the land-seeker returned.

"Margaret, it's wonderful!" His voice filled the house as he burst in through the front door, tossing hat and raincoat on the davenport. He kept right on to the dining room. "Twenty acres of land . . ."

"Hush, darling, you'll wake the children. Tell me about

it. Have you had your dinner?"

"Yes. but listen! It's about a two-hour sail up the inlet. Less than that, but the boat stops all the way along. Then you walk up quite a good-sized hill to a valley. The soil must be good. Probably old lake bottom. And it has the most beautiful trees on the back of it. It costs ten dollars to file. We could spend weekends there. It's just fifty cents on the boat. Oh, Margaret, a piece of land of our own! Soon there'll be roads and bridges connecting it to Vancouver. What do you think?"

"I think it's wonderful. But where do we get the ten dollars? Is it a down payment?"

"No, it's a fee to file. The land is a homestead. Every year you do improvements. I think it's a hundred dollars worth a year. Then after so much clearing and work on the place, you get a Crown grant to it. From the King. I've seen them."

"Well, it sounds too good to be true. There must be something the matter with it. How far up the hill did you say?"

But George was running down the basement steps. Presently he called upstairs, "Who did you say you loaned that tent to?" He was already lining up the Murrays' first weekend at the homestead.

At nine o'clock the next Saturday morning, the four of us were aboard the *New Delta*. Besides string bag and valise, a pack sack was brought along for easy carriage of the infant in "making" the hill. Two hours on the water sped by quickly. Then the long walk up the floating dock, to the beach, to the timber line, and finally the hill.

"In the name of God, how long *is* this hill?" asked Margaret, as she caught up to her husband on the first level. The other settlers, hardened to climbing, were out of sight ahead. A huge wooden reservoir covered with cool green moss and, dripping constantly into the gravelly road, made this spot an attractive resting place.

"George, this looks more like a gravel pit than a land proposition," said Margaret, half-way up the steep hill.

"Yes, but of course, the land lies in the valley above, my dear. Listen to the birds! Smell that good air!" The small one had long since been picked up and was enjoying a grandstand view of the slowly passing countryside from her father's shoulders.

"You didn't say anything about the mosquitoes," said Margaret slapping her neck. "They're sure bad in the shade."

"After all, what are a few mosquitoes? You find mosquitoes only in the bush, and we'll have an acre cleared here in no time at all."

"Ummmmmmm," said Margaret, mopping her damp dusty brow.

And that was the beginning of the homestead. It was a mile and a half straight up from Burrard Inlet behind what is now the Imperial Oil Refinery's townsite. What a son of Ontario saw in such a landscape is hard to say. Great blackened stumps spoke mutely of the ravages of the timber-seekers who had logged the entire mountainside and the valley in the late nineties. Shalal grew every place, waxy, round leaves that would hide a stump socket big enough to drown the team and sink the wagon. The sockets were usually full of water. Salmon berries were everywhere. Except for the shalal, everything that grew on this land had prickles. Perhaps it was the thistle that sold George on this land venture. George found a unique use for these great purple-headed Scots devils. When old church or lodge friends died, the floral tributes often included one from the Murrays in which roses, shamrocks, or whatever were arranged around a giant purple thistle, carefully taken from the current homestead crop and made up by Ed Brown, the florist on Hastings Street.

George filed on twenty acres of land, and the man who loaned him the ten dollars with which to accomplish this transaction was Joe Martin. "My boy," he said, handing over the ten-spot, "if you make any contracts for clearing, see they don't leave a stone that won't go through a five-inch ring." Martin's warning was prophetic. Any richness that might be expected from an old lake bottom had been laid bare by the lumber cruisers and was rapidly running down the mountainside with the rain. Pit, pit, pit, pat, pat, pita-patta-pitta-patta — and the avalanche was on. Then pink, pink, pink, and there it was dripping through the chimney on the old black kitchen range. Phut, phut, phut. Quick, the wash basin, Danny's cot! The roof poured water for a few minutes, and then the weather settled in for a day of it. Or a week. Or two weeks.

Some stumps took ten years to burn.

For many years, the Murrays waited for that nine o'clock Saturday *New Delta* — and not infrequently Captain Brewster and his alternate, Captain McLean, waited for them. They always watched for them, for the arrival of the Murrays was something to behold — children crying, lard pails swinging, George shouldering a canthook, Margaret desperately trying to hold a valise closed.

Once they were safely aboard, the little steamship took on an excursion atmosphere. If the day were fair, you sat on deck and watched the waterfront pass. You knelt on the seats and looked over the side at the grey green inlet while your mother held your coat tail or anything grabbable. The harbour was busy enough but once beyond the second narrows, the pilot could relax and just smell his way up the inlet. You called in at Dollarton where the lumber schooners lay and were entranced by the big sawdust burner that belched ashes and sparks. Dollarton smelled of creosote and new lumber. You called in at Carraholly where little girls in frilly dresses and nurse maids attending them strolled down the tidy landscaped walks to the fenced wharf. From there the boat followed the odour of rotten eggs to the chemical works at Barnet where scows of yellow sulphur lay in the inlet. Then on to Port Moody and the big lumber mills, and from there to Old Orchard where weekenders and berry pickers were consigned, and finally to Sunnyside Wharf, where the Murrays got off.

Sometimes if weekend clocks were slow at the homestead, or if the family didn't listen carefully for the shift whistles, the Sunday night descent to catch the boat back to Vancouver was a genuine spectacle. The children would run ahead, reach the clearing above the beach, and yell back that the *New Delta* wasn't in sight, or was just coming in.

"Hurry, Mama! We'll miss it, Mama!"

Patsy the Airedale would strain at her leash and Danny would jerk on down the gravelly road, restraining her. Presently Margaret would emerge from the woods, loaded down with a coal-oil can and a suitcase, the children's coats, and a string bag full of sundries. George brought up the rear with possibly a cross-cut blade for sharpening or a piece of a stump puller or whatever was the greatest burden up for repair at the moment. Once or twice the little steamer had left the dock and was churning white water to turn into the stream. With shrieks and commands and the grabbing of small hands, the whole tribe would disappear down the railroad track and madly leap ties to the Imperial Oil plant gate, then down the refinery road to the oil company's dock, arriving breathless and voiceless, having expended both on attracting Captain McLean's attention to their plight.

Summer Camp, 1921

The year 1919 started off well enough. The *Chinook* was disposed of so that George's uncle could be repaid and his household secured. An acre of land had been cleared on the brow of the hill behind Ioco, and a tar-paper-covered frame cottage had been erected and furnished in camp style on the property. It had cost a thousand dollars to do the clearing. A new chapter in the life of the Murrays was about to open, and this was a good time for George to make a trip to Kansas to meet his wife's family and let his aging parents-in-law see the two Canadian grandchildren. Besides, he would be saved the embarrassment he knew he would feel in competition with returning soldiers who badly needed the few jobs that Vancouver offered.

In Kansas City, Father went to work for the *Post* and we lived at "Auntie's." Auntie was really Mary Kilkenny, a spinster, and she ran a boarding house. The most exciting people in the house were my mother and her three sisters. I could never quite accept the fact that Anne, Bess, and Helen Lally were my aunts, because they were such a contrast to the two aunts I had in Vancouver.

"How do you like your aunts?" Great-uncle Jack Kilkenny asked me the evening we arrived.

"Those aren't my aunts," I told him. "Those are my mother's people."

They were quite a far cry from the Murray women. Bess, whose independence of spirit had first expressed itself in the trip west with my mother, now worked for General Motors and drove a 1919 version of Chevrolet's Model T runabout. She wore black satin dresses with white collars and panels, and pretty shiny shoes with big ribbon bows on them. Helen was the "little sister," and had more time for my brother and me than the rest.

Aunt Anne looked pretty funny. She was getting over the 1918 flue and had lost all her hair, and it was taking a long time to grow back in. She had a watch which shone under the bedclothes and ticked a child to sleep.

I was the 'interesting' one of the two little Maple Leafs, aged five, and apt to say anything. Dan was a cherub, made to order for dressing up and showing off.

Between my gay young aunts, their "fellas," and my father's friends from the *Post,* life was wonderful at 3117 Thirty-eighth Avenue, Kansas City, Kansas.

Then suddenly Mother was ill. There was the doctor. There was Aunt Anne, clothed in white starch, not even laughing that her cap wouldn't stay on. There were tears in my father's eyes, no room in the hospitals which were full of influenza patients, the bedroom darkened, people walking on tiptoes, no jokes around the dinner table.

And father saying, ". . . and you, my darling little girl, are going to be brave and help Mama get better. You'll love the good Sisters. They're kind and there will be lots of children to play with, just your size . . ."

"Oh Daddy, do I have to? Do I really have to go away? Can't anybody keep me? Can't I stay with you?" Suddenly the lights all seemed to go out.

"It won't be for long darling. And everybody has to work hard to get Mama well. Get your coat on and you can go and kiss her goodbye".

I will remember being held down to kiss my mother until the day I die. The room smelt of onions. They used to wonder why I couldn't eat onions. Poor mother was lying in them — warm onion poultices from head to foot. And she didn't even open her eyes.

That night the little fair-haired girl with the sick mother couldn't eat her dinner at St. Benedict's and cried with loneliness in her little white dormitory bed until a vision in a white nightgown and a close fitting cap floated by.

"Come with Sister Margeret, poor little girl," said the vision, and held the child warmly and closely all through the night.

The crisis passed and the danger lessened, but my mother continued to be very ill. Little by little, she got some use of her hands again, but couldn't comb her hair, or even reach for anything. Her legs were useless, and for a very active young woman, the boarding-house bedroom became very dreary and hopeless.

"George, British Columbia is my home now," she said one night as my father sat beside her bed reading the paper and visiting. "I want to go home."

"My dear girl, I would love to take you home. But what are we going to? To my aunts? We have no home in the city. To the homestead? No water or electricity. How would we get you up the hill? Hell, I'll get a job, of course. I'll work pick and shovel, if I have to. But aren't you better off here with your family until you can get around?"

Mother thought she wasn't better off in Kansas City. And so it was arranged. By the time Aunt Anne's hair covered her head like a pickaninny's she was ready to take her sister Margaret home to Canada. One day my father came to see me at St. Benedict's and took me back to Auntie's.

The day my mother returned on the *New Delta,* she didn't walk up the Sunnyside Hill. She rocked up. Mr. Montgomery met her with the two-wheeled cart and Old Cleve's horse, and she was hoisted aboard in her chair.

At least there was going to be no rent to pay at the homestead. For food, my father talked someone out of a partial carload of flour. A thing about flour is that is must be consumed immediately unless there is ideal storage for it. In that soggy rain-swept valley, there was no such storage, so the flour was potlatched, and vegetables swapped for it.

Did you ever eat parsnip soup?

"If you're smart about the seasonings, it tastes just like clam chowder," Mother would say, as she mashed the long, white 'nips and added milk. Fifty pounds of navy beans were a great help, too, and it's amazing how many ways you can eat beans. We ate them all one winter.

"Pat Lally fed the nine of us on turnips for three solid winters, and there wasn't a smarter, classier-looking bunch of girls in Nemaha County," she said.

But poor Mother wasn't very strong-looking or very classy-looking then, shunting around the kitchen of that poor little house in her rocking chair.

Forty years isn't so long ago, but when the doctors found out what ailed mother, the operation to remove her tonsils was an elaborate affair, and she took three weeks to recover at Vancouver General Hospital before being allowed home to convalesce.

By this time, Dad was working for wages at the *Province.* He had published three papers — the weekly *Chinook* in South Vancouver, the Vancouver *Evening Journal* which lasted briefly, and the weekly *Standard* — and worked on half a dozen, including the Kansas City *Post.* He would come home on the Saturday *New Delta,* and sometimes during the week if he worried about us. On weekdays, he'd take the CPR to Port Moody and row across the inlet to Sunnyside wharf, then walk the hill. And repeat the whole performance to be back in the city room the next morning.

What a thrill to see him rounding the big posts at the gate! It would always be evening with the big hawks wheeling on the horizon with their ghastly "whoop whoop." I thought those hawks were the loneliest things in the world. The thumping of grouse was another lonesome sound, and the noise of a train, with its moaning whistle, which carried with ease across the water into the valley, was enough to make you cry.

Our fortunes had gone down about as far as they could go in 1919, so the Murray star seemed really in the ascendancy in 1921 when Dad took over the managing editorship of the *Vancouver Morning Sun* for Robert Cromie. He came to the *Sun* from *Farm and Home,* also a Cromie publication, a weekly journal whose name described it well. And although such a position must have been fairly important in a small city like Vancouver, we lived humbly enough.

When we moved back into Vancouver, home was a little

frame cottage, still standing on Templeton and Hastings, now nudged in beside a laundromat. I shall never forget the day we first saw it. The former tenants had kept chickens in the kitchen — or maybe the place was a chicken house altogether. Anyway, the prospect was pretty dreary. A cold house. Rain pouring. Aunt Esther directing operations from a step ladder. Hosing down the walls. Lye, water, and brooms.

"Mercy, get the children out of here, for any favour! They might get splashed," said Aunt Esther, who was efficient and professional and very spinsterish at forty-seven.

So mother sent us over to the neighbours, dear kindly souls who lived in a wee grey house next door. James and Mary Cormack took us in, cheered us with "a wee drap of yon mutton broth," and let us stand and watch the rain beat on the windows.

Weekends we fled to the homestead where we took piano lessons!

It was at this time that Miss Grace Kay came into our lives. She lived at the Blind Home, being practically without sight. We children used to think what a terror she'd be if she had it all. She was to teach me piano.

Mother had practically mortgaged her soul for a Gerard Heintzman upright in fumed oak, to match the dining room furniture, and the library table. I was going to play the piano if it killed her. It didn't kill her and I do play the piano, but just to be sure about it, mother took lessons herself for the first year so I couldn't put anything over on her.

"All right," she'd say, and start with the knitting needle. "First line? Second line? Third line? Now play! One, two, three! One, two, three . . ."

Some people are passive about the advantages they give their children because they didn't have them. But there was nothing passive about mother.

Because she could barely see, Miss Kay was a little old-fashioned about her dress, wearing very long skirts and high-necked shirtwaists. I don't know whose idea it was to have Miss Kay take over as governess for our summers at the Homestead but it was considered an excellent idea. It would give the children two solid months of out-of-doors and give their parents a rest during the week-ends. They even moved the piano to Sunnyside, boat, skidroad, wagon and all, so that the experience would be as rewarding as possible and music lessons would continue. They meant well but got a little mixed up on who was being rewarded.

And there we were, Dan and I and Miss Kay for two solid months, three years in a row. The first year Dan cried all summer. The second year he cried only from Sunday night to Thursday, drying up in preparation for Saturday when mother and dad would arrive on the brow of the dusty hill.

Those three summers made me old before my time. I was the big sister, aged nine, and had to be brave and comfort my little brother. I was expected to understand what Miss Kay was reading when we had our morning Bible hour, which was always accompanied by a large square of Baker's semi-sweet chocolate as a soother.

Miss Kay was a Russellite and would nowadays be as a Jehovah Witness. However my father was all for the Bible reading and my mother was all for my father, and Miss Kay's particular persuasion regarding it never dawned on either one of them. Anyway we were used to my father reading to us from the Bible. He knew it back and front and he read, loving the words, as his mother had read to him and his grand-mother had read to her. But Miss Kay didn't read the same at all. She read, to begin with, with her nose, feeling the text, we thought as we'd sit watching her. She was very fond of Genesis, especially the verse about various creatures — so many lambs, so many doves, so many oxen and so on.

When the reading was concluded, she would take this particular verse and add and multiply and subtract the numbers of livestock, always coming out with 1922, the year the world was coming to an end, she said. This made a deep and disturbing impression on me. I knew all about cemeteries, having taken my first steps practically at Mountain View with Nellie and the thought of people knocking down the Angels and pillars as the trumpets sounded, of Jehovah and his great white beard and of all those strange relatives having a reunion on the golden streets, was terrifying. And with your parents away off in Vancouver, at that.

But if Miss Kay needed her sight to deal with us children, she had no need for it at the piano. She played beautifully, and often for us. She would first pull herself up to her full five feet two, smooth her hair, expectorate into a handkerchief (She was a caution with handkerchiefs, owing to germs) and assume her place on the piano bench. Then she would pause for quite a long while, until the audience stopped rustling, and then Attack! And then the Spring Song or Rachmaninoff's Prelude would get a going over like you've never heard.

Beefing up a Daily

My father became Managing Editor of the Vancouver *Sun* in 1921. Its publisher, Robert J. Cromie, was a lot of things, none of them dull. Back in the old *Chinook* days, my mother had delivered printing to a firm whose accountant signed the ducats for the big brown parcels. He was a sandy-haired man who signed "R.J. Cromie" with a flourish and then went back to his railroad construction journals and ledgers. He worked for Messrs. Foley, Welch, and Stewart, builders of the Pacific Great Eastern Railway.

Now he ran the *Sun,* and he was tough on his managing editors. You got the idea that he was a dynamo of energy, a man of vision, a financial wizard, a patriot, and a philanthropist. However, he was these things only on those days when he was not an unprincipled rogue, a nut or a cold-blooded, calculating scrooge. Just the same, he put together a great newspaper.

The *Sun* kitchen in those days was unofficially at our house on Templeton Drive. As a family we personally tested all the recipes for beefing up a lively morning paper. My father shared Mr. Cromie's views that dope addicts could kick the habit if they could be filled to the brim with a series of appetizing meals. I don't remember the cure for kidnappers, murderers, and other varieties of criminals, but in the early twenties Vancouver abounded with them all. Almost at once there started a procession to our back door of dejected, beady-eyed men who trembled and sniffled. One wept on the piano keys when his rendition of Beethoven's First became too much for him, and mother wiped up after him with alcohol. Extra house money was earmarked so that the best and most attractive food possible could be prepared for these derelicts. The experiment was a complete failure and a waste of good beefsteak. Not one of them could eat a thing.

From the drug addicts we went to Dr. Coué, the mind-over-matter specialist for the ills of the twenties, then a featured *Sun* columnist and much admired by the publisher. Dr. Coué, was a pioneer in the positive-thinking school.

"Okay now, let's hear it, children!" Father's muffled voice would emerge from the bed clothes and reach to the front of the house as the youngsters would be getting off to school.

"Oh, George, for goodness sake. They're late now."

"It only takes a minute. Come on. 'Every day in every way' — louder, please — 'every day in every way I'm getting better and better.' " The children would shout it and Patsy the dog would join in with a howl.

From Dr. Coué we plunged wildly into Dr. McCoy, another of the publisher's favourite people. Dr. McCoy went for orange-juice diets in a big way, and devoted whole columns of his syndicated daily feature to the elimination of body wastes. We were thoroughly purged and growing daily weaker when my teacher at school put a stop to the orange-juice era.

"Sister says that Danny will have to stay home tomorrow unless his trouble clears up", I reported one night after school, having had the word on my little brother. "She says it's comic what he has. But she wasn't laughing."

"Maybe she means chronic but there's nothing the matter with him that I know of," said mother, eyeing her youngest.

"I unbuttoned him three times this afternoon in front of the whole class." Everybody laughed.

We children attended St. Ann's Academy next to the big Cathedral downtown. This was to keep my scalp clean, owing to the melting pot of humanity that went to the school near home.

"This one," mother said to new friends, indicating me, "Is a catcher. Let there be an itch between here and Burrard

Inlet and she'll have it." So the 'Catcher' and her small brother went by streetcar downtown to school. Dan was barely five years old and suffered prolonged attacks of homesickness, which could only be eased by sitting on Sister Mary Adelina's desk platform and playing with milk bottle caps. Sister had her class collect milk caps which she traded back to the Fraser Valley Dairies for premiums. She raffled the premiums and thereby became the avant garde of all organized church fund-raising organizations in the west. She had a big organization. It took in the whole school.

She was a large woman, middle-aged, French Canadian, with dark complexion, dark eyes and flashing white teeth. "Now class," she said one day, "My friends at the dairy are offering us a new way to thank our Lord for His many blessings. I want you to keep up with the milk caps. Don't let mother throw out a single milk cap — anyone can wash a milk cap — but on Monday we're starting something new. BUTTER WRAPPERS! Isn't that wonderful? Tell mother we want every single butter wrapper she has.

The shed in the playground out back of 406 Dunsmuir that spring bulged with butter papers, milk caps and used newspapers. Cigarette and tea packages were ripped open with abandon for the silver paper foil they yielded. "Flat," said Sister emphatically, "But if you do have silver paper in a roll we will not refuse it. Sister paid off in Holy cards or better. Sepia ones for fifty milk caps, full color for fifty butter wrappers, and a miraculous medal for a pound of silver paper — flat! Sister Mary Junk, as we called her, was persona grata with our friend, Mr. Feldstein. He called on Saturdays at the Convent playground, parked his horse and wagon at the east door of the Cathedral, lowered the big iron weight which kept his horse standing still, walked across the lane, and spent a mutually profitable half hour with Sister in the little grey shed under the huge Maple trees which encircled the playground.

"I am a poor man. Four dollors I get only for one ton of newspapers. I should haul them maybe for nothing? Three dollors, my final price . . ."

"Three fifty, Mr. Feldstein," said Sister evenly. "You should see the dozens of poor old men that come to the kitchen door at mealtimes . . ."

"Sister, you are looking now at such a man."

"Come with me, Mr. Feldstein and see how worn the Chapel floor is."

"Ha. Always the Chapel. Okey. For the Chapel floor, my last word. Three dollors . . ."

Between Mr. Felstein and Sister Mary Adelina, St. Ann's on Dunsmuir Street had the most beautiful Convent Chapel in British Columbia.

The early days of Bernarr Macfadden were hard on us, too.

"Children, get up here!" said mother at the porch door one morning. She stood over us bundled in an overcoat of Father's. The rain was sheeting off the verandah roof, and the wind soughed damply around the corners of the little brown shingled house. "Quick, here are your slippers. Into the house before you catch your death!"

What were we doing out there in the first place? We were sleeping outdoors because it would make a man and a woman out of us. It was pretty hard to see Dan as that figure in the ads with the tight underpants and the bulging calves and forearms, but there it was.

"Your dad didn't come home last night and I'm worried sick," said mother one day. On a morning paper, an editor went to work about two in the afternoon and returned when the paper hit the street about the same hour in the early morning. "They said he went to the club about midnight and didn't come back. I hope he isn't sick somewhere."

We had been through this before. After mother worried about him 'being sick somewhere', father usually turned up full of conversation and jokes, with his eyes very bright and his hat on just the tiniest bit crooked.

"I think I'll call the Terminal City and just see," said mother. "Life the porridge and button up Danny." She was quite a long time at the phone. Was Mr. Murray there? He was, one moment. please. And there they were talking.

Mother said 'yes' six times. Then she asked, "How far is it. Six or seven miles you think?" Long pause. "All I can say is your back is stronger than your head." Bang went the receiver.

"Well," she turned to the breakfast table in somewhat cheerier voice, "I guess I shouldn't have scared you youngsters like that. Your father is alright. He just walked home for supper with Mr. Cromie last night to get an appetite. A little stroll of fifty two blocks. He went to the club for a snack at ten, and laid down for a few minutes. He's had ten hours sleep, so he's just dandy, I'm the one that's tuckered out."

My parents were young and gay in the twenties, and life was very exciting. The big CPR hotel, the Vancouver, was the centre of the social and cultural life of the city. We sometimes had family dinner at the wonderful place, but otherwise it seemed to be a sort of step-out from my father's regular office. If you couldn't find anybody, you always tried "the Hotel." Celebrities, statesmen, heads of government, balls, banquets, conventions — all were found at the Vancouver Hotel. On the other hand, my father frequently dug his reporters out of the Spanish Grill following their evening lunch break. For they too were gay, and not much younger than he. And like him, they did their best to be loyal to the current health authority being featured by their newspaper. But instead of walking seven miles for their supper, they chose to dance their way through it.

We children attended Highland games at Brockton Point, and patted the tiger skin on the police pipe band drum major at exhibition time. We saw Madame Pavlova round herself into a ball and roll across a stage and watched the veins stand out on the temple of Mr. Paderewski as he thrashed furiously across the piano keyboard. We looked hard for the wire that held the fairy up in Peter Pan and never saw it, and I got hysterics in "Uncle Tom's Cabin" and had to be taken home after the lashing scene.

We attended parades and Liberal picnics and were taken to the arena to hear our dad make speeches about Sir Wilfrid Laurier and William Lyon Mackenzie King. We heard the same speeches shortened down for McMahon Park in North Vancouver on July the First, and waved our fried chicken drum sticks in the air for the sheer joy of being first a Canadian and second a Liberal Canadian.

Although our housing arrangements were always modest enough, owing to our homestead retreat on Burrard Inlet, we had trips to Victoria to see the Legislative Chamber from the visitors' gallery.

On one such trip I was taken by my father to the studio of Mr. Victor Long, a fine portrait artist. Upstairs in his room on Fort Street, he was working on a huge canvas of a man with a beard. Who was the man? He was the late Premier of British Columbia, my dad said, 'Honest John Oliver. Mr. Long had been commissioned to do a posthumous portrait of the great Premier, and if I would just sit down and be quiet . . .

"Look, Victor," said my father, "The hands are not right. He had enormous hands, the hands of a ploughman," and he drew a sheaf of copy paper from his suit coat pocket and proceeded to sketch a hand on a knee, large and square and rugged. "Now the jaw. Under that herbiage, it was this way . . ."

Every time he went to Victoria, my father visited the Long studio to watch the progress of the portrait which would one day hang in the Legislative Buildings. Finally the great day came. Mrs. Oliver and her daughter were invited to tea with the artist to view the finished work.

"Victor's reward, and mine, for the small part I played in helping him with the portrait, was that afternoon," dad reported. "Ah, the dear man," said Mrs. Oliver, with a catch in her voice. "He looks as if he might speak . . ."

"And that's how for forty years, the Murray household has been under the watchful eye of old Aunt Tean, a beautiful oval portrait of my father's favourite aunt, done for him as a token of thanks from Victor Long.

A Hard Day's Journey

It was in 1921 that Dad and the *Sun* promoted the International Peace Arch at Blaine on the United States — British Columbia border. The school children of the province — and of the State of Washington — each gave ten cents to have their names engraved on the scroll which was sealed within the monument. The whole thing was planned from the big double bed in our parents' bedroom, where Dad read his own morning paper, the Seattle and Portland papers too, and made phone calls into the long-necked instrument beside the bed, with the receiver hanging on the side. His office day didn't start until afternoon.

My brother and I heard all the long distance calls to Seattle with Mr. Hill, the son of the famed railroad magnate, James J., who had a great deal to do with the Peace Arch undertaking. We heard the arguments of Italian marble versus B.C. granite, and saw the plans a good year before the monument was finished. But our names weren't in the capsule. The day the collection was taken up at St. Ann's, we were home with the effects of a ghastly business called smallpox vaccination. We had arms like footballs with little red crosses pinned on them.

Those were the days when the World Series results came in by telegraph wire and telephone, and news-hungry citizens who couldn't wait for their papers went down on Pender Street and blocked traffic on the wide bricked thoroughfares, as they watched the hand printed bulletins go up on the front windows of the *Sun's* offices.

Two young priests at the church we attended were mad about baseball. They were from Chicago, and often dropped over to our house to have lunch with my father.

"If you boys want to come down to the office," said dad one day, "And listen to the squawk box we have down there, you're welcome. If you can glue your ear right up to it, they say it's pretty good — if the weather is right. They have this man right out on the field, describing each play. Our sports writers listen but we get so much wire copy on the world series that we don't rely on the squawk box. A novelty, you might say." Dad was describing the *Sun's* first radio receiving set.

Old Joe Fortes died that year. Joe was a coloured lifeguard at English Bay, who rowed around in his boat, close to the shore, and watched children as they swam. When he passed on to his reward, word came in from the undertaker's and set my father thinking. And the more he thought, the brighter his eyes got.

"Margaret," he finally called to mother, "What would

you think of a civic funeral for old Joe?" Mother came into the bedroom with a dust mop in her hand, and worked away at the dark shiny floor.

"I'd say if anybody deserved a civic funeral, it would be old Joe," she said.

"Who's that fellow with the big voice down at the Cathedral?"

"You mean old Joe was a Catholic?"

"That's what the funeral director said. Hand me the phone book." It was such a good idea that it woke my father up immediately.

Several hours and phone calls later — to Joe Morris, the tobacco man who was also a big Elk, ('Jeez, George, who's dead?'), to Mr. Jordan who sang at the Cathedral on Sundays but was a printer on other days, to the rectory of Holy Rosary and Father O'Boyle, to the Parks Board for free flowers, to the mayor of the city for his co-operation — the civic funeral was on it's way.

A packed Cathedral, uniformed Elks, the City Council, a couple of bands that played "Old Black Joe", "Old Folks at Home" and a half dozen negro spirituals — all these were on hand at the appointed hour to usher the old life-guard to his last resting place. The crowning touch, of course, was the old rowboat, hoisted on a gun carriage, and filled to the brim with beautiful flowers. Vancouver never saw such a funeral and there wasn't a dry eye on Hastings as Old Black Joe wheeled slowly down the street.

The tall young man in tweeds who stood outside Billy Dicks clothing store on Hastings street had his little girl, me, with him. They were just two in a crowd. As the cortege passed, he squeezed her hand and said; "Georgie, wouldn't Old Joe just love this if he saw it?"

"Well he was a wonderful man and people loved him. And I wanted a story on him but we couldn't talk to him anymore and in order to get the story I had to create it. I had to make something to write about." He was so pleased with it all. "Come on," he said, "We'll go over to the chocolate shop for an ice cream soda."

The *Sun* was going through a hectic period of making ends meet. Wages were low because income was low. The publisher, who had acquired the newspaper because he was the clever accountant of a firm that wanted to subsidize a Liberal newspaper, gained control when party and newspaper were at low ebb. He then turned up at the newspaper office and took charge, dismissing the editor and, under the guise of being an independent party man, menaced the party at every turn. Running the only so-called Liberal newspaper in the community, he exercised great power. At every election campaign he exacted high tribute from the party funds, and lashed leaders, provincial and national, with such relentless fury that fund collectors were kept busy buying him off — and for twenty years only a handful of Liberals were elected to Ottawa.

But R.J. Cromie, to whom the end justified the means, got the *Sun* on its feet. And politicians, who had the year before violated "the code" by exacting tribute from Cromie's railway firm with one hand while abusing it with the other, knew with whom they dealt. He played hard with his enemies.

George Murray was its first managing editor, as the *Sun* merged from this hurdy-gurdy era to pause and assess its potential and future. The machinery was paid for, but the reporters were a poorly paid, inept lot. The business manager was a clever man with figures but had little use for the editorial side of the business, and less money to spend on wages for that department.

This offended George's fine reportorial sense. He had the ability — and relished the flair in others — for making the most of a story, using lots of colour so that it was not merely a record of events. But you paid for that sort of ability. You didn't find it wandering in the door broke and slap-happy. Editing the *Sun* in those days was a continual battle.

Two small boys went into Spencer's Department Store one day and carried away a five hundred dollar fur coat. They simply took it off the rack and proceeded to carry it out of the store. The *Sun* carried eight lines on this item, picking it up through police files. When asked by the police why they had stolen the coat, the item said that the boys replied that their Mama was always cold and she never had had a fur coat.

"Mr. Cromie," said Murray, "how can a reporter turn in a story like that, and how can a news editor handle it and not realize the wonderful material there. Why, this isn't the story. The story is the family. The mother that's cold. The little boys who love her and want her to have a fur coat!"

"Hire somebody then, goddamit," said Mr. Cromie.

"What wage can I offer him? I have a man in Ottawa in mind. A good, live, sound newsman who handles the desk at the *Journal*."

"Get him and we'll pay him. Tell Salter that I said the cashier was to wire him his ticket."

"My gosh, Jimmie, I'm glad to see you," said Murray a few days later. As their bare hands clasped in greeting, big furious rain drops splashed down to wet them. The place was the Vancouver waterfront down near the ferry slips. Jim Larkin had arrived from Ottawa the night before, a Saturday, and was up bright and early to nose around the waterfront and see what he could pick up on the Britannia disaster — a burst water tank had taken out the townsite of the big copper mine on Howe Sound and killed twenty-two.

"When they told me you were not in the office, I figured you might be somewhere in this vicinity," grinned Larkin.

"They're just now going to let me have the use of a harbour board craft. This story I'm doing myself. You get up there to the office, tell Cromie who you are, hang up your hat — and go to work. There's a woman telephone operator up here at Britannia who's the heroine of the hour. She has remained with her board all the way through by hanging on to a log, they tell me. I don't know how I'll get the stuff through to you. But I will somehow. It's great to know you'll be at the other end."

"You can count on me."

"And if they wonder where I am, tell them I'm out getting subscriptions."

Larkin, the slim young Ottawa Irishman, who ten years before had been Murray's boss, now went to work in the *Sun's* news slot, and little by little new men were hired and trained and polished and the paper grew in stature. It grew in wealth too, and not always according to the rule book. Once when the bank account was precariously low, the *Sun* simply went to work and printed a voter's list for the Oliver Government covering the entire province, ten cents a name, cash on delivery. No one ordered the list to be printed but if you don't like it you know what we can do to you.

Or Mr. Cromie put on his hat and went up the street to Spencer's, a department store in the city, then making a bid for the working man's dollar. He laid it right on the line. "I want the money for this month's advertising NOW — or no newspaper." Spencer's needed the *Sun* to Woodward's and Hudson's Bay, as much as the *Sun* needed Spencer's account. A cheque was made out, the overdraft lifted, and the payroll was out on time.

But such violent machinations on the part of the Publisher hardly made for a serene crew. A reporter never knew when he might be embraced or shown the door. And the society writers had an even worse time.

Doctors Coué, McCoy, Dorchester and Jackson may have annoyed the medical profession but the Vancouver doctors kept their own council and put up with the large advertisements which dwelt on the joys of orange juice, breakfast food, seaweed and etc. But when Painless Parker got his outdoor girlie show on the road, accompanied by large ads testifying to his painless dentistry, the Medical Association rebelled and took formal exception to the testimonials of this fakir.

For my father, the last straw was added about now by Crepo, a physical culture expert from Seattle who was talked by Cromie and his advertising manager into a full page advertisement which was to serve a dual purpose. It would advertise Crepo's method of manipulation and massage which was guaranteed to turn a man into a lion. And it would at the same time draw attention to a big hockey game with Seattle which was scheduled to be held the same night at the Vancouver Arena. The advertising manager, one of the hockey greats of a decade before, had sold the publicity to his old colleagues, the Patrick boys, who later established the New York Rangers, completely overlooked the effect Crepo might have on a large block of their ticket holders. Vancouver's medical and dental professions contributed great support to sport in the twenties, and filled a section of the arena with wives, brothers, sisters, nurses, technicians and friends in the pharmaceutical firms.

Crepo was admitted to the dressing rooms the afternoon

of the game, and with unguents and lotions, sweat baths, ice packs and his own two bare hands, he worked over the Vancouver team. The unfortunate part of the thing was, that after a series of defeats, the team skated out on the ice, fresh from Crepo's hands to display some of the fastest skating and fanciest stick work ever seen in the Vancouver arena. They won a smashing victory. But the Doctors and their friends never, as a group, darkened the doors of the great arena again.

Back in the little brown house on Templeton Drive the morning after the game, I drew pictures on the vapoured window pane against the rain drops and listened while my father talked into the telephone beside the big bed to Mr. Patrick.

"Repeat that, Frank . . . I don't follow you. Am I your friend? Well now, Frank, we've known each other for ten years, boy — why would I not be your friend? Crepo? Yes. I know about the advertisement but I couldn't stop it. It's a matter of revenue, Frank you understand, coin of the realm. That's too bad. Surely we can do something . . ." Dispiritedly he hung up the phone.

"Well there is nothing I can do, Margaret," said my father later that morning. "Nothing. Except leave the *Sun.* How would you like to have a little trip to Ontario? Some of Granma's good cooking might brighten up the little lady-bird over there drawing pictures. What do you say. Call up the CPR ticket office!"

When we returned from Ontario in the spring, we children had added to our knowledge the geography and economy of the five provinces we covered, as well as Treasure Island going and The Five Little Peppers coming back. Father had added a trade journal to the family assets, "The Western Lumberman", a Hugh C. McLean publication in which he shared a partnership with Stewart M. Read of Vancouver.

Roaring with Dynamite

During these years the homestead had taken on a new look. Friends came for weekends, occasionally bringing with them some of the first cars the neighbours on the hill had ever seen. They backed up the dreadful rocky slide so that the gas could run down and reach the engine and keep it turning over. There was a Miss Heinz, from Chicago, who drove a Stutz and may even have been one of the fifty-seven varieties, and the nobleman, Sir F. St. John Milmay. Milmay used to write a little for *Farm and Home* to keep in groceries. He once forgot his teeth on a rock during an assignment and by the time he found them in a cow pad, he and his wife were our firm friends and regular visitors. One day they arrived in a limousine complete with speaking tube and liveried chauffeur. The chauffeur was in such poor shape, having negotiated as terrifying a twenty-mile stretch of road as you'd find around Vancouver in the twenties, that he had to be allowed to lie down to gain strength for the railway ties that had to be negotiated on the return trip. A reasonable road around the head of the Inlet was still years away.

Invariably a group of my parents' newspapering friends were aboard as we travelled up Burrard Inlet in those early days. The little harbour craft took on more of a picnic atmosphere than ever, and good humour and hearty laughter issued from every hatch and porthole. Mostly they sat forward of the fo'c's'le on fine days while Dan and I climbed the sacks of chop-and-chicken feed, steered the boat behind a wagon wheel or played hide-and-seek inside the coils of steel stump-puller cable bound for an up-inlet rancher.

Mother and the dog Patsy — all our dogs were called Patsy — sat still out in the open air. This was because of the tendency of both ladies to sea sickness. Above, in the wheel house, Captain Brewster's peaked cap was visible as he peered over the choppy waters.

This was the end — or near it — of an era in which a newspaper was rated by the excellence of its home-created journalism. Vancouver, for its size, embraced a wonderfully brilliant, if erratic, colony of writers, artists, poets, and scholars, and many of them were our friends.

During these weekends, the little brown Sunnyside schoolhouse opposite our land was the social centre of the community. The desks were moved along the walls of the schoolroom and made handy shelves on which to lay sleepy children.

It's amazing how customs change in forty years. No one on the hill ever heard of a baby sitter, and to my knowledge there was never a bottle of liquor on the premises. But the Saturday night socials were the highlight of the week. About eight o'clock, the district would be alive with flickering lights, converging on the schoolhouse. These lights came from "bugs," home-made lanterns which were cheap, simple, and efficient. But I haven't seen one for thirty years. A "bug" is a jam tin or lard pail with a hole poked in the side of it, through which a candle is inserted. The handle, of some wire, is looped the long way for carrying, so that the candle remains upright. In the bottom of the can, the owner punches his initials with a nail, and through these nail holes comes sufficient light to show the way to children who drag behind.

The Farmers' Institute ran the Saturday night socials. In the twenties, this organization was the PTA, the Board of Trade, and the Elks, Owls, and Eagles, all rolled into one. It was the only burr a small community had to insert under the tail of a recalcitrant Public Works Department, and it provided many a benefit to the man struggling to improve his homestead. The Institute enjoyed many an old knock-down-and-drag-out, but members managed to lay aside their arguments for a few brief hours at least once a week.

Talcum powder would be generously sprinkled on the floor, and Laura Johnson would bang out postwar hits. Everybody danced and, taken as a group, they were pretty bad dancers. The salmon sandwiches took an awful beating usually, and extra coffee was made over on our big black stove and carried across to the school on the uneven foot path in a water pail. Even the cake with the lard icing was eaten completely.

On alternate weekends, when there would be just family and heavy land clearing was indicated, a box of stumping powder would be put gingerly ashore with the groceries on the old Sunnyside Wharf. At these times, my father occasionally hired a pipe major he knew to accompany us. "Just walk up and down, Donald, and give us anything you can think of. A man needs some cheer in his heart when he's battling these stumps." And wee Donald would step off, hair blowing and Seventy-second Highlander ribbons flying from his pipes, and the echo coming back from the mountains would make you swear a second piper was just emerging through the glen.

No doubt that we brightened the landscape, but the Murrays were regarded with suspicion by the hill folk. My dreamy young father they considered a crackpot. Besides, he did his dreaming out loud.

"We'll sow this field to alfalfa," he'd say to anybody who would listen. To the neighbours this could mean only a waste of good land. Kale, rutabagas, turnips, potatoes — maybe. But what good was an acre of alfalfa? Alfalfa, however, it was, just to see how it would yield, and the four of us ended up weeding it by hand.

"We'll shove a tennis court out here," he'd say, and wave his hand toward Old Baldie, the mountain. Neighbours listening to this kind of talk, particularly those apt to lay up for a rest after merely walking around one of the stumps, were bound to report that the daft Murrays were off again. But several hundred sticks of dynamite and a few years later we got the tennis court.

We also got a water line. It came from Ikey Porter's creek, right under old Baldie's eye, and was a gravity deal running about three-quarters of a mile. Every once in a while someone would have to go up and take a trout out of the intake pipe, or wrap the various leaks in old underwear and tar, but we had a water line which proved a blessing, for in spite of a small fortune spent on water diviners, and other assorted experts, we never brought in a well on the entire property.

Another thing that Father "shoved out here" was a north wing to the house. Ours was probably the first split level on the Coast. It was a very ambitious addition, and for years the stairs were finished only to just above eye level, where the cull shiplap took over. The unfinished upstairs didn't bother anyone. We just called it our Abraham Lincoln Room. If the wind whistled the candle out or the guests crashed one leg through the ceiling (as one once did), it was all part of the weekend.

The kitchen of the new wing had seven doors in it. No two were alike. One was formerly Room 409 in the old Vancouver Hotel, another was off the writing room at Glencoe Lodge, and so on. Or take windows. Dad would be resting while the new wing was emerging. Suddenly from his chair, he'd spot between the open joists a particularly rewarding view. "We'll have a window right here," he'd tell the carpenter. And "right here" it is today, a solid sheet of plate.

Or driving around Vancouver, he'd spot an old mansion being dismantled, one perhaps in which he had been a visitor, or a house which had been built by some great idol of his when he was a young reporter. He'd stop the car and go over and bargain with the wrecking foreman, and if possible load up the stained glass, the leaded door, or the fancy newel post right on the spot. A trip through the new wing was like a trip through history, built with bargains in colourful wreckage, each bit a conversation piece. It didn't matter that the cellar steps constituted a death trap that would do credit to a terror novel, or that anyone not tall for twelve years of age couldn't open the library-cum-bedroom door. All the bits had a story and represented the lives and times of people worth remembering.

When Mother joined the Murray family, she was so impressed by them that she spent the first half of her life doing what she thought they wanted her to do. Cheerfully and gladly, she entered into the land-clearing, the shake-splitting, the berry-picking, and, later, the weekend house-building.

As soon as the children were old enough to go to school, she plunged back into publishing and for eight years brought out *Country Life in B.C.* with an office in downtown Vancouver, near her husband's. She threw her energy into bee-keeping, potato-growing, fruit-raising, poultry-marketing, Women's Institutes, and all the other things *Country Life* was interested in as a magazine. Our dinner table echoed with talk of aphids, "bott weevil," rust, erysipelas, Oatha Scott, and contagious abortion — all in exactly the tone most mothers would use to talk about their housework or their bridge. Some nights we got off agriculture and talked lumbering, for Dad was publishing *Western Lumberman* at the same time.

Any trouble Mother had with dangling participles and split infinitives was, at that time, never revealed to the public eye. Her husband's editorial pencil was sure and fast, and he did half the writing anyway. Expeditions by motor car gathering copy for these two magazines were also joint affairs. A third party, however, would usually be invited along to keep the children from annihilating each other in the back seat. The safari started off from New Westminster over the old Fraser bridge. You hit the Pacific Highway, a narrow, solid concrete ribbon, at a giddy twenty-five miles an hour.

The anticipation of the border encounter at Blaine kept the back seat quiet for the next fifty miles or so, and then adding up license numbers would be good for another fifty. At that point boredom set in.

"This half of the seat is mine," Dan would suddenly announce. And that was all that was needed for a plunging, shrieking free-for-all in which hats flew out the open side, the dog got her chain caught under the foot rest, and the car had to be pulled over to the side of the road and justice meted out to one and all.

The endless mills we visited, waiting while Father promoted a product or sold an ad. The dingy hotel lobbies with coal oil lamps burning on night desks and lighting lists of "rooms open, settle in the morning". The trips back in the rain when the car curtains would be safely stowed at home in the garage, and the lap robe soggy and your feet cold and damp!

We attended all the swine growers' picnics, the Jersey breeders' luncheons, and the bee-keepers' conventions ever held in the Fraser Valley in those years. I became so agricultural and wholesome that they gave up taking me along. The decision followed an encounter in the show ring at a Jersey breeders' field day. A breeder-member of the old school pointed his cane at me as if I were set up right in the pin bones and suggested to my father that he had a nineteen-year-old son, and how about it?

Although rustling printers' bills and keeping up a running battle with the reclaiming forest at Ioco kept the Murrays constantly on the prod, George saw to it that he made time to keep his hand in on the affairs of British Columbia. "Your father," Margaret used to say to the children, "has just put politics on his long finger. He's just vergin' on the verge." But our father took on a new dimension for us at this point. We heard him on the radio.

This was the crystal-set era, in which earphones were connected to a radiator and the purring you heard behind the squawks was the Philadelphia Philharmonic. True, Vancouver's first radio station soon followed, but few people had radios. They were big oblong boxes on stands. The first one I recall belonged to neighbours, a deForest Crossley, a gleaming mahogany box of magic in a room of dark over-stuffed furniture and lampshades of pleated orchid chiffon with tassles and beads. These people were Imperial plant employees, most of whom had everything first. In such a living room we three gathered one weekend to hear Father speak on the radio.

He had driven down to Seattle to address a Lumberman's convention and his speech was to be broadcast. The children knew all about their father's prowess on the platform. We had been fed lower freight rates, bigger grain elevators and more railway extension with our porridge and orange juice.

The announcer came on with the station break, then introduced the guest speaker from Vancouver. And there was Father, talking to us as clearly as — well, Mother burst into tears. The children jumped up and down in their delight, jiggling the machine and losing the station, and the host and hostess agreed that the wonder of it all was almost too much to bear. George talked that night about the need for a highway to Alaska. "The darling man," said Margaret to the children, later, "has only one fault. He was born thirty years too soon."

Whereas television had radio to draw on for early programming, radio had nothing to draw on. Stations would come on in the afternoon and keep going as long as they had time sold and material to broadcast. Down at CNRV they scraped bottom every so often. Once George Wright, the first manager, asked Mother to talk on Women's Institutes. Her dangling participles didn't show in a speech and Wright had heard her talk somewhere. I was taken along because it was an educational experience to see a broadcast studio.

Although she has reduced strong men to tears of laughter with speeches she has delivered since that time, her first radio appearance was another story. She never got off the launching pad but stood frozen to the spot after the "Good evening, ladies and gentlemen" as the peculiar quiet of an early radio broadcast room came crashing in on her. The place seemed full of cotton wool, and indeed the walls and ceilings were padded with quilted material, hung with heavy velvet drapes, and carpeted wall to wall. They looked like drawing room sets from the early movies. The only furniture was a grand piano and a couple of metal music stands, left behind by Calvin Winter's band. And Mother froze.

She opened her mouth, but nothing came out. The engineer looked pained but patient. Fifteen seconds . . . thirty seconds . . . forty-five seconds . . . eternity.

Finally she recovered her voice, and her presence of mind. There was the piano keyboard staring her in the face, and me dangling my legs over the bench.

"I think I'll have my little girl play something for you," she said weakly.

I played. But I'll spare you a description of that.

Dad stayed young and handsome long after Mother began to show the wear and tear of some of the family projects. But the time was not far off when he would plunge into politics, and then she would be the one to stay youthful for a while.

A Kansas Education

Margaret Murray said that for most people the crash came in 1929, but for her family it arrived in 1928. That year they lost both magazines, *Country Life,* which had beautiful covers and slick paper and tried to provide British Columbia with a first-class magazine about what went on beyond the Vancouver city limits, had to be given up. The fledgling agricultural industry at which it aimed could not back up the magazine's rich editorial diet with the essential advertising support. *Western Lumberman,* on the other hand, booming along on the economy of the era, was doing so extremely well that the Hugh C. McLean interests sold it.

"I wasn't sold out by the sheriff this time," says Margaret grimly, "but I was certainly advised to close up. On top of everything, we almost lost your father that summer managing Heath's election campaign away up in the Mackenzie riding."

Heath was the candidate who managed to get "indecent," "indignant," and "indigent" all mixed up while discussing widows' pensions at a public meeting, aging poor Father ten years. It was a bad night altogether. Coming back through Dean Channel in an open boat — donated by a political worker at $50.00 a day — most of the Liberal leaders nearly drowned.

"And here we were in Vancouver without any money, with a lot of big ideas and a lot of big debts to go with them. I was thrashing my one-cylinder wondering where we'd move to from the fancy apartment, trying to collect old accounts I knew we'd never get, and thinking about how we were going to educate you two youngsters and just eat," says Margaret.

Father was never a man to let a few debts discourage him. When the election was over, he came back to Vancouver and sat down in an empty office and put his eight years experience in agriculture and lumbering into neat rows of statistics. The day he handed the office keys into the management, he took the last ten-dollar bill in Mother's purse to buy lunch for H.R. MacMillan. MacMillan was in the papers that week regarding a subsidy he had received from the Dominion Government to build up trade with Japan. He was then just creating his great empire. His ships were going out with lumber, but coming back with things like lily bulbs and hot-water bottles. Why not British Columbia meat in those ships, frozen poultry, Pacific milk and thoroughbred breeding stock? Dad asked. Why not indeed?

If the Port of Vancouver was to fulfill its destiny, Father was convinced B.C. would have to look for its own markets, or it would remain a one-elevator grain depot for the next fifty years. Forget the mountain differential, the freight rates — B.C.'s market lay across the Pacific!

The far-seeing Mr. MacMillan concurred, and Father was on his way to the Orient to write trade articles and do some persuading on the side. The small matter of eating and providing the necessities for us children Mother solved by extending a feature of her now-defunct magazine. She clapped the two of us into boarding school and took off around the province to demonstrate the making of comforters and the hooking of rugs to farm women. She bought a lot of hooks and canvas and wool and bats, and then proceeded to make the finished product for which she hoped she had customers all lined up. When she didn't, she sold some to her well-off relatives, who certainly received some weird creations, and have never forgiven her to this day. But Mother could justify it all in a sort of Robin Hood philosophy she had in those days about the "haves" and the "have-nots."

By Christmas, she had a few "shekels," as she called them, gathered together, and she got Dan out of an isolation ward at St. Ann's, Duncan, where he was languishing with smallpox. I continued at St. Ann's in New Westminster.

She then proceeded to deal with the Depression.

"George was away four months, and I kept the pot boiling until his articles started to roll," she says. She did it by laying hold of a cow, a sow, some baby chicks, and a hired man — in that order. She grew a garden, cultivated kale and turnips for the swine, got a separator and fed them skim and buttermilk. Meanwhile Dad's articles were running in all the Southam papers — forty of them — and when he came back he kept them coming from the Peace River country, making a complete survey of the trade potential down the Peace as far as Fort Vermillion.

He had returned from Asia excited and imbued with the idea that China was a wonderful country, and our real market. He met Chiang Kai-Shek at the first China Trade Fair in Shanghai. He was loaded with gifts and tentative orders. But it was on the very eve of 1930, and too late. He was lucky shortly to have just a job.

Depression was just a word to me until my father came to call on me at the convent one day, lugging a dressed pig over his shoulder to pay my board bill.

"We haven't the cash, and they have to eat," said Mother firmly, as the decision to take the meat was being made. St. Ann's wasn't Sacred Heart, but my pride hit a new low that day. It was the vulgarity of the thing — a pig. And over his shoulder!

"Which way is the kitchen, Sister?" asked my father in that big boomy voice that brought all the music boarders peeking out of their practice rooms. I almost died of mortification.

We lived out the worst of the Depression at the homestead. A road of sorts now connected the hill behind Ioco with Vancouver, twenty miles away. It was narrow, winding, and rough, and in foggy weather my father could be all night getting home through soup along the Inlet, so thick that you required a passenger with you to get out and lead the car on foot. My father's day started at 6:30 A.M. and was twelve hours long. He worked for Southam's, on the evening daily, the *Province*. Mother's day started at the same time, but if the day had embraced thirty-six hours it might have been about right for her many activities. Father laid on the projects over the week-end.

I came home from boarding school in June because Father's salary, cut in half, just wouldn't cover tuition. To make up for not being able to return another year to my beloved school, I was to be allowed to drive the car. I got my first licence that summer at age thirteen.

"Officer," said Mother to the clerk in the New Westminster police office, "I want this child to have a licence to drive. She's fifteen and I'll sign for it." She justified this barefaced lie because she had the car all worked into her plan for beating the hard times.

"Which is your right and which is your left?" asked the officer of me, in a deadpan sort of voice. Sick with nervousness, I gave him the wrong answer.

"Well," he said, "it's one or the other, isn't it?" and wrote out the licence. Things were so uncomplicated in 1930.

"Now," said Mother when we got down on Columbia Avenue, "Drive!"

The car was a monstrous-sized Willys Knight touring with jump seats in the back. It had driven President Warren G. Harding around Vancouver on the historic occasion of the visit of the American president to Canada, and it had class. It was a *cafe-au-lait* colour and had a black top and black wheels with large wooden spokes. The hood came down in summer and folded neatly, and in winter there were black curtains, held in place by rods, and it was altogether splendid because it had a sleeve-valve motor, whatever that was. On the other hand, it was half a block long, hard to steer, so heavy that you had to double clutch it on steep hills, and the very devil itself to park.

Were the weanling pigs to be taken to market?

They were gathered into the back seat of the Willys Knight, all eight horrid, squealing, snuffling, smelly little pink things and chauffeured there by me, with Mother coming along to see that the mission was accomplished.

Was the heifer due?

By all means, said Mother, just shove in the jump seats, take out the cushions, and there you were. Blossom, being a maiden cow, and a neat little Jersey, could be stowed in sideways so that her head hung out one side and her tail out the other. This arrangement wasn't too comfortable for Blossom. For me it was a disaster. Her stern end was right behind the driver's head. Heruerves. The green grass she'd been on. The tail thrashing in the stiff breeze, and the twelve-mile journey to the Hindu's pure-bred sire all combined to make the memory live.

Turkeys? You bet.

And not just ordinary ones, but White Hollands, bred for the host who enjoyed carving the choice white meat. These turkeys had breast works like Fort Knox, but any further allusion to strength stopped there. They were the sickliest, most colicky and delicate bunch of necks and legs you ever saw. Just let the wind change direction for an hour, and the entire family and any available neighbour was called upon to fetch the turkeys because wet feet were murder. Messes of hard-cooked eggs, buttermilk, and chop were doled out three times a day, along with castor oil for any bird that looked peaked. They snapped legs and broke wings right and left. Basket cases were given names, and the end came when Louis Phillippe, teetering on an old antique tin bathtub full of liquid manure, fell — in the only way a turkey would be likely to fall — in. Plop went the bread dough Mother was into, bang went the screen door and across the garden she streaked. Louis was going down the last time, when a firm right doughy hand jerked his great ugly purple neck from its aromatic grave. He was dunked in a sack, hustled to the oven door, probed, squilled and dosed. But he died anyway. Out of fifty eggs, three turkeys made it to the Christmas table.

Goats proved unsatisfactory as soon as they got big enough to reach the ankles on Father's Stanfield underwear on the clothesline. While small, however, they were great little beasts of burden in diminutive harness, hauling small boys' red wagons. By far the least destructible of the farm creatures were geese. Those were the result of the co-habiting of a goose and gander which we called John and Mrs. Oliver, after the current premier of B.C. Mrs. was a tough old girl who produced so many children that she lost her egg bag and it dragged behind her all one summer until Mother performed an operation and removed it. John the gander was keeper of the guard on our acres, only he got a little mixed up on who he was guarding. He attacked everybody.

"You hear me, Danny, now?" Mother would warn. "Watch you don't come outside the toilet with your panties down! If you can't do them up, hold your overalls up. You can never tell about geese."

The only dull times on the hill were when the kids were tethered to the cow on a fifty-foot chain, especially if the oily, salty inlet smells wafted up on the breeze. After Blossom's first calf, she put on weight and assumed more matronly proportions. No longer, thank God, could she fit into the back seat of the Willys. When she required to be bred, she walked to the Hindu's. The journey took three days and Dan was our boy.

It was quite a rustic sight, watching them take off.

Blossom, true to her breed, had an enormous bag which swung giddily as she walked. Hip and alternate shoulder lurched with their alternate members, her head swinging back and forth keeping time with her tail, the cowbell tankling (ours never tinkled) and Dan padding along beside her, raising little poufs of heavy dust with his soft shoes, his overall legs flapping and his lunch in a paper sack. If Blossom knew she was off to keep any romantic engagement, she was certainly bored with the whole deal. And Dan fitted her mood perfectly. The journey was accomplished by parking Blossom overnight at various small farms on the way, and driving the reluctant herdsman home at night, and back to the job in the morning.

All that the early thirties did to the Murray youngsters was to make us fat, suspect Conservatives, and give us a good Kansas education on twenty acres of British Columbia stump land. Chickens were caught, killed, plucked, and cleaned before unexpected company had settled in the living room. A good hot-biscuit cook is never stuck, Mother would whisper, giving Dan the eye for some fast kindling, and at the same time browning the flour that went into a milk gravy that turned fried chicken into a connoisseur's meal. The geese yielded filling for pillows and cushions. Those Saturdays on which I didn't manage to break the thermometer into the churn, through drowsiness induced by the bee-loud hum in the clearing around us, we had fresh butter, buttermilk and cottage cheese. We butchered pork, rendered the lard, fried down the sausage, and made head cheese. Washing was accomplished with tubs and board and copper boiler and a roaring fire in the old black kitchen range, later spreading tea towels on the grass, rags on the fence, "rench" water on the roses, and wash water on the back porch for its weekly scrub-down.

Thirty people for Sunday night supper was routine, and the back seats of the visiting cars had little remembrances tucked into them like cabbages, carrots, lettuce, flower bouquets or a bottle of cream. At these rustic Sunday "salons" of my parents, all professions, religions, and politics were represented. It was nothing to have a revival meeting carrying on around the big square grand at one end of the living room, a political argument going on in the other, and a car deal being put over in the library. It took a lot of finesse and tact to moderate an outsize panel discussion around the old fireplace, but my father handled this department beautifully and never lost a panelist.

The day Gerald McGeer's small niece and the daughter of his publicity chief mixed it up over McGeer's stature as a candidate in his coming election, came nearest to ruining those Sundays. The McGeer child had been backed into the honeysuckle bower which covered the outside plumbing department. No McGeer child that I ever knew was backed into anything for long.

"Come one step nearer and say that," said Uncle Gerry's champion.

"He's no good," said the advertising executive's daughter, promptly. Thereupon, the fair-haired little McGeer angel dipped into the hole behind her and in a flash vindicated her uncle, all over the Sunday dress in front of her. That afternoon, the guests left early.

After our livestock-express expeditions, the back seat of the Willys would be washed down with carbolic solution which — even in a Lifebuoy and Listerine era — was almost as bad as the smell of piglets. The car would then be ready for Father to take his old aunties to the Central Presbyterian Church in Vancouver. For the earlier and unwashed expedition to Mass in Port Moody, Margaret pointed out that if any taint remained on our clothes after the freshening Inlet breezes, it was a good honest smell and nations had been built on it — and anyway, the important thing was to just *get there*. "Of course," she finished, "with your father it's different,"

And it was. He often wore a boiled dress shirt to church on Sunday, with wing collar and black silk bow tie. If he were staying on for some social engagement, he might wear the whole dinner-jacket outfit. This saved business suits and wore out formal clothes no longer needed. Mother, however, was proudest of what she wore on these occasions. "Her heather mixture" went through two elections and a miners' riot and ten years later ended up in a bundle for Britain. It was a knitted suit, and the wretched thing from the sheep's back to her own never left her hands, except to rest briefly in a whiffy stew of horse urine and golden rod which dyed it.

"Don't you dare say what colour it is. It's a darned

smart little suit, if I do say so. And it cost me just forty-three cents for the buttons," she said, and posed proudly in it for the *Province*.

Time was marching on and civilization reaching out. We got electric power. One reason was to get more eggs out of the hens. The other reason was radio and convenience generally in the household. In the thirties, the B.C. Electric was not exactly taken with the idea of running power lines into a handful of poverty-stricken homesteads such as we had on the hill. Mind you, high-tension wires, carrying power from Lake Buntzen to the City of Vancouver ran right past the door, but a transformer was required to step down the power for domestic use.

"What about the appliances they'd sell?" asked my father. "Did you say anything about that?"

Well, no, Margaret hadn't, but it gave her an idea, she said.

So she and a bright young salesman named McDonald visited every house and shack in the neighbourhood, signing every homesteader who could afford to pay a light bill on a contract to buy one electric appliance on terms. With a sheaf of contracts in one hand and a sizeable fistful of down payments in the other, she sallied up to the B.C. Electric, and how could they say no?

The night the power was turned on you could hear the "Campana Italian Balm Theatre" from one end of the valley to the other, and every housewife was a first-nighter. Every dwelling was lit from attic to basement and the windows thrown wide. Instead of washing machines, irons, pumps, and other labour-saving aids, most people bought radios. Mantel jobs, and they looked like squatty gothic windows.

It was the heyday of commercial radio. Billie Brown of CKMO was wide awake and rarin' to go away up here in Lil Ol' Vancouver. It was Billie Hassel at the *Province* Station, and "Good Evenink" Kelly who gave the news. Ray Mackness got married and two thousand people turned up to the wedding in New Westminster, he was such a celebrity. It was Amos 'n' Andy, and Eddie Cantor and Jack Benny and Fred Allen.

It was the beginning of the end of an era at the homestead.

Dad's Election Costs

British Columbia is one of the richest and most diversified provinces in Canada. Sprawled across its 366,000 square miles are four mountain ranges and all the major rivers which flow into the Pacific. Between are the lush valleys. It abounds in every natural source of wealth — timber, mineral, water power, fur, fruit, fish. It enjoys every shading of climate except tropical. It has grandeur and beauty unmatched in the world. Its potential is only now being recognized.

In 1933, fifty miles out of Vancouver, where the forty-ninth parallel meets the Pacific Ocean, the wilderness started. There were not 100,000 people spread over those 366,000 square miles. But within the southern perimeter, six times this number made their homes, with more arriving daily from the drought-ridden or frigid prairies. The jobless, lured by the mild Pacific Coast winters, were putting a disproportionate burden on Canada's most westerly province. The penitentiary, that year, was three-quarters full of men under twenty-one years of age, and the public high schools in Vancouver were about to matriculate four hundred students for whom there were no jobs. The province was broke. And, as usual, the unhappy electorate blamed the government then in power.

George Murray, whose dream of fulfillment was as bright as ever, in spite of the cloud of circumstances which dimmed it after World War I, had managed Liberal election campaigns and written about their candidates. While Mother was trying to beat the Depression on a stump ranch, he was dealing with it on the farm, editorial and feature pages of the Vancouver *Daily Province,* and at the same time by taking a fervently active interest in politics. He had ghost-written speeches, and as chief executive of the party in British Columbia, had helped formulate Liberal policies. He had littered the house with miniature sacks of wheat in a brilliant — for those days — publicity campaign to further his man, and he had watched the victory refreshments moulder in their boxes when his hopes for a candidate were crushed.

But this was not enough. He longed to get across his dramatic ideas for the development of the hinterland of British Columbia from which wealth for the cities had to come, and on the loyal Conservative *Province* for which he was writing this couldn't be done. All good Liberals were rallying around their chief to upset the reigning Tolmie Conservative government, and George was in the front row. His decision was no surprise at all.

"Margaret, I've got to get into politics," he announced at the dinner table one evening in early summer, "and we've got to get back to publishing. A newspaper like the *Province* is all right, but somebody else can put a blue pencil through your stuff any time they like. I'm going to get myself a nomination. The kids are almost out of school. The time has come." And Mother, who had been saying that Dad would never be happy until he had his chance, never batted an eye. The area he wanted to represent must lie somewhere up behind those mountains. And when two months later he secured the nomination in Lillooet, he was sure that the pibroch was sounding for him again. Lillooet — in the Southern Cariboo district of British Columbia, 232 miles up the Fraser River from New Westminster, where this mighty system emptied into the ocean.

Dad always said that Mother needed only three or four items with which to make a home livable in double quick time — even on a sand-bar. These included a butcher knife, an iron skillet, and a feather bed. This was particularly fortunate in 1933, because the Lillooet campaign took three months and cash in hand amounted to one hundred dollars.

The old Willys Knight was brought around to the front door of the homestead and was well and truly packed with a typewriter, bedding, three thousand blotters urging the voters of Lillooet to elect Murray, and a case of whisky. There were also stowed aboard the items mentioned for home-making. The back of the big touring car was then wrapped in a white cotton sign with letters a foot high reading "VOTE MURRAY," donated by the Hall Sign Company, and the Liberal campaign headquarters for the sagebrush riding of Lillooet was ready to roll.

To the one hundred dollars in the kitty was added a personal check for $100 from Victor Ross, the President of Imperial Oil and an old school friend of George's. A chap named Pat Russell of Pacific Packers, a casual acquaintance, matched the Ross contribution. Russell said the donation was for luck and to help clean out those bastards at Victoria — "his very words," Mother staidly remembered.

"Leo Gregory at our regular filling station filled us up with gas free," recalled Margaret, "and Frank Cummings, a fierce Liberal and family friend, scrounged the whisky from somewhere. It was called "Whistle" brand, and it was well-named. Pretty raw stuff. But we were glad to have it just the same. It did us for the whole campaign."

The day was beautiful. The birds sang. The Fraser Valley community of Sumas sparkled in the sunshine with its dykes holding up grazing herds of cattle, hopyards, tobacco barns and vineyards. Then Hope, the gateway to the Fraser canyon and the southern end of the old Hudson's Bay Brigade Trail. Beyond Yale, the terrain stood up and looked them in the eye. Boiling Fraser to the right, cliffs scraping the old Willys on the left. That wall of rock hanging halfway over the road was only the outer guard to the temple wherein lay the secret of the Cascades and the records written by men with powder and steel during the past century. The Royal Engineers took four years to build this amazing 96-mile road to Lytton in 1860. One dollar for the toll gate, please — and then Hell's Gate, Jackass Mountain, Kanaka Bar and Cisco. They could almost see among all this grandeur that Scottish factor, Simon Fraser, canoeing down the river in frock coat surrounded by his voyageurs.

"Have those lookouts been standing there a hundred years?" Margaret wondered out loud at one point.

"Not lookouts, but Indians, watching for their supper. Watching for salmon."

"Of course, what else? There's a squaw, tending the drying rack."

In August, in the Fraser canyon, nature provided the bake oven that cured the winter's food for the native people who lived along its banks.

Suddenly there was the dry belt. Brilliant sunshine, sage brush, irrigation ditches, cantaloupes, apples, cattle and sheep. In Lytton you saw the heat as well as felt it. It shimmered. The old Willys headed down the hill, over the railway tracks and on, twisting and turning with the rest of the narrow, winding and hazardous road to Lillooet. The lead cayuse in the Mucumchin outfit which scouted it back in the fifties must have been given his head to wander up hillside, down valley. The trail, later widened, meandered up and down like an endless snake with acute indigestion, here writhing in the agony of passage, and there limp from the effort.

"Put her in low, George," said Mother, who'd never been over a road like this in her life. She was inclined to be a back seat driver, which always made Dad angry. For in spite of the conversational flourishes, his right hand was powerful, and he was, in fact, a splendid driver.

"All right, Mrs. Murray," he'd say icily.

"Well, I don't care. Less talk and more attention to the road — or we'll all end up down at the bottom of this cliff." And she'd accompany her words by either bending forward to assist the machine up the hill, or pressing backward into the leather cushions and driving an imaginary brake into the boards.

In days to come, Mother was to enlist "helpers" to negotiate those roads and never failed to take them along. These were "the good little people" of which she had a bottomless supply for friends and relatives setting out on a journey.

"Good-bye, Duff," she once said to Premier T.D. Pattullo, after he had stopped in Lillooet for lunch. "We were right pleasured to have you with us today." She slipped her hand into his suit coat pocket. "I'm putting the good little people in there to take care of you to Lytton!"

And then there was St. Anthony, the patron saint of those who lose things. Mother used the widest possible interpretation of the "things." She put the good old saint to work on everything from lost causes to lost business.

One winter night as they prepared to make the long drive to catch the CPR at Lytton, Dad came in from putting chains on the little Ford which succeeded the old Willys Knight.

"That front left tire looks a little weak to me, Margaret," he said.

"Well, it's too late to do anything about it now," she

answered. "We'll just have to pray to St. Anthony to help us find a smooth track in the road."

"That's the trouble with you!" said Dad with some heat. "Why make a garageman out of God? Is it very fair to your precious saints and your Creator to expect them to intercede for you and save you from your own carelessness? How can you ask the Saviour of the World to concern himself with your oil pan or your left front tire?"

It was a good point, but it was lost on Mother, whose approach to the heavenly throne was absolutely intimate, whereas her husband's was from a respectful distance.

Now they were negotiating an unforgettable spot on the road known as the Big Slide, a ledge chiselled into the mountain, halfway between heaven and hell. Lillooet was twenty miles farther along.

From across the river, the old gold town looked like a Wild West theatrical set with none of the players on stage. Just the props. The pit was the Fraser River in front, heaped with untidy gravel beds, left by gold dredges at the turn of the century. Railway tracks — the P.G.E.'s — outlined the apron of the stage while the backdrop was the dark blue of the mountains edged halfway up with the silvery green of sagebrush. Entrance was gained by a bridge to the right.

Presently they were on the boards, and the old car was rattling to a stop outside the hotel. False fronts. Plank sidewalks lurching and heaving up on their spikes. Old frame churches with sagging fences at each wing. Beautiful leafy trees missing occasionally, decaying here, solid there, but once a splendid even row, like teeth in an old man's head. Old residences built with the fortunes that followed the gold rush, and titivated with the gingerbread of the period.

This was the oldest town in the great interior plateau called Cariboo. This was Mile 0 on the Cariboo Road where the gold seekers of the 1858 rush rested after their arduous journey by water and portage, to gain strength for the tortuous miles which lay ahead up the river. There are three or four main thoroughfares in British Columbia which may be older, but civilization has rendered them unrecognizable. Lillooet's remains as it did in 1858 — wide enough to turn a span of oxen on, without backing, wide enough for the boys from the creeks to race their horses right down the middle

—close to the bars — and not waste time getting out to a race track, wide enough to accommodate the hordes of gold seekers and the thousands to follow.

Margaret thought she had never seen such a place. A few Indians in their wide-brimmed felts sat on their haunches in front of the false fronts, wordlessly enjoying the excitement of regarding the Murray caravan. Their women in bright head scarves stood around with papooses slung in plaidies over their backs. The quiet of the street was interrupted here and there by the jingle of harness, or the snort of a cayuse, or the wham-bam of the saloon-type doors at the corner of the hotel.

George stepped down from the car, and a round figure of a man emerged from the hotel to meet him. He had the look of the oldtime political supporters and gold inlay flashed through his smile. "Got here, eh?" said Joe Russell, softly. "I expected ya yesterday."

"My wife, Margaret, Mr. Russell," said George.

"Ummmmhum," said Joe, giving an acknowledging nod of the head, and regarding here while rolling his cigarette holder against his teeth from side to side. "The women get scared," he nodded his head, indicating the road across the river. "You scared?"

"No," said Margaret. "My husband is a good driver.'"

"Ya gotta be," said Joe. "It's a son-of-a-bitch. But the election will fix that." He turned without smiling and went out to spread the word.

That night the beer parlour did a roaring business. The hotel lobby and pub were the only lights visible on the street, except for the odd lighted home. The racket from the tavern was, in fact, a dull roar two blocks away.

"Draw twelve . . . shuddup . . . hey, Frenchie . . . Goddammit, have a beer . . ." Now and then a voice would pierce the hubbub. Strangers, in self-defence, unable to sleep, went down to see what went on, if not to join the strenuous celebration. It really wasn't a celebration at all, just another warm evening in Lillooet. But Margaret and George had an election campaign on their minds, other things to think about.

"Well, my dear, what do you think of it?" said George. They had climbed down through the window and were enjoying the cool of the evening from a balcony that ran above the sidewalk on the hotel's first floor.

"It sure as hell isn't much of a town," said Margaret, "but it's pretty. Has atmosphere. You couldn't help but like it. But did you see that place down there?" she pointed toward the noise.

"Never mind down there," he answered. "Have you seen the wonderful old Fraser in the moonlight?"

That was like him. If it was unpleasant, ignore it, and maybe it would go away.

They looked across to the flat and the gravel-covered glaciers, across the sagebrush, silvery in the moonlight, down the Fraser toward Lytton. They may even have looked across the years, those ahead to be fulfilled, those behind that had enriched their experience so generously. It was one of those magic dark blue nights, and Margaret thought she had never seen anything as beautiful.

Suddenly a yell arose from the din in the suds dispensary below them. The double doors on the corner of the saloon opened up, and a heap of arms and legs were flung out on the sidewalk underneath.

"You Indian bastard, I'll show you!" came a man's rough voice, and the brawl was on. Margaret climbed down through the window into the room and fetched the big white china pitcher full of water.

"You young devils," she yelled, climbing out again, "clear on home!" She poised the water on the railing. "Clear on home and let decent people get some sleep!" Splash went the water on the thrashing *melee* below.

The fighters moved into the darkness.

"So far so good, eh?" She squeezed her husband's arm. "That racket can't go on much longer down there. It's eleven-thirty. Let's go to bed."

The Murrays had arrived in Lillooet.

"Darling, You Made It!"

The election wasn't accomplished without effort.

Mother recalls painfully difficult decisions: should they go to Big Bar with a scattered population of perhaps sixty or seventy people? Or keep an engagement at Bralorne the same evening to talk to more than 150 miners?

"He has to go to Bralorne," said Dan Hurley.

"He promised those people in Big Bar," said Mother. "He can't let them down. This country isn't all mining."

Big Bar was where they had the wonderful stampede every year and everyone seemed to smell of cake. It was a community rather than a village, and at stampede time the Indians and ranchers rode in for miles around, bringing the children, the cow, the home-made brew, and the grub. When they ran out of brew, they drank whatever they could get, including extract. When they ran out of *that,* they went home. Meanwhile, they had been stampeding and dancing in relays for two or three days.

Well, the upshot of that argument was that Mother went to Big Bar and Dad went to Bralorne. Forty people, an unheard-of crowd, were waiting for her as the old car chugged over the top of the last little hilly place.

What did she talk about? "Well," she says, "I don't remember. But it had plenty of zing in it. I think I told them what a smart candidate they had in your father. What he hoped to do for the Cariboo. How he had longed all his life for this chance, and how they damned well better give it to him."

Then there was the night at Pioneer. The candidate was scheduled to speak at 8:00 P.M., and the community hall was full of miners waiting to hear him. Mother knew that he was flying in by chartered plane due to land on Gun Lake. He was to be met and driven up to the top of the valley for the meeting.

8:05, no George.

8:15, still no George.

In 1933, commercial flying was still fairly basic. A pilot flew with the aid of an altimeter, a compass, a gasoline gauge — and, sometimes, in the mountains, an empty whisky bottle filled with water, the level of which indicated the angle of bank on the wings — and not much else. A week before a ghastly accident had occurred on Anderson Lake.

"Oh please God, keep them safe . . . St. Anthony, find them that little Gun Lake. Those trees . . . getting dark . . . his big chance . . ."

8:25. The crowd was getting restless. There was nothing for it but for Margaret to get up there herself and hold their attention.

"Dear God, what will I tell them? Mining Act? Don't know anything about it. Widows' pensions? But these are all men."

Mother cleared her throat, and this is what she said:

"Mr. Chairman, and all you wonderful people: I don't know where my husband is. He's flying in and they're meeting him and I'm sure he'll be here any minute. Perhaps you'd like to know something about the candidate."

She breathed deeply: "George Murray is a fifth generation Canadian. His people came here from Sutherlandshire in Scotland, and you know how it is, they never get over it!"

No one laughed. Here and there talking persisted, and boots scraped the floor as the miners squirmed in their seats, adjusting to the unexpected prospect of being addressed by a mere woman.

"Mr. Murray is a Presbyterian, a newspaperman for twenty-five years."

"I want to hear what the Liberals are going to do for unemployment," sang out a deep voice.

"Ha abaat a batter break far passpacting," came a flat tone.

"Has he the Gaelic now?" jeered a Scottish one.

For as long as I can remember, my mother has always had the ability to size up an audience and give them what they wanted. Maybe this was the night she learned how.

"If you boys will shut up and show me the common courtesy of listening, I may tell you," she flung at them.

"My husband thinks that he has something to offer. He thinks he can save the people, but I tell him most of the people" — looking right at them — "most of the people don't give a damn about being saved."

And now they laughed.

"He started his career as a cub reported on the Ottawa *Journal* in 1908, waiting for his day. He used to tell me his hopes and dreams for this beloved province of his, and me with only the R.C. Catechism and *Hale's Almanac* for a background."

More laughter. Then a hand clapped somewhere in the back of the hall. When the applause died down, Mother was in command. She could have talked all night, she had that tight a grip on them all. But presently the door of the hall burst open, and there he was — handsome, confident, hurrying up the side of the hall, hat and briefcase in hand.

It was a knockout of a meeting. The unexpected. The Dramatic. And it was the same everywhere.

What where the issues in 1933?

Unemployment camps, the prairies a dust bowl, collections of shoes and sugar for Peace River people, every other family on relief, including doctors and lawyers and trades people. Vancouver office buildings and stores and harbour empty, and taxes ever going up.

"In this community," said George Murray at a Pemberton meeting of thrifty farmers, "we get an appropriation for public works of twenty thousand dollars. But it costs ten thousand to administer the spending of it — too many engineers and supervisors. We spend two hundred thousand a year enforcing the game act, yet a lot of unfortunate gentlemen of the Metis persuasion are harassed when they shoot a little for the pot."

"Bravo," said Pemberton, which boasted about twenty miles of public roads altogether. "Cut the spending. By God, he's right!" And that was Pemberton in the bag.

To PGE railroad men at Squamish: "Make this railroad go someplace and bring something back. Extend the PGE into the Peace River. That country has enough natural wealth to keep us all busy for the next fifty years." And they said, "Damned if he's not right. Let's give him a try!" And they did.

"Why should a *bona-fide* prospector have to pay the toll on the Cariboo Highway at Spuzzum?" Mr. Murray asked at Lillooet.

"Why should a prospector not be grubstaked for the hills instead of given a relief cheque in the town?" he asked at Bralorne.

At Pavilion: "With goat trails like these for roads, why should farmers not work out their taxes on a public-works crew?"

At Clinton: "Let us build this highway to Alaska and use our idle men to do it, and in this way open our arteries to the cities with commerce from the great north country."

"Let's give our railroads something to haul besides down-and-out prairie farmers," he argued at Spences Bridge and Ashcroft and Lytton, all mainline railroad towns, with a clear view of the boxcar Pullman traffic.

"Let us forget about town roads and make money available for mining trails. If the mines make it, the towns will take care of themselves," he said to anyone who would listen.

"Hear! Hear!" they all cried, and clapped and stamped their feet.

Only the Alaska Highway was remote to these people. With the dreadful roads, which served the populated end of the province, where would the money come from for two thousand miles of road on which only ice worms would travel? But long, long before a war and the needs of defence dictated it, George Murray had a vision of the great road leading north to Alaska.

That September, Margaret Murray handed out three thousand blotters that were still being used ten years later. She walked the PGE track from Squamish to Shalalth, taking rides on the little come-to-me-go-from-me rigs which plied between sections. These got her over the trestles which are many and treacherous along the PGE, and she left blotters everywhere, met everyone, and forever after knew who had rust in the wheat, erisypelas in the hogs, or milk-leg after the last baby. She knew every rock on the line, every sliding mountain, every rotting tie, and which section-hand wanted a raise. Everything she could find went into her notebook, including the everlasting state of confusion because someone called the valley of the Lillooet River after the well-known

Victoria family, Pemberton, while the town of Lillooet was sixty miles away on the banks of the Fraser.

Who before had ever heard one single word about the colourful construction days of the PGE? About brawny teamsters who could lay a whip around a gnat's ear? And cussin', sweatin' foremen who bossed picks and shovels, donkey engines, stump pullers, blasting crews, and six-horse teams? The railroad wasn't twenty years old in 1933. Construction was still going on with horse power as well as motor power. Nothing was too recent or too dull for the little black book. In the meantime, Dad was out on the rim of the riding, covering the miles, talking to ranchers, visiting the creeks, holding meetings.

Mother's way of meeting people was like a dog wagging its tail. You might not be really interested, but it was such a nice friendly wag, and such a persistently good-humoured wag, that you just had to stop and speak. Of course, there are people who just don't care for dogs that are wagging their tails. Mother took the odds as a calculated risk, and came out with more pats than kicks.

Dad was different. He was blessed with a formal education, polished in his manner, and quietly spoken. He could send the drinks around with his compliments, but he couldn't set them up and be part of the treat. He was the last man on earth with the first-name touch so necessary to a politician.

Where Mother had graduated in the art of cussing before she was ten years old, and had a carrying voice to go with it, Dad never swore. He was well-tailored and groomed. Mother got by when she gave it thought, but she was really a do-it-yourself artist who could be relied on to purchase the wrong kind of hats. He was sentimental and sensitive and hid it with brusqueness. She was smart and down-to-earth and never forgot a name. With absolutely no self-consciousness, she would tackle anything, talk to anyone, write anything, and let the dangling participles, the mispronunciations, and all other impedimenta fall where they may.

They met on the last day of September, 1933, at Shalalth, where Dad had ridden down from the mines on a five-ton truck.

"My dear girl," he said, taking her hands on the little freight platform that afternoon, "I have missed you so much.

How is it going? Do you think we'll be successful?"

"Of course you'll be successful. You can't miss. My, that was a wonderful speech in Squamish. I heard about it all up the line. The worst, the very worst they can say about you is that you're a carpetbagger. But we'll talk on the gas car."

Crumpled and dusty, needing a bath, and dog-tired, the two discussed the campaign as the gas car galloped along Seton Lake on the sixteen-mile journey to Lillooet. "What's that iron thing?" asked Mother suddenly, looking at the luggage on the seat opposite.

"That's a piece of the first railroad in British Columbia, seventy years old."

"What are you going to do with it?" asked Margaret, eyes laughing. "It's a little big for a paperweight, isn't it?"

"I'm sending it to the archives in Victoria," said Dad, whose sense of history loomed large even when he was pressed by the exigencies of the moment.

But it was all over two nights later. George had spent election day in Squamish and had ridden up to Lillooet on a speeder when the polls closed. The wind in his coat-tails almost extinguished the coal-oil light which fell equally on happiness and disappointment as the supporters of the two candidates waited in the little telegraph shack for the late dots and dashes bearing results from creeks, and mine, and ranch outposts. And George Murray was the winner. At Big Bar, where his wife was the only speaker, he got every single vote.

"Darling, you made it. You wonderful man! I'm so proud!" She didn't finish. The defeated candidate had just walked in the door and conversation stopped. Suddenly, like the snap of a bullsnake, a sibilance cut through the room at the newcomer. "Sssssssnake!" hissed old Dan Hurley at the defeated Conservative. "Ssssssnake I say." The fury and hatred behind the word dispersed the gathering.

My father was so stricken by this lack of sportsmanship by one of his own supporters that he went outside and was sick. Not that the other side didn't give it back as good as they got it. But until that moment he hadn't realized what a serious matter politics was in Lillooet. It split families and set ground rules for the stores at which you dealt and the company which you kept.

The effect of elections on the temperament of their new

acquaintances was not all they learned. When the campaign was over, between them they had enough information, local colour, and facts about the district to start a weekly newspaper, fill it up with some of the most colourful journalism in the west — and make it pay.

A Country Weekly of Their Own

How do you start a weekly newspaper in an outpost of civilization with no cash? First you had to see the vision of your community fifty years hence, as the Murrays did. They cared about its future and its potential. The present — the meagre population, uncertain mail service, creaking transportation facilities, inaccessibility — all these placed second. Advertising revenue placed third, because George and Margaret aimed to make their publication so good that the local business people and their suppliers in the city couldn't help but support it. They knocked on doors until they had the first printer's bill in sight and one edition printed and folded to show what they meant. Within two years they had saved enough to establish their own shop.

Lillooet in 1934 was experiencing its seventh gold rush. So although the biggest news in forty years was the new price of the precious metal on the world market, no one, unless actually engaged in mining, was too excited about it. Nor were they very excited about a newspaper. All the merchants but one were Chinese. The most venerable of these was old Wo Hing who sat on the porch of his dark, cool, almost empty premises and dozed. But his son, who had children at university and lived in a comfortable home in Vancouver, had come to Lillooet to measure the effect on those empty shelves of the current excitement in Bridge River, and he understood advertising. The copy was no problem. Six words. "Wo Hing, Provision Merchant, Lillooet, B.C."

At See Hing Lung's restaurant, the difficulty was communicating. "It will say you serve good meals," said Margaret, exhausting her best pantomime, and waving her dummy sheet for emphasis.

"Oh, ho, ho, ho. Velly good meals. Loas' pok, loas' beef, loas' tulkey, laisin pie, appo' pie." And all the old celestials peeling potatoes in the back door sunshine joined in the laughter. "What you want? Laisin?"

Jim Brothers' office was a counter packed in with onions and potatoes and cartons of coffee. But Mr. Jim put aside his abacus and joined his wife at the single plate-glass showcase in the store to hear about the newspaper. He would have to talk it over with friends, he said.

The third Chinese store in a row made Margaret's day. Fred Hunt, whose Oriental name had long since been Anglicized, had been waiting for her to call, he said. He would have a weekly advertisement of twelve inches. As they talked in his poop-deck office with a railing around it, they looked out on a sea of sacked vegetables, Sunlight soap cartons, and boxes of canned goods. Over at the meat block a single customer stood waiting while an animated panel discussion was going on in Chinese, lengthy enough to be settling the meat situation in all of Western Canada. Presently, Fred Hunt silenced the argument at the shopping block. "No beef until this afternoon. The truck isn't in," he said to the customer, then turned to Margaret. "We might consider a second advertisement for our wholesale meats," he ventured.

As Margaret headed down to meet her husband at the gas car and learn what he had accomplished with similar calls around the mining camps, she didn't even go into the town's only white store. Its owners were Tories and she wouldn't be welcome.

Bridge River in 1934 was so alive with opportunities that people were falling all over each other scrambling to seize one.

"Where the hell is the Hotcha Lunch?" asked one of Evans Transport drivers at the Gold Bridge Townsite office one day in March.

"Let's see," said Mr. Harris, the manager. "Hotcha

Lunch. Sure sure, that's Mrs. . . . ah, well, it's right over there, by the lumber truck. Little kiddie playing beside the truck . . ."

The driver wheeled his big diesel over the most direct route across the lava ash to the unloading lumber. "Hotcha Lunch? I gotta a ton of freight for ya. Where'd 'ja want her?"

"Oh my goodness. The stove? Not already," said the nervous proprietess. The only visible sign of the establishment was a two foot pile of white shiplap on the bare ground.

"S'okay kid," her husband reassured her. Then to the driver, "Put 'er there Mac. We'll cover 'er with a tarp. Where do we sign?"

Within a week, the Hotcha was in business with eight stools, two oilcloth covered tables, and a washstand for truckers nice and handy to the back door where the contents of the tin basin would settle the dust out back.

Would they advertise?

Of course, but you'd have to call around about three a.m. to explain it to the management. That was the time of day they counted the cash, hauled out a mickey of rye from behind the breadbox, then relaxed for an hour before hitting the sack.

With Billy Bell, the barber, it was different. You could talk business while getting your hair cut. "Why sure," said Billy, "I'll have a professional card. Run it every week. Things are good."

Neil Trout, Gold Bridge provisioner, would have a little ad, sure. Best time to see him was when the Vancouver *Daily Province* news was on, at eight thirty in the evening. The gas lamp hanging from the rafters over the counter shone on a relaxed group of truck drivers, wayfarers and Gold Bridge citizens who relied on Trout's radio for news of the outside and the daily stock market quotations.

It was at Trout's that Vaughan Dubois, the garage owner and taxi man, signed for weekly space. His two-column three-inch advertisement in 1934 in the Bridge River Lillooet *News* rather startled the district when it declared that Dubois had the best and most reliable tools in the Bridge River Valley in his garage. This was fine, except that the proof reader failed to catch the missing 's' in the critical word.

And the churches? Of course, notices. Twenty five cents a week for a classified would be very satisfactory. It made no difference that they hadn't yet built the churches.

"But Mr. Murray," said the little French priest with the heavy accent whose parish was Gold Bridge, "I do not know about this place. It is so noisy at night. Where do they all go? The car headlights wake you up through the trees. The dust choke you." The good padre went on to say that he was sure that the kind of woman who endowed St. Margaret's, Gold Bridge, would be most unhappy.

Indeed she should have been. For as it turned out, the church was being built smack alongside three new sporting houses, though no one, including the town commission, knew the destiny of the three frame houses on which work was proceeding furiously. On the other hand in the Bridge River valley, all hours of the day and night, the little town of Gold Bridge jumped with activity and its accompanying traffic and revelry. Cars and trucks plunged wildly down the rough, new roads, twiglets snapping, stones flying, dust billowing, and axles bending on a low poplar stump here, or a high centre there. Gasoline lamps hung in trees, lighting the labours of men with hammers who were in a hurry to get homes or business premises put together. And all night long those mammoths of 1934 motor transportation, the big Evans' diesel trucks, groaned in the distance as they climbed into the valley with supplies to keep all these people going and the mines producing.

The two big gold-producing mines were Bralorne and Pioneer, whose townsites were not, in 1934, properly established. From an advertising point of view, Gold Bridge offered the only support the paper could expect at that early date in the mining community, with Lillooet the only sizable town in the entire district.

But it was the women of Gold Bridge who finally assured the establishment of a newspaper. One of the busiest thoroughfares in town was that leading to the establishment of "Les Girls" — who had become quite a tricky problem to the town commission of Gold Bridge. The question was whether to live with them or live without them. The Board of Trade figured they were good for business, meals, haircuts, broken springs, blowouts, beer, shopping and banking. But the school board wanted to be rid of them. The children were endangered by the frantic drivers, their health threatened by the clouds of dust, their attention taken by the visitors across the road. And this wasn't mentioning anything at all about the morality of the thing or the embarrassment to the teacher.

Even the Ladies Gold Nugget Club was divided on the issue.

"They gotta go somewhere, dearie," said Virginia Martley at a regular meeting.

"Well, it isn't decent," said Mrs. Billie Bell, to the vigorous nod of half a dozen heads.

"Charlie says the streets wouldn't be safe at night without them," said Mrs. Hodgins of the hotel.

"My husband says that what we need here is a newspaper to fight for a decent camp," said Mrs. Neil Trout. "And if all of the businessmen in this town would get behind Mr. Murray, we'd have one."

The first member of the Bridge River — Lillooet *News* staff was myself. Actually, my Father had rather fancied me as a potential concert pianist. He had gone so far as to accompany my piano lessons with a course of tuition in voice.

"Good lord, George, that's another ten dollars a month," said Mother, coping with a fresh salary cut, a new hired man, and a second hand separater. We were then still on the homestead.

"Well, I know it is. But she's a big girl and it will teach her to breathe properly and to stand gracefully. Did you ever figure out how much poise is required to just enter a room and wait to be greeted or introduced?

So Madame Bellos and I 'shot an arrow into the air' every Saturday morning on the third floor of the old Williams Building on Hastings Street and I learned to breathe and stand.

By the time I had had two advanced piano lessons from Mr. Tripp, I knew I would never make it beyond the living room as a pianist.

"Ah, my dear girl, Debussy is lacy — like fine filigree — now let us have that passage again."

But my Debussy was limp and stringy, no matter how much I tried.

It was then that the old maestro would straighten his shoulders, toss his white mane behind his ears and say resignedly, "Just play on." In a moment he would have disappeared out the door, wrapped in his opera coat. The homberg would still be on the hall tree, the silver headed cane in the umbrella rack. It was years before I learned that Mr. Tripp, faced with a trying pupil, regularly required a quick one at the Arctic Club next door.

Following my Father's election I returned from a year at school in California. My Mother's sisters considered this their contribution towards their brother-in-law's political future. Mother was delighted, hoping it would round out my education. Nothing else about me needed rounding out, a fact discreetly pointed out to me as my aunts steered me, almost upon arrival, towards the corsetry department of the 'City of Paris' in San Francisco.

"We'll get that long hair of yours cut, and put away that Harris Tweed coat. Then Bess, I think black patent leather pumps, don't you? She has the Lally legs for which God be praised, and lets not hide them."

When I got off the Seattle bus a year later, the family hardly knew me. I was bruised around the rib cage, but had a figure like Mae West. I had rounded out my education by washing dishes and keeping house for my board and room. This followed a disastrous 1934 teener's resistance movement. I had the last word. With aunt. The last words were, "Do you hang up your halo when you have a bath?"

After that it was the want ads in the Oakland *Examiner* for me.

Mother's cup was flowing over. In her view, no young woman's education was complete without a tour of duty in someone else's kitchen. "If you're not born to servants, then you better be one yourself, if you're ever going to handle them, my lady," she said. "Look what McAtee's kitchen did for me!"

All the Meredith's kitchen in Oakland did for me was to strengthen my desire to be a newspaper woman. My Father greeted this decision of mine with about the same enthusiasm you might expect if I'd suddenly declared myself for a career in chick sexing. Perhaps he had in mind the bobbed-haired, aggressive young women who turned up writing sob stuff in the dailies after World War One.

I started on our paper while it was still being published in Vancouver. At Mitchell's Printing, I learned type faces and sizes. I learned to read proofs and handle copy. I studied the daily papers to see how they wrote mining news, then copied their style. In fact, the first year's Bridge River — Lillooet *News* looked more like a miniature *Wall Street Journal* than anything else.

"The Reliance Gold Mine is not the South African Rand, for goodness sake," my father would say to me. "You write that over again and don't overwrite it. Stick to facts."

"I copied it straight out of *Time* magazine, and I did so stick to facts. That's just how they write directors' meetings."

"Yes, but don't you see the difference? *Time* deals with famous — or at least established and important — producing properties. No one outside this province, this community, has ever heard of Reliance. It's a prospect, a penny stock, possibly just a manipulation. How do we know?"

It was the same with weddings. I at least aimed high. *The New York Times* or *Mayfair*.

"Well," said Mother, "I absolutely defy Mr. Timothy Eaton to recognize the outfit you put on that girl. I saw that wedding party as they were going into the beer parlour on the way to the ceremony. A cathedral veil? It looked more like a net curtain to me. And where did you get the organ music? They played her in on an accordian."

"An accordion is a hand organ, isn't it?" said daughter primly. "And besides, they liked it. They ordered twenty extra copies."

"Well, I must say," said my father, "she's got the idea of what sells newspapers."

But if I caught on fairly quickly to reporting, I was certainly less than distinguished as a proof-reader. At Mitchell's the contract said that the newspaper would be responsible for its own proofs. And in those early days, all the mistakes seemed to be disasters.

"Things are brisk at the mining camps in the district," reported the "Run of the Mine" column from Bridge River. "Storks are moving fast, and Jimmy Pollard is getting the lion's share of all the business." "Stocks" had been set "storks"! Jimmy was a Howe Street stock broker who had opened a sub-office at Pioneer Mines for his very dignified and reputable firm.

When the telephone rang at Mitchell's a long, long ring the next morning, I knew who it was right off the bat.

"I have a long-distance call for Miss Murray routed

through McGillivray Falls from Pioneer . . . go ahead, McGillivray . . . go ahead Pioneer . . . go ahead Mrs. Murray."

"Georgie! For God's sake!" the voice came in waves with McGillivray Falls pounding in the background. "What are you trying to do to me down there? This Pollard thing. He's pulling his ad. Did you read those proofs, or didn't you?"

"Yes I did, Mother. But I didn't notice it, I guess. I'm sorry."

"Sorry! What good is that? Being sorry. What have you got a head on you for, may I ask? I'm the laughing stock of the whole valley."

"I really am sorry, Mother."

"You'll be sorry when your carelessness loses us every ad in this paper. Vaughn Dubois. And now Pollard . . . hello, hello . . . and what about this applesauce at the school concert? That's almost as bad. In fact it's worse."

"Applesauce? I don't remember anything about applesauce at the school concert."

"You wool-gatherer, you! It was *applause* . . . . . a-p-p-l-a-u-s-e . . . children reciting . . . school concert! And you made it applesauce. The mothers are furious."

The proofs were read twice after that. But the worst was yet to come.

"Ollie," it should have said, "Had just finished two hours of his afternoon shift, when the door of the cage came unfastened and fell on his foot, breaking it in several places."

Guess where they'd left out the "f"?

Those papers sold for five dollars a copy, and Ollie headed out for Northern Ontario soon after.

After lining up the local advertising, the Murrays went off to Vancouver to see the wholesalers, the mining people, and other suppliers of goods and services to the Bridge River and Lillooet districts.

George took the mining companies, the automotive suppliers, and the banks. Margaret took the breweries, the distilleries, and the rest. One of George's headaches was the horde of people wanting beverage-room licences for hotels, nearly all of whom were more interested in selling beer than in accommodating possible guests. He found out what even his best friends were careful not to tell him — until after his election — that all their lives they had entertained a secret yearning to be hotel proprietors. And those who did not want to cash in on the miners' thirst certainly wanted mining trails to properties in which they were interested. Or they were keen to sell the government trucks and equipment, stationery supplies, office furniture, grass seed, or any other conceivable item required in the administration of an up-country riding. Father was careful not to ingratiate himself personally with such prospective advertisers. Rather, he felt he should sell the newspaper and district on a higher level — to service clubs and other organizations welcoming a guest speaker, or to newspapers and magazines eager for feature stories on British Columbia's exciting new gold country.

Mother, though, got right down to cases. "The most wonderful country in the province, Mr. Willis, Hard-working miners work up a gosh-awful thirst in that lava ash . . . brought you a little sample here of what they dig for." And while she dug from her bag a small piece of gold-bearing quartz, United Distillers' Number One Man was deciding that perhaps, after all, he could work one more weekly newspaper into his budget. Today the liquor interests build theatres and art galleries, subsidize authors, and such. Thirty years ago they often contributed the only sure cash on which a weekly editor could depend.

Mother didn't always score. Not only did the businessmen who were Conservative Party supporters give the paper a chilly reception, there were other non-believers as well. Every head in the Pacific Great Eastern Railroad office turned toward the counter as Margaret went round and round with the purchasing agent. Mr. Williams was a Scot and was taking no chances.

"I'll have to talk it over with the President," he said, "The railroad does very little advertising."

"That's the trouble with the PGE," said Margaret. "It doesn't do enough advertising. It runs through the most beautiful country in the world."

"Aye, that may very well be," said Williams. "But how can we be sure that this paper will come out every week?"

"Because I tell you it will," said Mother. "And you very well know the record of the Murrays regarding the PGE for the last twenty years."

"Aye, so you say," said the unconvinced one. "But I'll still have to take it up wi' Mr. Wilson."

Copy for Volume One, Number One, of the Bridge River — Lillooet *News*, March 1, 1934, was no problem at all. One page was taken by the Gold Bridge Townsite Company, and the rest given over to my father's maiden speech in the Legislature, a good speech, made better by dramatization. He stacked the carpeted floor around his desk in the chamber with 150 reference books — every single one a reason for extending the Pacific Great Eastern Railroad to the Peace River Corridor, as it was then called. "You can't afford not to," he thundered from behind his improvised fortress.

Even *Saturday Night* magazine in faraway Toronto wrote an editorial of approval: "George Murray, a Vancouver newspaperman, is up to date the chief 'find' of the British Columbia Legislature," it said. "He burns with ardor and an undimmed faith in his newly adopted constituency, and his maiden speech was an earnest plea for encouragement to pioneer settlers."

The desk-thumping had hardly died away at Victoria when a second issue of the *News* was in the works, three weeks later. The third issue came out the middle of April. The paper has not missed an issue since.

Wednesday was press day at Mitchell's where the *News* was printed, and every Wednesday night through fog, rain, snow, or sunshine, a little red Ford runabout skidded into the freight shed at the foot of Columbia street not far from where the *New Delta* used to be, and drove over the wooden oily planks to the PGE office. The cartons of papers were loaded from here onto a Union Steamship train boat, to be transferred onto the PGE express car at Squamish for onward passage to Lillooet.

The Murrays usually relied on the mails to carry the week's copy to Mitchell's. Important or last-minute news was telegraphed to Vancouver, the telephone connection between the city and the Bridge River country in the thirties being expensive and not too reliable. Occasionally, however, one of the Murrays would bring the week's budget of news and ads into the shop himself.

"Well, how's everybody this morning?" Mother would clarion, oozing the aroma of sagebrush, lava ash, and Cariboo. The two secretaries in the office would answer "fine" in practically a whisper. The accountant would acquire a pained expression and go on adding. The rest would close their doors quietly. Only George Beattie would amble out of his office and encourage the conversation that was bound to accompany the visitor whether he liked it or not. George had never got Ashcroft out of his blood, nor the *Journal,* whose old flatbed press he used to turn by hand when a lad.

"I got a coupla pars here to write," Margaret would say. 'Pars' were paragraphs in her lingo. "Guess there's time to get it in this week's issue, eh, George?" She would then launch into a complete rundown on what the pars concerned.

"Our travelling dentist, Dr. Lowe, had this plate grinning in his hand, it's owner in the chair," said Margaret. "He was shooting the breeze, when 'BOOM', the mountain started to slide. Well sir, the folks around Ogden didn't know whether Doc had drilled right through his patient, the floor and the mountain side, or whether he'd changed bits and was practising for the miner's hand drilling contest . . ." By this time Mother would have the reluctant attention of the whole *Financial News* staff.

"So then what happened?" George prompted.

"Well they sent a search party after the plate and found it down on the Native Son property. And according to what I hear, the gold in that plate may be the only gold Native Son will ever see around there . . ."

Two years after establishment, the Bridge River — Lillooet *News* moved to Lillooet and its own printing press. John Jackson, then mechanical superintendent for a Vancouver daily, had saved up a week of his holidays to give his old friends a hand, and under his guidance fifteen-year-old Frankie Tomado, a singing, whistling cut-up of a youngster who used to sweep up at Mitchell's, produced much of the type for the first issue in Lillooet, and for many more after Mr. Jackson returned to Vancouver.

Billie Reese was the compositor. He got to Lillooet by virtue of being on duty at a car wash on Pender Street in Vancouver one morning when the Murray car needed service. Billie was just finishing off the last wire wheel on the little red Cabriolet when my father congratulated him on a good job.

"How much?" asked George Murray.

"Fifty cents," said Billie, "twenty-five for the guy that owns the station."

"I haven't noticed you here before," said George.

"Oh I just work here when the other fellow is away," said Billie. "I'm a printer. Leastways I'm going to be a printer. I got laid off."

"My boy," said the publisher of the Bridge River — Lillooet *News,* "you've just got yourself a job."

"But George," said my mother in desperation a few days later. "Did you find out how much experience he's had? What is he — a pressman, an operator, or what? How old is he?"

"He's a compositor," said Dad. "Eighteen. He's had a tubercular spine, and he looks to me like he could stand some of this good Lillooet sunshine. Besides the boy has character."

"How much did you say we'd pay him?"

"I didn't. I said we'd decide that when we saw what he could do. I told him he'd get a good clean bed and good meals. And maybe a horse to ride."

"God help us all," said mother, with feeling.

We got Mr. Dibben the same way. Dad met Dibben on the gas car to Shalalth. He had been a printer a half-century before in England, he said, and would like to work at his craft again.

"Good," said George absently, taking in the scenery. "You may be of great value to us." But he didn't project any particular time, and Mr. Dibben turned up the next Monday in a white smock, black bowler, and carrying a bag full of his tools.

Besides the drawback of a fifty-year time lapse, Mr. Dibben had lost two fingers. The end came following a catastrophic day in which Jackson had the linotype laid down all over the shop, with Frankie cleaning parts. Billie was sweating over a pied-up case of second-hand wood type older than Confederation, and Mother was getting off some colourful language as she hunted for streets and cities among the jumbled slugs of the newly arrived mailing list.

Suddenly Frankie's fifteen years rebelled. In one leap he attained the composing table, pulled his hair down over his brow, extended his hand in the Fascist salute, and in the language of his race went into Mussolini's Rome balcony scene. While Mother lectured Frankie about behaviour on the job, Mr. Dibben was led off to the kitchen for a sustaining cup of tea, and the next day he caught the gas car home.

Mother always said that her husband hastened the termination of his son's formal education by presenting him with a tuxedo at seventeen years of age. Between the tux and the sporty little convertible we owned, Dan's mind was anywhere but on his trigonometry.

"Look, Son," said Mother, as she laid down the Vancouver College report that Christmas. "You're learning the printing business. I'll call up Mel Bryant at the North Shore *Press* and see if he'll take you on over there and teach you something."

Dan took to printing with complete ease. In a few weeks, he could operate the linotype slowly, had learned the type case, could feed a press, cast a mat, and understood fairly well the principles of the craft.

Success — of Sorts

The Lillooet Publishers started life in the depths of the Depression, and it would be hard to duplicate the conditions under which the family and their helpers lived and worked in 1934. George, as M.L.A. for the district, received a pass on the railroads and twelve hundred dollars a year indemnity for his services. His hand was continually in his pocket for prizes, trophies, or gratuities of one sort or another for a hundred mine and farm activities in his district. The newspaper, when it moved to Lillooet, was six and sometimes eight six-column pages. From the beginning, any profit it made after the printer's bill was settled went into machinery for the home printery. None of the family took wages.

The shop itself was on Lillooet's main street, in premises which had been abandoned for many years, but which had been designed as a boarding house for railroad-construction workers in 1912. It was a "box" house, big, plain, and "toothy." Two windows under the gabled roof on the second floor for eyes, and three windows and a door on the main floor for teeth, with the verandah turned back over the dentures like lips in a grimace.

Dad discovered it by being charming to a constituent early in his political career. This good citizen wanted a beer-parlour license and went into business anticipating approval of his request. His first improvement on the property was to install one Wong Yenyee as *restauranteur*, and move in a gramophone. The idea was that Wong would cook chow mein and the gramophone would play records and he would have a fine flourishing nightclub. He did — until the police caught up with him.

One hundred acres of sidehill and sagebrush flat went with the boarding house. A log barn sat alongside. A garage stood on a tired foundation next door. The upstairs had ten cubicles called bedrooms. There was a coldwater tap in the kitchen, which was downstairs, and the rest of the main floor was lobby, card room, dining room, and office. You could sling a cat through the door frames and window sill, and the place was in a musty, dusty condition. But the lobby *would* accommodate a press, partitions *could* come down, and the bedrooms would be necessary for the staff in the 1934 economy. When money was available, a bathroom would be added.

We move in promptly and acquired a boarder, a Mr. P.J. Wilson, and his law office. P.J. Wilson had been in the country only a few months, arriving with the new town mechanic, Charlie Friss and his wife from Chilliwack. Charlie was a big man with a wooden leg. He overcame his driving disability by the simple expedient of affixing a tin can onto the clutch pedal of the truck he drove, and into this inserting his peg leg. It worked fine.

Mr. Wilson had boarded with the Frisses in Chilliwack and had paid his board bill only a few hours before the decision to move was made. Seeing as P.J. always paid in advance, he was somewhat shaken to awake the next morning to an empty house. Hurriedly he dressed and went to the window, just in time to see the last rope securing the kitchen stove to the load, and Mrs. Friss in hat and gloves issuing orders nearby.

"What about my twenty five dollars?" wailed P.J.

What about it indeed! The Frisses needed the money for gas for the trip. So P.J. went back, gathered up his law books and notary seal, thrust his few effects into a suitcase, and grabbing his hat, joined the safari. Thus on the back of a truck load of household effects did Lillooet's first lawyer (and the Murray's great and good friend for the next quarter century) ride into a career in jurisprudence in the town of Lillooet.

With a paying boarder to feed, Mother decided to hire Ling, a Chinese cook. Ling's contribution to the culinary department was to keep a gallon pot of coffee on the stove, emptying it on Saturday night and starting the weel's brew Sunday morning. He just added to it the rest of the week. Otherwise he followed purchasing and other instructions to the absolute letter. After Mother's orders to buy in big lots and save money, Ling was feeding permanent residents and all guests for about a dollar a day, dairy products extra.

It became necessary to straighten him out regarding the odd items of livestock found lurking in the raisin pie or macaroni, but otherwise in his white jacket he gave the dining room quite an air and visitors were sure the Murray's were on their way up as soon as the furniture arrived.

Ling lasted until the Owl episode. Down the precipitous bank behind the house slithered a dead owl one winter. The boys found it out by the wood pile, frozen solid. Delightedly they picked it up by one wing.

"Hey Ling!" Billie called the old Chinaman out of the kitchen. "You cookem?"

Ling rubbed his hands, bowed and took the owl.

"You take feathers off him. Clean him. Cut off wings alla same turkey."

"O ho ho ho. Tulkey . . . Loas tulkey!" Ling understood.

That owl was dressed, stuffed, trussed and in the roasting pan before the pranksters were found out.

That first winter — as so many "firsts" seem to be — was the coldest in Lillooet for many years, but the winter was partially relieved by a bright and youthful idea conceived by Dan. Why not ice the north side of the house and seal it in? A hose was brought through the kitchen, and a second fifty feet was attached to it. The house was sprayed until the ice sheeted it like a giant mirror, and it twinkled and blinked reflections of the sunlight on the Fraser River road across the river miles away.

There were rats to plague us. We had spotted their nests when cleaning out the old building, and traps were set along with poisoned bait in an effort to eradicate them. Every night we could hear them down in the print shop, scurrying around, skidding on newsprint, "wittering" between themselves. But by the time you got down the creaky steps from the second floor, all was quiet. They conventioned under the big press, and the new cement showed up the inky imprint of their feet.

"Have you checked those rollers?" asked Dad. "Do you know what printing rollers are coated with?"

"Gelatin, aren't they?" said Mother.

"Yeah?" Everyone was learning around the fledging newspaper.

"Take them off," ordered George. The rollers were removed. "What did I tell you? Ruined! This one, too. They'll have to be recast."

"You get them ready for the morning train, Billie," said Mother. "And the ones that aren't chewed, set them carefully on end over there against the wall."

That night the thermometer went away down, twenty below. Fires were stoked during the night to keep the machines warm and workable. Twice someone got out of bed to push another great pine log into the big drum of the stove which heated the shop.

In the morning Mother was the first downstairs. She went over to the comfort of the long rusty heater, and stood rubbing her hands. Suddenly her eyes were attracted to three giant licorice drops on the floor. Quickly she looked to the steel cores of the rollers standing behind them, and her eyes travelled up the wall. The side of the rollers that faced the stove had melted and slipped to the floor. The licorice drops were pools of congealed gelatin.

Despite the labour pains, the first issue of the paper printed in its own shop was delivered, thanks to the improvising genius of John Jackson and Glen Miller. Glen, who kept the PGE around Lillooet lit up in the thirties, often by pure invention, transformed the worn old Miehle press so that it turned by electricity instead of man-power, to which it had been built to respond. Soon the stops and starts were coming more frequently, all the proper parts were touching, the paper clean and shining. Everyone stood around and waited, everyone but George. He was upstairs in No. 5 — a little editorial cubbyhole — getting next week's editorials ready.

"Ah," said John Jackson, as the press delivered the first legibly printed four pages, "this is what we've been waiting for!"

Five pairs of hands reached for this wonderful first sheet.

"No," said John, "this one is for the publisher. George, where the hell are ya?"

And suddenly there he was, running down the creaking old stairs, shirtsleeves, hat on back of head, be-pencilled waistcoat, eyes shining.

"I knew you'd do it John. By George, eh?" Dad put everything into that expression — gratitude, satisfaction, pride, and that special thrill that creative newspaper people know when they see their work in type.

Several other people helped us through our first year at Lillooet and remained to become our friends.

On press day Toody Cahill came in to feed the press. Toody not only helped out at the *News* office. The big oak tree which enfolded her house across the street provided Mother with a lead for her annual spring weather story. "It's true. Spring. It started at four a.m. this morning with the birdies ball in Toody's tree and wakened all the neighbors in this end of town . . ."

An Indian boy looked after wood. Alex English worked fine when hungry, but better when thirsty. However as his family multiplied, he settled down and did fine for our forty seven woodboxes.

"George," said Alex in the woodshed one evening — only the Indians called my Father by his first name — "My woman tell it to me dis kids need school."

"They do need school. Didn't you go to school?"

"No," Alex grinned as he adjusted the thong on his moccasin.

"Your grandfather was an educated man Alex. He was also a clever man. I've read lots about the English boys of Ashcroft. Which was your grandfather? Was it "Doc" English or his brother Bus?"

"Dunno," said Alex, picking up the axe again. "My

Mother tells it to me they wuz both around that winter."

The Van Horlicks drove up with bennet buggy and team every Saturday with vegetables. Mr. Van had such an accent that we once took delivery of a gunny sack full of cream cheese and one pound of green peas in the pod.

Martin Chenault, a tall rangy son of Kansas, delivered ice. His ice machine was a glacier, tunnelled into by gold seekers. Long before refrigeration, Martin was in the quick freeze business, taking a little meat or fish for himself for payment. In the thirties he cut the tops off five gallon cans, filled them with water from his spring and froze them solid. He sold blocks of ice for fifteen cents — use your own sledge hammer.

And we had alternating washwomen to keep our printing family clean.

We loved both Pauline and Jenny Ann — Jenny Ann just a little bit more maybe, being the frailer of the two, and landing every so often in the iron boarding house at New Westminster.

"How long for Jenny Ann this time, Pauline?" I once asked her.

"Dunno," said Pauline. "She tells it to me she not like it good this time. Them guys gives her cold room down there."

Jenny had run afoul of the 1st of July. If every drunk Indian were sent to gaol following Canada's national holiday, the place would be choked. But Jenny Ann when apprehended on this occasion cussed the police for ninety-two seconds without stopping and repeating herself, which was such a record that admiring throngs gathered around at the stampede ground and embarrassed the police officers into taking her into custody.

The youngsters in the Bridge River — Lilloet *News* plant got a very solid grounding in the publishing business. Father was the editorial mastermind, and mother was the ways and means, adding a few salty columns of her own only — at first — when the forms needed filling up.

George had a sort of Roycrofters vision for Lillooet; he loved saving type from a particularly good article and doing it into a booklet. He experimented with moose hide for covers and illustrated the work with linoleum cuts. Enough battleship linoleum to do a destroyer's wardroom went through the Lillooet plant during the thirties, half of it ruined by amateur hands.

Flour paste was made to mail the paper until it was discovered that a dry commercial mixture lowered the screams from the post office several hundred decibels. Mailing was done with a bone-handled kitchen knife, each name cut off the long strip directly onto the corner of the paper. The papers stuck together and names were lost. Often mother not only rewrote the name by hand but she also added a note to subscribers: "If you can't pay your sub in cash bring in a chicken. We got to eat, too." Or: "You're behind six months. Send Harry in after school. The woodpile looks sick."

The paper's editorial office was upstairs in cubicle No. 5 – a former bedroom. No. 5 was furnished with a good solid Underwood typewriter as old as I was. Two home-made kitchen tables were set against facing walls so that a swivel chair did for both "desks." A black telephone on a stem, with receiver on the side, gave the place its only city room "prop." A hole was cut in the floor through which a cord and clip let down copy and pulled up proofs. And a fourteen-foot length of garden hose, with funnels on each end, allowed instruction, abuse, and sometimes certain other material to flow freely from linotype to editorial desk or vice versa.

After Frankie sprouted his wings and left for greener fields, the *News* was visited with a series of linotyping characters which included the last of that colourful breed known as tramp printers. These men were brilliant in their work when sober; they were well read, and they had handled the copy of famous writers in their day.

Dusty Warnock was one of these. His real Christian name was Medford, and we used this when he consented to stand for Mayor of McGuire — a mythical town on the PGE from whence the fictional "Chezacut Locals" originated. This feature was sometimes quite hilarious. Views on the current scene were at times far more safely attributed to the lips of Mayor Warnock than to the local M.L.A.

Dusty taught me to write columns by the simple process of picking up a stick of stove wood and clunking up the stairs with it behind his back, knocking on Number 5 and demanding "Copy, by God, in ten minutes." As well as being a superb operator, Dusty was a great critic of the entire family.

Behind his rough demand for copy from me was the fact that he thought I could write a very agreeable column.

"For one so young, and a girl, you understand," he used to tell me so as not to inflate my ego too much.

"This week, he'd say to me, "we'll do a Winnipeg *Free Press* front page, since we have a good headline and a picture. Picture here . . . building the heads along and down like this. A box there . . . now why is that a good front page?" While awaiting an answer, he would slip around the stove, grab his jacket, and briefly disappear. "It's interesting looking, that's why," he'd resume, wiping his mouth with the back of his hand, and screwing the top on the mickey of gin. "It's heavy in the right places, here and here, above the fold. Small items at the bottom, lots of small heads. And balanced whether folded in half or whole sheet. D'ya catch, kid?"

Dusty thought my father was right up there with the best of them. "By God," he said one day, "do you kids realize the vocabulary a man has to have to write a half-column editorial without a single *t* in it? So my *t's* aren't dropping, for Chrissakes, and I'm fumin' and cussin', and calm as can be, he says "Okay, Dusty, give that back and I'll rewrite it without any *t's*. Why, the guy's a genius. It's enough to make you cry."

And that's just what Dusty would be doing a little later that evening, crying. Into his beer, spiked with whatever fitted his hip, and talking about his boss's vocabulary to a bunch of bleary-eyed kloochmen in the local pub, who hadn't the faintest idea what he was trying to tell them.

Aunt Nan Easson was a beloved house Mother — actually she was a cousin of my father's. Dusty was our guide and mentor out in the shop — at least from Monday until the pubs opened Thursday evening. So George and Margaret were free to move around the province, attend the sessions at Victoria, speak at meetings, make trips to the advertising agencies across the country, and be sure that all was well with "the family" at home.

Lillooet is populated with the sons and grandsons — and now great-grandsons — of the Royal Engineers, and of the first gold-seekers and adventurers, who arrived up the Douglas trail a hundred years ago. A few have kept the line Anglo-

Saxon, but many have mingled their blood with that of the native. The woman cheerfully washed the gold, drove the team and hewed the logs, raised the children, and kept the house. She smoothed the road for her fair-faced successor, whose chief hardship was homesickness in a strange land, and the lack of those amenities to which she had been accustomed. Some, like Eliza Copeland, laid the foundation of a fortune for their men. Eliza, out picking hoosim berries one day, reached too far out for the succulent fruit, hurtling herself into Cayoosh Creek. She was still regarding the piece of root and moist earth in her hand when a pebble rolled down the bank after her. It turned out to be a gold nugget — the first from the Golden Cache Mine, a fabulous find in 1896.

In our time, however, Charles Tupper, M.L.A. for Similkameen, and a director for some years of the PGE railroad, wrote an article for a tourist magazine describing the scenic beauties of the country through which his railroad travelled. "Lillooet," he wrote, "half-asleep with the torpid vicosity of its half-caste blood . . ." He thereby gave the *News* the only peg on which to hang a discussion of the mixed-blood situation. We moved our editorial guns around to Similkameen and burst out round after round of ammunition at poor Charlie. Mr. Tupper was an old railroader and could be expected to know about the word "viscosity" in oils, the paper editorialized, but there was nothing slow-moving about a district that produced five million dollars a year in new wealth, whose government office yielded a hundred and fifty thousand dollars tax money annually to the provincial treasury, and on and on.

Tupper, of course, was not talking about the Lillooet district, but about Lillooet town, and he was dead right about its torpid viscosity. No one moves very fast when the thermometer reaches 110, as it does through July and August. Nor do people generally move very fast in a climate that is mild in winter, where people live to enormous ages, where fruit and vegetables rot on the ground in their abundance, where salmon abound in the rivers, and game roams the hills, and where if all else fails, a man can still take a gold pan down to the banks of the Fraser and pan himself a couple of dollars a day.

However, by the time the incident had passed, the paper was enriched by one good news story, two editorials, and six letters to the editor.

"A good reporter, sweetie," said my father, "must know a great deal about a great number of things. But his copy will have double the punch if he has a peg to hang it on."

Dad never ran out of pegs.

In the old gold rush days they said that the towns of Lillooet and Lytton were cursed. They were known as the Sodom and Gomorrah of the mainland. True or not, the fact remains that seventy years later Lillooet rejoiced in a mighty relaxed moral code. In the thirties, priests and ministers of all faiths laboured in vain in the vineyard. A congregation of four at any of the three churches was par for the course. And a dozen people on an average Sunday morning was a sure sign that Hitler had reached the borders of another country.

At the *News* office, we knew about this first hand. Father and Aunt Nan attended the United Church every Sunday. Mother and Dan and I scrambled off to the rancherie, or the town church, depending on who was saying Mass. If it were "der Fadder" Rohr — Victor Rohr, O.M.I. — it might be at the rancherie up the hill. Father Rohr was the Indian missionary and his territory took in the entire PGE line from Skookumchuck to Williams Lake. It was a tradition with train crew and passengers that someone always looked out for Father Rohr, including the engineer. He never bought a meal in the diner but never failed to have full privileges. Many times Big Angus McRae, one of the old-time hoggers, backed a train of thirty cars of mixed freight, concentrates, cattle, and passengers a full mile up the track to the straggling party of Indian guides and the old priest as they emerged from the Leon Creek trail onto the tracks. It took almost a mile to stop a train on a grade like that. No station. Just a flickering light, bobbing on horseback through sagebrush and pine trees.

One reason that Catholics gave for not attending church was Father Rohr's limberger cheese, which the old man loved. He took this, honey, and Baker's chocolate with him for nourishment on the trail and the rest of his food was provided by the Indians. Occasionally he was careless and left some cheese on the rectory's pantry shelf. When a fresh supply arrived in the mail from Father's family in France, Postmaster Wilson buried it, they said. It was further rumoured that Father Rohr himself buried it under the town church to get even for the poor example set by the whites for his beloved Indian children. In any event, very few attended the poor little church into which half the town had been baptized.

Mother saw to it that — come fire, flood, or blizzard — we got there somehow, even finishing dressing on the way, having been stirred awake by 6:00 a.m. Not until eleven o'clock, however, did the head of the house emerge, immaculate, shoes polished, grey lounge suit, and big wide hat — while little Aunt Nan was all a-jingle with double silver foxes, flowers on the hat, earrings, white curls and black eyes dancing. Together they walked in the sunshine the few steps to their church.

Margaret maintains that Catholic children with loving Protestant fathers or mothers can't help but be schizophrenics. Our personalities weren't split observing Father lying in bed those early Sunday mornings: They were fractured!

Grandmother Murray visited us in 1936 and accompanied us to Mass at the Rancherie. The Indians sat on the floor with their children playing around beside them. The choir sang two hymns to the only tunes they knew, "Go Tell Aunt Rhoda" and "God Save the King." It was First of July, a Sunday, and Father Rohr had a dinger of a sermon for his people, warning them about the coming celebration and the danger of strong drink. This he delivered in Chinook and Pitman shorthand with some *commedia del 'art* thrown in. Grandma, a charter member of the WCTU in Zorra, couldn't help but get the message.

"Well," she said as we started down the rancherie hill. "Well," she said again, more or less stumped. "Well, anyway," she said, "I'm going to phone Mrs. Farrell when I get home and tell her those CWL ladies in Woodstock better forget their foreign missions and see what they can do for the Catholic priest up here in Lillooet, Canada."

Dad used to write up the Reverend Mr. Daly's sermons at the United Church as though it were St. Andrews Wesley and a thousand people were listening. But Mr. Daly had his troubles too. There was the local tax collector who took offense at the text for the Christmas Sabbath Sermon, "There went out a decree from Caesar Augustus that all the world should be taxed." Mr. Daly grew eloquent about the wickedness of those in authority in ancient times. "And to the wicked tax collectors," he said, pausing for emphasis. But his thoughts were ruined. A great commotion was taking place in the third row left as the local government incumbent got heavily to his feet, urged his wife to hers, grabbed his hat and left — never to darken the door again.

Mr. Cowan, a peppery little Englishman, was Rector of St. Mary's Anglican, the prettiest and most beautifully appointed church in town. St. Mary's was built in 1861, the second oldest church on the mainland of British Columbia in which miners found rest if the inns were full, and P.G.E. construction men did likewise fifty years after the gold rush. It had been endowed by Lady Burdett Coutts — the altar plate, vessels, organ, vestment and liturgical books all were the finest and most beautiful. It had a lych gate and beautiful garden. But except for marrying and burying, no one came to the church, Mr. Cowan tried. Was it a wedding?

"Dearly Beloved," he would intone as the bridal party took their places, and the organ music died away. "We are gathered here today in the sight of . . ." Then he would look around and shift gears and launch into a real blast. "How many Anglicans are in church this afternoon? How many were here Sunday? The Sunday before? And proceed to tear a strip off the congregation that blistered them for the rest of the year.

Mr. Cowan did even better at funerals.

At the *News* office we felt sorry for them all, and gave the ministers editorial space whenever they felt like putting their feelings into print. Mother was so upset at the Anglicans for ignoring their lovely little church that she did even better. She wrote a history of St. Mary's and had Ethel Ronayne, one of our helpers at the *News* office, make beautiful linoleum cuts to illustrate it. This she turned into a booklet, having saved the type from the newspaper, and with it the Anglicans raised five hundred dollars to restore the church and place above it's chancel a stained glass window.

Ma's Lurid Journalism

After we were established a year in Lillooet, Mother decided that the exchequer needed a boost with a special edition of the young newspaper. The PGE had given the editor a pass, as was its policy along the line, and several trips to Vancouver and a basket of nineteen-ounce pears later, Mother got Mr. Williams, the railroad's purchasing agent, on the dotted line for a regular timetable advertisement in the paper.

Then, loaded with cantaloupes, gigantic tomatoes, hunks of quartz, and a hind quarter of pork, she hit Vancouver on a round of the advertising agencies. Most of these were located in the *Province* Building, and they could all hear her coming as she and Peter, the elevator operator, brought each other up-to-date on the vital statistics of both while ascending in the ancient lift.

She would usually start the calls with a stop on the second floor, the *Province's* editorial rooms. "Peter, I'll just leave this carton with you here in the elevator if you don't mind. I'll be right back." And off she went down the hall with the quarter of pork over her shoulder.

Mother wrung every ounce of shock and drama out of every situation she was ever in. "It's a nice day, R.J.," she'd say to Mr. Jamieson, the music critic, who would allow that it was, and then do a double-take and turn and peer over his glasses at this apparition going down the hall.

Every other person she met spun around, eyes fixed on her as she marched to the office of Torchy Anderson, the Managing Editor, who, naturally, wasn't in.

"Tell him," she said to his stunned secretary, "that Margaret Murray called. We're printing a special edition in Lillooet about a month from now. I'd be pleased if he'd give me a little squib on it, oh, say a week beforehand, in your paper. And don't forget this. I'm leaving him a little something for the pot, and this pork is just a sample."

Margaret Murray was a public-relations expert long before people knew what the words meant.

Sometimes the combined ears of the family burned a little red as she handed out Lillooet produce — the biggest and showiest fruits and vegetables she could find to busboys, bellhops, pursers, hostesses, But she was always right at home in the public eye. And the haughtier the gaze, the better she liked it.

There was an awful to-do one night in the Georgia Hotel concerning some dressed turkeys meant for the Province Building advertising offices. Despite the long journey, Dad somehow always looked unrumpled. Mother, however, with her hunks of ore, fruits of field and stream, rolled-up newspapers and other impedimenta, was completely sublime in the ignorance that her hat was askew, her belt hanging or her overshoes flapping.

"A double room, if you please?" asked my father.

"Yes, Mr. Murray," said the clerk, "on the sixth floor, overlooking the harbour." He held the pen for Dad's signature in the register. "That is, you did want twin beds?"

"Young man," mother said in a loud voice, "We want a double bed. We're old fashioned. If people used double beds more there would be less trouble in the world today. Save your twin beds for a gal you can see daylight through her withers."

"Margaret!" thundered my father.

"Well, it's the truth." The voice had come down several hundred decibels, but the conversation had already been thoroughly enjoyed by all and sundry. That night Mother got her box of turkeys taken up to the sixth floor by two bellhops. The first bellhop carried them, the second went along for the laughs.

Upstairs, the Murrays sat a moment to consider the morrow's errands — and the turkeys. The restaurant was closed for the night, it was past ten o'clock. The manager's 1935 refrigerator was of modest size. The room was too warm for fresh fowl.

"What in God's name am I going to do to keep these things from spoiling?" asked Mother.

"What about cold water in the bathtub?"

"You can't do that — it would spoil the flesh overnight."

"Well, what are you going to do?"

"Get me that cord off that cardboard box," said Margaret. The fifteen-pound birds were released from their carton. "Now, tie their necks together."

"The necks were tied.

"All right!" she said decisively, making for the window and raising it softly against the dark night. Carefully she tied the twine holding the turkeys to the radiator inside the room so they would dangle outside the bedroom window. "Now let's go to bed."

By dawn's early light, every seagull on the Vancouver waterfront had heard the good news, wheeled up to the side of the Georgia Hotel for a look, and woke everybody on the north side of the building and in the buildings around. As the hotel switchboard lit up with irate calls from guests, and the air outside whirred with gulls screaming their signals for a landing on the adjacent sills, Mother gently opened the window and hauled in the birds, which in spite of a fishy peck or two were in prime condition.

With the odd exception, management at the two big producing gold mines was downright hostile to the little paper, and to the family that ran it. They were particularly cold and rude to my father for daring to suggest a better break for the miners and muckers. My mother they refused to receive at all. But who cared, said Mother. If the shift bosses were for us and the men in the valley hung around long enough, to hell with the rest!

A weekly newspaper in a small town is great only if it mirrors the town and community it serves. The "Letters to the Editor" column is still the least expensive and the surest reader-interest rating available for weeklies. In all our papers, the "Letters" column has always been an outstanding feature. The paper at Lillooet was no exception. And no *bonafide* letter was refused.

With the publisher a provincial Member of Parliament, and he and his family avowed Liberals, this policy was not followed without teeth-gnashing. In Lillooet, politics was a deadly serious affair. I well remember creeping into a Conservative meeting, my first political assignment, one night after the chairman had called it to order, and hearing my own father referred to as the (censored) carpetbagger from

Vancouver. I went outside and wept.

In 1937, in Lytton, three went to the hospital as a result of a fight between the Conservatives and the CCF's. The only reason the Liberals were not in on it was there were not enough Liberals in Lytton that year to get a good scrap going. Fifty or sixty votes each had been cast for the Tories and Socialists. Only ten were recorded for the Liberals. And we went through the agony of trying to figure out who the ten were! Of course, that was not as bad as at Alta Lake in the same election. One Liberal vote was cast there. If that was Alex Phillips' vote, what happened to Myrtle?

We accepted the Conservatives as a necessary evil, but the Socialists we distrusted and disliked. We were great free enterprisers in our paper, sounding off weekly about the opportunities waiting just outside the city for willing hands and strong backs. And when readers wrote in and called our editorials pie-in-the-sky and dream-bait, it was almost more than we could bear — especially if it were near spring and we were sick of beans and canned tomatoes, or the woodpile was low and all the subscriptions paid up!

But print them we did. We printed brickbats from the mine managements too, who took a dim view of the paper's support in 1935 for the striking miners at Bralorne and Pioneer.

"Four-fifty a day," said the paper, "is not enough for these men." This was followed by a table showing the cost of food and fuel in the Bridge River Valley, and the gold production table of that month, which ran into several hundreds of thousands of dollars.

And four-fifty a day to keep you in Victoria, answered the bosses at Bralorne and Pioneer, to the editorial writer, is six times too much! They thereupon withdrew their advertising support, started their own mimeographed sheet, and made it clear that the Bridge River Valley wasn't big enough to hold the newspaper, its M.L.A. publisher, and the producing mines at the same time. The miners, however, never forgot. Not that it much helped the Murrays: being miners, most of them eventually drifted away.

Not all contributions to the paper were of such vital importance. Some of our correspondents had problems clearly about the news from their district. One wrote, "To Whom it May Concern: I have the highest regard for our volunteer fire brigade, and was not being sarcastic when I reported that they were all wet. They were." Reporter Nina Anthony once offered her side of an argument with the Squamish readers in solid verse, which went on for two columns and ended with two immortal words: "I quit."

The paper, the odd time, was useful to lawyers seeking divorces for clients. "Please send us the April 15 issue of the *News*. We are interested in the guest registry at the Mines Hotel. Our client is anxious to secure the report that her husband registered himself and wife at the Mines Hotel that week. Having just returned from six months in the East, she is, as you will understand, puzzled."

This certainly made spicy reading. So spicy that, very shortly, we were forced to discontinue publishing hotel blotters in the news columns.

Sometimes the letters demanded retractions. The paper was death on wildcat promoters and dishonest practices, and sometimes our parents went a little overboard in their anger. "My client," wrote Angelo Branca, a young struggling Vancouver criminal lawyer, to the *News*, in 1936, "is not a crooked horse-trader and he is not a gypsy. He therefore demands full retraction for your statement regarding him in the last issue. He further demands that the retraction be given the front-page prominence given your reference to him."

The retraction, however, was not made, and the paper barely squeaked out of that one with costs, the judge doubtless aware that plenty of hanky-panky was going on in the mining industry at that time in the Bridge River.

There is no doubt that the British Columbia liquor interests were a great help to the newspaper's budget in the thirties. Bridge River, of course, was also a great help to the liquor interests. The first government liquor store at Gold Bridge sold out clean as a whistle before Christmas the first month it was open. And at this festive season, Mother would get thumping at the typewriter about what a bash you could get out of Vin Supreme, or a jug of UDL's brandy-gin cocktails. Maybe she would even do a couple of inches about the new tissue wrapping for Teacher's or McCallum's, suggesting at the same time other uses for the tissue. Once, she wound up, "Down here at the *News* office, our favourite tipple is overproof rum: $1.25 for a mickey. Mix with honey and nutmeg and boiling hot water, and you can get fourteen people smiling, seven people chuckling, and four people slapping their thighs, which is good mileage out of five bits."

The letters broke about fifty-fifty for and against the paper's stand on the Gold Bridge sporting houses. The controversy had raged on from 1934 until there were five or six hundred miners living in bunk houses in the valley, and more than a year had passed. The paper was for a fair shake for the sporting women, and said so.

"They were here first," maintained Madame Editor. George was away in the United States, drumming up interest in a Highway to Alaska, or the editorial might never have appeared. "If you want them to move, let's get in and help them move. Allow them uptown on mail days to shop. Stop harrassing them. After all, Gold Bridge was happy enough to sell them the lots and the lumber for their houses. They don't bother anybody. And it's fine to adjust your rose-coloured glasses and say these houses shouldn't exist. But until the six hundred single men in this valley can build themselves homes and bring their wives and families here, you may as well relax and face the fact that sporting houses are necessary to the safety of the women who do live here."

Running a newspaper in Bridge River in the mid-thirties called for a strong stomach. First of all there were the roads, which were incredibly bad. Passing cars and trucks slowed to a crawl and inched by each other. Even front-seat passengers got car-sick, and covered lard pails were standard equipment in cars. In winter, with heaters going and windows frosted, even the drivers got sick. But in spite of usually great care on the part of everyone who drove, a car or a truck was over the bank every day, sometimes twice a day; and after a big dance or celebration, every hour.

Dust blinded the Bridge River traveller, snow slid on him, rampaging rivers washed over him, mud engulfed him, and the unexpected ice spun him around like a top, but nothing stopped him. They winched him up onto the road, and away he went on his own steam, if there was so much as a sputter left in the old machine.

In the mines, it was a different matter. There were blasting accidents, and few walked away from those. The *News* reported: "He shoved the stick of blasting powder into his pants pocket not realizing it had not been properly extinguished."

And falling rock. "Bill had just said to me, "Send the tram along a piece, mate,' and then I heard it coming . . . whump. All I could see was his hand. His fingers moved once . . ."

And carelessness. "It was a harrowing experience for the witness to see his companion disappear down the shaft. Evidence shows that only the lower doors of the cage were closed and that the deceased had fallen out. They brought him up in powder boxes."

There were plenty of coroner's inquests, with the doctor bending over the cadaver in the back of someone's garage, chewing tobacco, and spitting freely in the course of the operation. "It's the only time the Doctor chews — at autopsies," said his wife to her friends.

After the inquest was as good a time as any for a drink. This was usually of indifferent quality, straight, and obtained from the local bootlegger, at least until the end of 1935, when the liquor Control Board opened a store in the valley. If you could stand the inquest, you could stand the drink.

"God Almighty, Mrs. Murray, did you hear about the cook at Pioneer?" Curly Lonetti, the barkeep at the Zarelli Hotel still had his apron on when he bounded into the Gold Bridge office of the *News*.

"What about him?" said Margaret.

Curly panted with excitement all through the story: "Charlie Cox just told me. This cook fella, name of Lee, has been on a bender, so he walks up the road towards Pacific Eastern. He gets dizzy and sick, see. So he goes over by this tree and shoots his cookies. Then he scrunches his hobnals over the leaves and dirt to cover it up and he sees something shining. He figures he's lost his teeth, but he feels, and the teeth are okay. So he bends over and touches the shining stuff, For Chrissakes, Mrs. Murray, it's free gold. Just sticking up there like grapes, and it's all over the place . . ."

By the time Margaret is in Curly's little flivver, and they're careening off up the hill to Pioneer to see the gold-encrusted quartz, obviously planted in the ground by high-graders — miners who smuggle rich gold ore from their work — to await an opportune moment for onward passage to a black market dealer in Vancouver.

Who planted the riches beside the road was never known. But that summer, Pioneer had struck ore so rich on the three thousand foot level underground that the miners could bend it, and it was brought to the surface in boxes.

High-grading went on all the time, and was duly reported. The men carried the gold out of the mine in their lunch boxes, their mouths, their ears, their noses, their navels — and yes, *there* to!

"Hey watsa matter with Ollie?" Ollie was out cold.

The men were emerging from the dry room after shift, and walking down a flight of wooden stairs to the ground below. Ollie had slipped and sat down hard — on about eighteen dollars worth of nuggety quartz, no bigger than your thumb. He was off work for about three weeks. And at the *News* office we were about the same length in time arguing how to write the high-grade story and not have subscriptions cancelled.

On one of these return trips from Pioneer, Margaret one day spotted the Public Health Officer who was making his first trip to the valley — and not before time. Townsites were building up a house, or a business a day and sanitary troubled brewed. Now a knot of people had gathered in front of the still-unfinished Truax Inn at Fish Lake and were going at it.

"Pull up here a minute, Curly," said Margaret. "Let's see what's going on."

"Believe me, Mrs. Skillicorn, your privvy ain't no honey pot either," the wife of the hotel proprietor was saying with heat.

"It may not be a honey pot, Mrs. Mac," said Thyra Skillicorn, "But if you would put lime in yours . . ."Thyra was a nurse.

"The hell with that. Why should I spend good money for lime when every sonofabitch on the road uses my privvy. It fills up faster 'n we can dig holes . . ."

"Ladies, ladies . . ." pleaded the Sanitary Inspector.

"And right there, Margaret had the background material for a good earthy report on the sanitation situation in the valley.

When my father was at home to edit and instruct, there was never any problem concerning good taste in writing. The youngsters around the *News* office were learning. But Margaret's lurid prose, from the looks of things, was going to need a firm blue pencil for the rest of her life. And my father was away a great deal.

While she was mixing it up at accidents, inquests, high-grading trials, town meetings, construction projects, and camp socials, George was busy speaking to service clubs in the city, making frequent visits to Victoria, and keeping warm the seats in the outer offices of ministers and deputies and others responsible for administering the Lillooet electoral district.

It was George who dreamed up packaged holidays at the dude ranches and lodges along the PGE railway — train fare, cabin, meals, and a horse — at fifteen dollars a week. Business for the lodges and ranches, passengers for the railroad, and wonderful publicity for the district!

"When we get all those little Vancouver stenographers and bank clerks interested in a Cariboo holiday, maybe we can charge for this space and have a holiday for ourselves," he said to Mother. The clerks and stenographers of Vancouver flocked off to the Cariboo at holiday-time for the next thirty years, but by the time there was money enough in the family treasury for the Murrays to try out their own medicine, they were at the cruise-ship age.

Every year George arranged a businessmen's tour of the Bridge River Valley. Another package deal. Twenty-five dollars covered everything, except his time and everyone's work. A pullman of Coast businessmen agreed to go because the area was so important to the economy of the province just then, and because they could make the trip and be away one day from their Vancouver desks. It was a big sales job — first to the businessmen themselves. The tour left at the close of one office day on the Union Steamships for Squamish, where the travellers boarded sleepers to awake refreshed at the foot of Mission Mountain the next morning. So you started early on the government-owned railroad, selling the idea to them. Being civil servants, the key men always had a built-in sales resistance! Then you talked the Steamships into quantity rates for dinner and passage. Next the taxi companies, which met the trains at the foot of

Mission Mountain, were enlisted for reduced rates for twenty-four. Hotel rooms were lined up free to provide washing and rest facilities in the afternoon of the one-day visit. At night, the visitors returned the sixty-odd miles to the railroad station for the return trip to Vancouver.

Since the members of the tour were mostly bankers, stock brokers, and manufacturers, the great and wealthy Pioneer Mines usually picked up the tab for a banquet at night. But the noon meal, my father said, provided an opportunity to rub shoulders with the truckers, storekeepers, telephone operators, and road gangs who were just as important to the industry as the miners.

Communications were primitive, telephone lines strung along trees on the roadside. Once, the lead car stopped *en route* and rang in about lunch from an emergency telephone box on a big tree. No answer. The caravan stopped again at Minto mines. No answer. The line was down in a windfall. There was nothing to do but take a chance, and the Stopping Place at Fish Creek put up good meals.

"Could we have dinner for twenty-four?" asked my father politely as he came up the path.

"Twenty-four? You talking about dinner, or you talking about lunch? Gawdammit, George Murray, you have sure took me with my pants down. I'll see. Fred!"

Presently, she bore down on the kitchen door. "I got pork chops for seven, lamb stew for ten, and rest gotta take poached eggs. Make up your mind. Them as wants to wash, line up out back. The can is behind the woodshed."

Such small crises notwithstanding, the twenty-four always got their money's worth on these tours. They returned to their firms not only more knowledgeable about the physical situation regarding the mining companies they handled, they saw also the crying need for an increased annual government budget which provided trails and roads, bridges, communications, and facilities generally. And what really topped it all off for George, they came back aware that many stout hearts and backs helped to produce gold — the life-saver of the thirties in British Columbia — and most never saw the inside of a mine.

Being a B.C. M.L.A.

My father was re-elected in Lillooet in 1937 with no trouble at all. He had kept his district on the front pages of the Western Canadian dailies with at least one good news story a week carrying a local dateline, and during the legislative sessions, Lillooet and Bridge River made daily copy by the columns. The mines were producing almost half a million dollars a month in new wealth. The Bridge River-Lillooet *News* was established in its own plant and turning out an exceedingly live and interesting little paper.

And the Murray children were learning — fast.

"Hey, why don't we print VOTE MURRAY on some of that scrap bond, put a staple in 'em and give 'em to the kids to wear?" asked Dan who even then was developing the Madison Avenue touch.

"Say, ya got somethin', Dan. What about printing some without staples and asking Mrs. Wilkins to wrap them around the bread?" said Bill Hambly.

The VOTE MURRAY caps were a great success and turned up on every rancherie and in every section-man's yard in the district. With the addition of mailing-list paste, they were applied — without the staple — to truck boxes and rear car windows

George was solid with the miners, owing to his support of their struggle for more wages, and the fact that management never forgave him was not an issue, until the miners moved away when war broke out.

He was the author of the first plan in British Columbia to compensate miners for the consumption which was an occupational disease for underground workers. A nine per cent tax was put on the industry to pay for it. It didn't come easily.

"Bralorne could possibly pay one hundred dollars a month to silicotic miners," he said at a mass meeting in the valley in 1934, "but no fledgling mine could pay that much. Even Britannia could not pay that much. Agree, therefore, to sixty dollars a month and maybe I can get it for you," he pleaded. "Hold out for a hundred, and you're likely to get nothing at all."

"Yea, Murray!" yelled the perspiring muckers and miners. They had agreed to the sixty-dollar pension, and the next year it was written into the compensation law of British Columbia.

In 1936, he won the regard of the PGE employees by fighting to change their status from that of civil servant to brotherhood. He was king on the farm owing to a bill he shepherded through the Legislature which allowed farmers to work out their taxes on the public roads. And on the creeks, there were loud hurrahs because prospectors could take their relief in grub-stake, thanks to Murray of Lillooet.

One of his dearest dreams remained the Alaska Highway. Promoting it on a speaking trip through the Pacific Northwest, he had received columns of publicity in the American press.

"You have to hand it to your father for getting mileage out of twelve hundred dollars a year," said Mother, sighing over the family books one hot afternoon. "Seven thousand miles he's travelled in six months this year so far — doing what? Promoting a highway that only the Americans care a damn about. That man Murray was born thirty years too soon. Just mark my words."

The summer before the election, the Los Angeles *Times* sent a reporter up to discuss the highway which would cut through the top of the province via Hazelton, *en route* to the Arctic Ocean. The visiting journalist was loaded down with mowich, fruit, fresh-baked loaves, butter and cream, road maps, books to read, and a three-hour pep talk — all courtesy of the Bridge River-Lillooet *News*. And away he went over the tortuous road to Hazelton to see for himself the route the Great North Road might take.

Another expense was the lively correspondence opening up about then with Lord Henry Paige-Croft who was shortly to be Under-Secretary of War in the British Government. A letter to England cost thirty cents. Sir Henry had a dream about settling Great Britain's unemployed in British Columbia's wide open spaces, notably the Cariboo country.

Besides opening up the north with roads, George's other pet project was immigration. "Land" was a sacred word around our newspapers. It never ceased to anguish my father that so much of it was vacant in his beloved Pacific province. "It's basic," he said in editorials, at the dinner table, during political speeches, or to anyone who would listen. "It's the old story of demand and supply. Use it or don't count on holding it."

Already he could hear the war rumblings in the Far East. Since 1929, when he had visited the Asian countries on the Pacific in the interests of trade with British Columbia, he had kept closely abreast of affairs in this theatre.

"There lies our market, out beyond the Pacific. There's where the Peace River wheat must go. Until we can bring B.C. grain to our B.C. ports, just that long will prosperity be delayed. Extend the PGE to the Peace River corridor. What good is a railroad with nothing to haul?"

If we got a little sick hearing about the Peace River around the *News* office, it was nothing compared to the reception given Father's outpourings in the Legislative Chamber at Victoria, where he begged and pleaded for development of the hinterland as the only sound "relief" for the big cities.

Along about the end of January each year, the old PGE would snort into the station about ten o'clock at night, hoary with the frost of Prince George, Quesnel and Williams Lake. It would stand steaming and chuffing in the station while crew members went around hammering for hot boxes or flat wheels or whatever they hammered for. In a moment, the engine would be uncoupled for a short run over to the roundhouse and the passengers would come out of the Pullmans in overcoats and overshoes for a breather, or to swap pleasantries with the locals on the platform, and get a look at the dark velvet night and the moonlight on the mountain snow.

Presently, a square red coupe would round the corner and slide into the wooden station platform. The door would open and a large tweed posterior would emerge, followed by an unfolding six-foot frame with a briefcase, beat-up club bag, a raincoat and plenty of reading material. Finally, someone would hand out a large, light, rolled-brim felt hat. The local MLA was on his way to Victoria.

"Give 'em hell, George . . ."

"Hey, Mrs. Murray, you go too, and then we'll have two members down there!"

"Don't stay too long. Your feet might web."

George would smile at all the pleasantries and carry on. But Mother would stop and enquire about road conditions, the health and prosperity of the family, listen to a story or even tell one herself.

Once aboard, my father would join Donald McKay, Cariboo's MLA, from Williams Lake, and the Hon. Harry Perry of Prince George, Speaker of the House. The three were friends, fellow Liberals, and their ridings comprised the far-flung and storied Cariboo. Never has a district had a more colourful or effective representation, and never did the Cariboo need it more.

The MLA's gathered in the smoking room for a night cap and a little pre-session gossip. McKay was sandy-haired, a blue-eyed Ontario Highlander, softly spoken with a delicious sense of humour and a highly-directed sense of purpose. He was a surveyor, stationed at Williams Lake, where a young wife and three pretty little boys awaited his return from the annual six weeks at Victoria. The Hon. Mr. Perry was a north country self-made Englishman who took to black homburg and striped trousers — or cockaded hat and gown — as though born to them. A convivial sort, a wit and raconteur, he was still a man of enormous dignity. In Fort George, he published a weekly paper. His two boys were at the university but his wife shunned the hurly-burly of politics and remained quietly at home.

At Victoria, George joined forty-odd elected representatives, much like himself. There wasn't a wealthy member on the government side of the House, and most were without previous experience in the Legislature. The fledgling CCF party was making its first appearance and was hard-pressed to devour all the bills and proceedings and other House business so as to be equipped to discuss the issues of the day. Among the Socialists were two or three professional men, a streetcar conductor, a couple of farmers, and their leader, E.E. Winch and his son. All had been elected for the first time.

With this new blood, the sessions at Victoria in the thirties were so amusing that tickets to the public galleries were difficult to get when the House's star performers were slated to speak. Trouble was, nearly all of them were stars. And a reporter in the press gallery had plenty of "light" copy to intermingle with the heavier news releases on legislation.

Notable was Tom Uphill, Independent Labour from Fernie in the Crow's Nest Pass, who in fifty years was never defeated, and was a veteran even then. So outgoing and sparkling was old Tom that all the female lobbyists to the capital were certain of a sympathetic hearing from the burly coal miner. The hairdressers, of all the feminine trade and labour delegations, were his favourites. All were referred to as his nieces and made thoroughly at home in his private office and lounge.

"Mr. Speaker, I had a couple of me nieces in the office this morning. Hairdressers, Mr. Speaker. Beautiful. The thought of them getting gaunt and skinny brings tears to me poor old eyes." The House laughed, but the hairdressers were shortly announced a basic wage increase.

I once heard Mr. Uphill talking to a Victoria *Times* man, Les Fox.

"There's a good fellow," Tom was saying. "Set me down a good idea to lead off with. Soften them up for when I get down to the meat, Les. It will jolly them along a bit and I've got a big public building program for Fernie this year . . ." All Tom's important speeches had leads written by the press gallery boys, designed to jolly along the ministers from whom Fernie's MLA wanted favours.

Thus it was that the member from Fernie would rise in his place, with the galleries filled and waiting. Tom seldom let them down.

"This 'ere Royal Commission," he once said, in his heavy Welsh accent, "puts me in mind of an outhouse. They take their seat, make a report and let the matter drop."

Then there was G.G. McGeer, K.C., Mayor of Vancouver, and later Senator, who came to Victoria one year accompanied by a bodyguard of two police officers. This display of mayoral authority and importance inspired his opposite Conservative number, Mr. Herbert Anscombe, to go down to the five and dime and buy a small toy policeman, which he opened and placed on the corner of his desk for the rest of the session.

"As a former mayor of Victoria," said Mr. Anscombe to the House as he unwrapped the parcel, "I think I owe this to myself."

"Mr. Speaker," said McGeer, rising to answer, "may I ask the House's indulgence to shake hands with Anscombe's police guard and remark that it is by far the most intelligent and best-looking Conservative in the House."

Without stopping, McGeer then went into a harangue on monetary reform that lasted for two hours. He covered money-changers, coupon-clippers, and bond-dealing usurers. He quoted Biblical verses, kings of finance, and bank presidents.

Mr. E.E. Winch, the leader of the newly-elected CCF's, who was going short of sleep as the midnight oil burned in the Socialists' quarters in the Legislative buildings, became so bored that he dropped off to sleep and fell from his chair. This created such a sensation that Mr. Speaker was forced to threaten the galleries that the ushers would clear all spectators if the applause and laughter did not stop.

One of the ablest of the group was Dorothy Steeves, who bore watching. She had a tongue like a two-edged sword, and ripped the government up one side and down the other. When she spoke, however, no one left the House, enjoying to the full her clever thrusts and parries.

"The mountains endure birthpangs," said this pretty blockbuster, referring to the government's shelving of the Health Insurance that year, "and only a miserable mouse is born."

Thump, thump, thump went the desks, as the House gave her "A" for effort and fine delivery.

"I agree with the honourable lady member from North Vancouver," said Tom Uphill. "This budget, Mr. Speaker, it's something like the blanket on me poor old Grandmam's bed. She had just one blanket to cover all the kids. With the Honourable Minister of Finance, the budget is the blanket, and it's two feet too short. With the rest of the Cabinet, they pull it well over their eyes and heads and are perishing slowly of chronic cold feet. And when McGeer gets hold of it, he strips the bed."

In a flash, McGeer was on his feet, declaring that he had just coined a new word. "Hoomallymally" was the word, Mr. McGeer said, and the budget was full of it. In fact, the budget assayed one hundred per cent pure baloney.

The lady members of the House wore corsages; the Conservatives, to keep their spirits up, wore yellow primroses out of Harry Pooley's garden in their buttonholes; some Socialists wore running shoes. The government was making a cautious study of health insurance that year, and the budget for the whole province was less than three million dollars. The vote passed to take care of the booming Lillooet district, whose mines each month produced a quarter of a million dollars in gold, was thirty-three thousand dollars. It was considered a vast sum and a great improvement on the record of previous governments.

Dad was a past master at getting publicity for his district. Just as his wife proffered her fruits of field and stream among those whose help she needed in various aspects of running the paper, so did my father — in much more subtle ways — point up the wonders of his constituency with well-chosen gifts illustrating the needs of the district.

Once each session, members might arrive in the Chamber to find on their desks a beautiful, ten-ounce golden pear. This gave Lillooet's representative an opportunity to get on his feet, tell them who grew the pears, the difficulties of trucking them into the railroad over the frightening Texas Creek road, the need for major repairs on that road, and the need for new equipment on the PGE so that the delicate fruit might finish its journey to the consumer without blemish.

One year it was turnips. Waxed ones. A tremendous innovation, developed at Pemberton, which sealed in the richness and juice of the vegetable. "And Pemberton is a show place, honourable gentlemen! Wonderful farmers, beautiful crops, a prosperous co-op, outstanding people, but oh, Mr. Speaker, the roads! Oh, the dreadful, tortured, miserable roads! Give us two thousand dollars for the Pemberton Valley road, Mr. Speaker, and I'll show you one hundred thousand dollars worth of these glorious vegetables by next year."

Cantaloupe, apples, Ashcroft potatoes — even hunks of quartz to be incorporated into a fireplace — there was no end to the variety. Once it was stuffed baked salmon, sent especially for the members' dining room with compliments.

And then, of course, there was the alfalfa. Who could forget it?

My father thought alfalfa had certain therapeutic qualities and was delighted to report to us once on his return from Ashcroft that George Chataway had had an amazing experience with one of his Black Angus bulls. The animal, a registered princeling, had been failing and the Chataway herd was faced with a fate worse than death, while Chataway was faced with the enormous expense of replacing the animal. While thinking the crisis over, the ranch boss put the animal out in a stubble field of alfalfa.

"And do you know, Margaret, that in two months George tells me that bull has regained his potency. Alfalfa did it. Nothing else," said Dad.

"Well! Alfalfa tea doesn't seem to be doing much for me, or that is, for my rheumatism," said Margaret, eyes twinkling.

But he was already deep in thought about his gimmick. For the spring session at Victoria this time he'd bring alfalfa. He would also bring several sealers of ginger pear preserve, and he would host tea in the dining room for his colleagues, compliments of beautiful Lillooet.

"Muffins, preserves," he wrote in a note to the cook. "I am sending along a bag of cereal for use in place of bran in the muffins."

The tea party was a great success. Luscious hot muffins with butter, and the flavoursome preserve. Delicious tea. A pleasant half hour of camaraderie, gossip, boasting about constituencies, discussing problems.

"I am delighted you enjoyed the muffins," said George as the waitress crumbed the tables. "That unique flavour was ground alfalfa . . ." He then told about Chataway's Black Angus sire. ". . . and I will be interested to hear of any signs of added vigour in yourselves," he wound, laughing.

"Great kidder, George."

"It must be all right. You look healthy enough, Murray."

"Tell me. How do you think up all this stuff?"

Laughing and joking, the members trooped back to the afternoon session.

The muffins, of course, were a disaster. Some honourable members didn't even make the 1:30 sitting next day.

Syd Leary of Nakusp was the Liberal whip at the time. His job was to keep track of government members at all times. Next morning he was looking decidedly peaked, with perspiration standing on his brow. He held onto his desk for support.

"Say, Syd. You sick or something?" David Strachan of Dewdney had just come into his desk in the empty chamber to leave some papers.

"Never slept all night," said Syd. "George Murray served us alfalfa muffins yesterday afternoon . . . Say, where were you?"

"Alfalfa muffins!" Strachan was from the Fraser Valley and knew all about legumes. "You're joking!"

"I'm not joking," said Syd, evenly. "Florence just polled the wives. Six are able to stand. Six can't sit. Only five can make it to the House and George Murray is the sickest of the lot."

On the Road to Mandalay

One day in July of 1937, the telephone at the *News* office rang two longs and a short. There were only a dozen phones in the town and district, and we didn't get many local calls. This one was from Victoria.

"Hello Vancouver. Hello Hope. Hello Lytton. Hello, Mrs. Murray. On your call to Lillooet . . . hello Clinton, hello Ashcroft." In those days, a long-distance call brought every operator in southwestern British Columbia to the alert. And eventually, that morning, there was Mother sounding as if she was shouting down a convention of seagulls, with the waves pounding on the shore.

"Hello dear," she said, "how are things? Is Dusty keeping sober? You kids got out a wonderful paper last week, but your father wants to know what you are putting on page three in place of Evans Transportation. Who wrote that accident report? Never mind, but Jimmy Hughes is . . ." (heavy line-sing, lasting twenty seconds) ". . . for China probably Monday."

"Can't hear you. Repeat that about Jimmy Hughes and china."

"Jimmy Hughes is furious, is what I said. He is writing you."

"Oh. What about china? We have only four cups with handles."

"They say there are no winds this time of year."

"Look, Mother, that's not the right answer. I can't hear you properly. There's a line-sing. I thought you said you were sailing for China Monday . . . yes, well telegraph it. I just can't hear you."

"That was the worst connection I've ever had," I turned to the staff and announced. "She just talked garbage at the end. Evans are sure mad about that slide accident write-up. Dad says what are we doing to fill the space with?"

"Yeah. And what was that about China?"

"Oh I don't know. Some garbled nonsense. Maybe dishes. You know, chinaware?"

It had nothing to do with dishes. Mother and Dad sailed Monday, all right, in a lush stateroom on "A" Deck of the *Empress of Asia*. The CPR provided the transportation, and the Murrays dug up their own expenses. The first session of Dad's second term wouldn't start until fall, and he was eager to have a look at the markets across the Pacific on which he pinned his hopes for British Columbia's future prosperity.

In 1937, China was a world away, commonly known for flying fishes, the Great Wall, Genghis Khan, and Madame Chiang Kai-shek. And it was thrilling — and a little frightening — to think that our parents would have this great adventure.

Adventure was the word. They were gone four months, barely escaping with their lives twice. Margaret wrote fifty-five, twenty-one-inch columns of seven point type — fine and close — without spacing or subheads. The material came in on dozens of sheets of onion-skin paper at a time. At first it was — for Mother — fairly tidy copy, as relaxed as the sumptuous staterooms they enjoyed on the *Asia*. She talked about the people they met. The chap who looked something like the late President Harding turned out to be Colonel Dillon, publisher of the Minneapolis *Tribune*. He was accompanying a prize Holstein bull from the *Trib's* purebred dairy herd to its new home with the Japanese government.

As the bundles kept coming, they grew more dog-eared on the outside, more chewed up on the inside until, finally, they got completely out of sequence and bore marks of censorship. Some of them, which my father had revised and edited, had to be retyped. The boys in the shop complained about the mechanics of so much setting. How, asked Dusty, could you make a paper look interesting with such grey blobs of solid type?

That changed soon enough, however, and readers were suddenly backing up the Wangpoo River into the harbour of Shanghai, shouldering their way with the Murrays between British cruisers, American and Italian gunboats, and hearing the familiar "No momma, no papa, please missy, coppah" of the beggar children around the customs shed.

The British and American ships were in the harbour, standing by to protect their nationals, while the Chinese and Japanese governments settled a dispute concerning a lapsed pledge. This was a promise, made after the 1932 conflagration between the two countries, that all armaments and troops be kept twenty-six kilometres behind Shanghai. A Chinese "Peace Preservation Corps," patrolling the world's fifth-largest city, was, Japan charged, a fake. A larger and more meaningful reason was behind all this, but in 1937 — with Japan arming like mad, and China mortgaging next year's silk crop to flesh out its Air Force — no one was sure what it was.

" 'There are nine and sixty ways of constructing tribal lays / And every single one of them is right.' " Margaret tossed off a little Kipling, and proceeded blithely out of the Cathay Hotel with Vancouver nonchalance to have a look around. She passed a Hindu policeman at the front door of the Hotel who thwacked six rickshaw coolies over the head to clear a way "because Madame wished to walk," went on past the corner of Nanking Road, the most cluttered traffic corner on earth, and headed for the bridge across Soochow Creek. George, in the meantime, was off to arrange his various appointments and clearances.

Margaret dodged bamboo "freighters" along the street — bulky shoulder-burdens borne by native boys — elbowed her way among the masses of people in the thoroughfare, open-mouthed at the poverty, disease, deformity, and degradation in every alley and store front. She observed the food peddlers, with hot meaty messes sitting in beds of coals, the whole suspended from a bamboo pole and doled out judiciously for a few pennies into waiting bowls of rice. "If I were blind and deaf I'd have some. It smells good," she said.

At Soochow Creek, onions sizzled just below the bridge rails on a squalid sampan on which a family lived and died. She paused to regard her soiled shoes and dress, freshly changed not an hour before, and had some second thoughts about the practicability of walking in the streets. A basket of drowned ducks floated past on the incredibly thick and turgid yellow water. As she watched the floating confusion, a barge of do-do — the name given to human manure — took her attention. Whole families leaned against the matting which protected it from the sun, laughing, scolding, playing. This barge was bound up-river with the swank Shanghai nightsoil for market gardens and would return on the morning tide with fresh produce. She made a mental note to discontinue salads for the rest of the summer.

On the way back to the hotel, there was a formal demonstration going on for a famous Chinese general, just emerging from five years in hiding in Malaya. There were also transfer arrangements going on in the harbour. The British and American ships had moved back into the Wangpoo, and six Japanese war boats were replacing them and disembarking troops in full kit. The evening paper reported two Japanese naval officers had been run through with bayonets, and the Murrays' sleep that first night was restless with the sound of muffled gunfire.

Just that quickly, my parents found themselves in the thick of a full dress, undeclared war that the Japanese called a chastisement and the Chinese never got around to naming.

"Those guns last night were the Chinese sinking shipping to keep the Japanese from getting up the Wangpoo. Endless refugees pass below our window. Rather dignified lot with their household treasures, mostly clocks, in their arms. We will look for another hotel. The Cathay is a little sporty for plain folks. I came down in the lift this morning with Mrs. Roosevelt. Besides, we might be here longer than we expect.

"The Emperor's flagship, the Japanese battleship *Idzuma,* is out in the harbour not ten blocks away. Dinner tonight cost a dollar more than last night. Who can eat? The man at the next table has 'sprue,' the word here for dysentry. He is a skeleton. The tongue and stomach get corroded — like wrinkled tripe. Forget your liver extract in the morning and spend the day in the bathroom. What a joke this all is. No business can be transacted. George can't leave the settlement area until this is settled. We could see burning territory in three directions last night from the thirty-second floor of the Park Hotel where we danced a little and pretended not to be alarmed. Friends who are old China hands say a little boom-boom, a few dead coolies and ducks, think nothing of it.

"We're moving to the Metropole three blocks away and half the money. Our room has a terrace overlooking the harbour. The refugees are swarming in. Different from yesterday. Riding, running, rickshaw, wheelbarrow, coolie, motor, walking, crawling, they descend, clawing and fighting their way through the traffic. The alleyways are glutted. Where they won't be trampled to death, they will sink to the dirty street and fall asleep. I tipped that shiek at the door to let the poor woman rest on the step. She wasn't resting, she was squatting to give birth. He threatened her with his bamboo lily and she crawled around the corner. Mother of God, what is happening?

"I can't say which is weakening most, my hands or my thumping heart. They're shelling us. Three planes abreast came out of the mist over our Metropole Hotel and dropped shells on the roof opposite. We could see the pilots heads and the belly of the planes where the bomb-nests are. It must be an accident, they're Chinese planes. They're after the *Idzuma.* You can see them taking a run at it. The noise is deafening. I can count twenty-one Japanese ships in the harbour, all shooting. There are milling thousands on Foochow Road. George says come and look but the powder smoke odour makes me even sicker than that awful smell of human excreta this place is noted for.

"We have windows shut and drapes drawn. No ventilation. Can't stand the fan: motor is louder than the gunfire outside. We're sweltering but must stay dressed in case we have to evacuate . . . hear in the hall the ear-splitting explosion an hour ago was the top four floors of the Palace Hotel. We almost went to the Palace. Mother of God! They're bringing the people here. George is back to change shoes. He is white and sick and carrying one shoe, covered with bloody foam and tissue. He slipped off a fallen slate outside into a human chest cavity.

"What is all this anyway? Can it be possible the Chinese are such poor shots they shell their own? These shells seem to fall at a forty-five degree angle. The British Consulate says to stay where we are. Where is there to go? Will I regret writing this? I admit all the sins of my past life and pray to be forgiven and to accept . . .

"Darkness is falling. Heavenly Father, what a holocaust. The asphalt caught fire and is burning the paint, blood, entrails. The smell. Awful. Cars upside down. Fifty killed this afternoon at the Cathay. The American Navy has just taken Mrs. Roosevelt away. Those people from Chicago, the Valentines, can't find their Billy. The Cathay has been emptied and the Valentines are here. No Billy. Machine guns at the entrances of the Cathay . . . thank God for the size of the clothes closet. At every hit this mass of stone and steel quivers and wrenches. We'll sleep in the closet till morning. If there is a morning. The water and power are off. Every word impressed on these keys is a prayer, but now I can't see. George has the flashlight out and the Bible turned to the fourteenth Chapter of John . . ."

But morning came, of course. And with it, rain.

The *Idzuma,* having lost a few crew members, a little paint and some splinters off her lifeboats, had backed off about six blocks from the front harbour. Consulate offices and banks were taking advantage of the temporary quiet to move to safer quarters, their staffs picking their way through debris and glass and corpses with files and strong boxes. The streets were running with diluted blood and messed with entrails. Corrugated tin kept rain off stacks of corpses. Margaret went back indoors, but George carried on to a piano shop and steamship office on Nanking Road to see about a cheap-rate booking he had made their first day in the city — for Singapore. Six dead Chinese were piled on either side of the doorway, killed the day before, and not yet picked up.

During the bombardment, the cost of meals had risen twice in the hotel's grill. Today, the seventh day, the settlement went on cash. From chits for everything, now this. The banks had been closed for days. Even Shanghai dollars were impossible to get. A letter of credit meant something to a steamship agent, but nothing when it came to services of a lesser sort. The taxis had been out of fuel for days. And the Murrays were out of cash.

George hurried back to the Metropole. "The British are disembarking a thousand soldiers. The troop ship returns to Hong Kong at noon. If we can get to the harbour, we can board a lighter which will take us out to the ship. There'll be climbing. Can you do it? We have less than an hour." Already he was gathering papers into a brief case.

"Of course I can do it," said Margaret. "There must be other women in this fix my age." She yanked at a dresser drawer.

"Keep calm for God's sake. You can only take what you can carry anyway."

"Our clothes?"

"Leave them on the hangers."

"What about your beautiful big typewriter?"

"Leave it."

"We'll never make it in an hour."

"There are rickshaws down front . . ." he stopped. He remembered he had no money.

Mother has always maintained St. Anthony got them out on that occasion. She says she sat down suddenly and looked at my father in that hotel room. Surely it would all turn out to be a ghastly nightmare. His shantung whites, soaking wet, looked like he had suddenly grown a great creamy wrinkled skin. Feverishly he was going through waistcoat pockets for a stray quarter — even a dime. Mother was too mixed-up for any formality like prayers. But the good old saint, she says, anticipated her need, and suddenly she thought about her mending basket and the fifty-cent piece she had dropped in it as she sat on the old side porch at Lillooet darning socks six weeks before. Change from the ice man. Passport to sanity — and safety.

Luggage belts were fastened, shaving kit jammed into a pocket, briefcases swept up, and coats pulled from hangers. Jostling and skidding on the slippery streets, they were pulled madly along to the berthing stations by an eager native boy, who knew that fifty cents Canadian would be more than he would make in a week.

The ship turned out to be HMS *Falmouth* under a heavy coat of grey paint. Margaret was still gathering her wits and straining to see her husband waiting down on the lighter for his turn at the giddy, the makeshift gangway, when words from the ship's loud hailer seeped into her consciousness. "Will the Premier of British Columbia and Mrs. Murray please come to the bridge. Will the Premier of British . . ."

The incredible conclusion to their frantic morning was a suite of rooms — the executive officer's quarters — reserved for the Honourable Mr. Murray and his party. All hell could be breaking loose in Shanghai, but protocol would be observed on His Majesty's ship.

"Well," said Mr. Murray's "party," when the cabin boy had bowed his way out, "everything happens to us. Do you feel as silly as I do? We can't stay here. Those stretcher cases. The children. This . . . luxury, this space."

"I may not be the Premier of B.C., but it's our cabin," said George. "Open the door."

That night, bound for Kowloon, as their ship glided along the Yangtze, past dozens of warships strung out in a line, more persistent wings than that of the Chinese Air Force hovered over the refugees. The captain managed to out-navigate the old bird except for one landing. In the evil-smelling gloom of the XO's lounge, pressed in against sick children, frightened and ailing oldsters, a stretcher case, and just plain unhappy tourists like themselves, a child was born — practically on Margaret's feet. For the first time in ten days, Margaret knew exactly what to do.

In Sagebrush Country

Back in Lillooet, with none of these gory details and with all news weeks late, Dan and I were too caught up in what we were doing to worry about our parents. And if we were a little inexperienced in providing recognition for feature writers like our mother, we were progressive in other directions. Had the name of the paper been shorter, we would have sponsored the local baseball team and supplied jackets. But embroidering the name cost more than the jackets themselves. So we searched out other ideas.

Among the truly valuable people who contributed to our paper was the correspondent from Williams Lake, a man named Taylor, who kept the pot boiling with bright local items, the odd fiction story, and when the mood was upon him, the weekly news budget cast in rhyme. At this particular time, there was more news of Williams Lake and district in the Lillooet paper — 150 miles away — than there was in the Williams Lake *Tribune,* which served a town three times our size and, proportionately, an even larger surrounding district.

Why not start a paper in Williams Lake?

"Sure," said Dan, the practical one. "But what would you fill it with?"

"Well, to start, take Mr. Taylor's news, and put a ten-point cap head over every item." Taylor, that week, had an item on culverts washed out on the Horsefly Road, which we could extend out of the public works report in Dad's office. We could run the PGE schedule for free, throw in some Slinger's Wine copy, and use a harvest cut, advertising fares on the CPR.

"Change CPR to PGE, and make the caption read Williams Lake instead of Moose Jaw, Saskatchewan — you could fill it up easily. Tabloid, you know. Nice and neat and small." I was the idea girl this time.

"And then?" said Dan.

"And then take it up to the Williams Lake fall fair and sell subscriptions."

"Let's see that CPR cut," said Dan, picking up the intercom to Number Five upstairs. "Hey, Miss Going, how's the bank balance?" he asked into the funnel behind the linotype.

"It's wonderful," returned the bookkeeper. "It's $178.85 and only the paper company to pay." Then, more cautiously, "Why?"

"Come on down here, dearie. We want to talk to you."

Within an hour the Williams Lake *News* was on the make-up table. We voted thirty dollars in cash for the car trip north, and we hoped that George and Della MacKenzie would put us up. Friday we were off to Zone 6, Territory 13, Department 2 of the great Lillooet Publishers Limited.

The rumble seat of the Ford was loaded with papers, sheets of newsprint, hammer, tacks, crepe paper, VOTE MURRAY posters, special editions of the Lillooet paper, and samples of printing. And the two hundred issues of Volume One, Number One. *The Cariboo News!* At the last minute, we threw in a bakeboard out of the old kitchen cabinet which would serve as a drawing board.

Dan was to be the star of the show. He had once spent a summer on the fair circuit as valet to a two-year-old Hereford bull. The job wasn't taxing — the first half of each night he curried and washed the bull, and the second half he threatened him with a pitchfork to keep him on his feet, neat and shining for the morning's show ring — so there was lots of time to pick up and practise the skidrow sounds.

"Yell something, Dan," I advised him now when the crowd, ambling down into the fair grounds, paid no attention to the newspaper stand.

"Have a lunch, have a drink . . . have a cold cold drink . . ." sang out Dan. "Right this way, ladeez and genulllmen . . . right this way . . . and over in the snake pit we have Jo-Jo the dog-faced boy . . ."

The flavour of what he said brought the people around. And once we got them we handed out newspapers, talked up subscriptions, took names and addresses and social items. Inside the booth, standing on a box, Dan drew funny pictures on newsprint on the bake board, or caricatured faces. We still have somewhere a crayoned hen with the bubble in her mouth saying "Ouch" as she dropped an outsize Cariboo egg in the nest.

We returned to Lilloet with twenty-seven paid-up subscriptions and as many promised. Two advertisements were lined-up with six good-sized store ads to come when we put an office into Williams Lake. The hotel and drug store would take fifty copies each for their newsstand. Within a month, Dan moved a small card press and a desk into the basement of the Lakeview Hotel.

The day the teenage publisher left to set up shop in Williams Lake, a curious phenomenon occurred which, for lesser souls, might have been an omen. A plague of aphids descended on the village. They darkened the sun, made the board walks slippery, and required anyone outdoors to wear a cheesecloth mask over eyes, nose, and mouth. As lights were turned on in the print shop, some of the exuberance dwindled from the leave-taking preparations. What would our parents think of this new paper? In fact, what were our parents thinking, anyway? In fact, where were they? We had not heard from them directly for weeks. Newspaper copy arrived by slow mail from time to time, but so out of sequence that we were weeks getting the reports into print.

"Kiddo, mail these letters," said Dan drawing a chair to the lunch table for the last time in 1937. "I got such a great idea last night I couldn't sleep . . ."

"Another great idea? What? Thought we'd heard all your great ideas."

"Carrier pigeons," said Dan.

"Carrier what?" Every spoonful of soup paused in mid-air.

"Pigeons. Pigeons. Anything so funny about that? Pigeons will solve the problem of getting copy down here without waiting for trains. And these letters are to four breeders in the States."

"Eat your soup Daniel, before it gets cold," said aunt Nan.

"Listen, with carrier pigeons I could write a news story on onion skin, slip it into an aluminum tube, and have the pigeon trained to land here."

"Yeah? What about other pigeons?"

"No, I'm serious about this. Think of the publicity. By CP . . . get it?"

"Wouldn't Canadian Press just love that?"

"I thought about that but what could they do about it?"

"Harken," said Dusty, with dramatic hand movement to ear." The sound of wings. A messenger approacheth . . ."

"Okay," said the Williams Lake publisher when the noise died down. "They laughed at Edison and Franklin. Mail the letters."

"What happens when the aluminum tube is full? Continued by next pigeon?"

"Sure. Wait for the 5:20 or the 6:10 flight."

That night about nine-thirty, a long ring on the telephone indicated a long-distance call. It was the telegraph editor on the *Province*. Did we know that George and Margaret Murray were unreported in the Pacific for three weeks? Had we heard from them? What and where was the dateline on their last copy? Did we realize what was going on over there?

When I'd answered as best I could, the faraway voice said, "The Red Cross will keep checking, so no real worry — yet." And hung up.

The young Hearstlings at Lillooet had been too busy with their own small empire to consider the real one. Thirty years has blurred the anguish endured around the old Cariboo print shop for the next two weeks. But the Murray kids grew up that fall.

And then, like a Pat O'Brien movie, there they were! It was a typical Murray arrival home — they opened the door and we all started talking. Bags dropped first, overshoes kicked off, top coats flung, and hats tossed. Conversation and outer garments marked the progression into the centre of the house. Everyone talked at once and continued talking for hours.

Hori coats, kimonos, brocade slippers, and ivory cigarette-holders were being modelled and admired while the Christmas week's paper forms sat on the press. Coats, hats, typewriters, boxes, newspapers, and luggage sat on the office counter and cluttered the floor.

"And now," said Mother, when the great day was finally over, "let's have a look at your books. Surely this can't be the bank balance."

"Williams Lake *is* a little behind with the printing bill," apologized Miss Going.

"Bring *him* here," said Mother. "Dan, what's the meaning of $75.00 in arrears on your printing bill? And why the spurs?"

"Well, gee, ma, I was just saddling up for a little ride."

"Don't 'gee-ma' me. What are you kids thinking about, starting a second paper in a little jerk-off place that can't support the one it has?"

"But you should see them read it on the post-office steps. It's great."

"If it's so great, why isn't there more advertising in it?"

Brightening, "We sell more than three hundred every week, and I sure got a lot of promises."

"Answer the question. How many subscribers paid up?"

"Ninety-eight last week. Forty promised for January."

"Yes, well, the day after tomorrow is January. Get packed. You're riding yourself back to Williams Lake this afternoon to do some collecting." Then she turned to me.

"Now, Madame Editor, we deal with you. You've been getting out a not-bad paper. I wouldn't say it was any better than it should be. You're not ready to be syndicated, but generally not bad. Aunt Nan says it's time you had a change of scenery. So here's your birthday present. You're on your way."

"Where on my way?"

"To Ontario. The pass is in the envelope. One way. I'll get you the return when you need it. And, Miss Going — as for you, here's yours on the Great Northern. Go home and see your folks. I want this Number Five cleared by this afternoon. Because I'm home and I'm here to stay for the rest of my life."

Famous last words, those!

When Dan got the replies from the pigeon breeders, he tore them up. But it seems to me less rational ideas worked out just fine around Lillooet. George hardly had his coat off that Christmas after their Pacific experience when he found an unusual way of solving a problem in type. The Chinese Relief had sent in a large advertisement, aimed at their people in our district, asking them to support a fund drive for war casualties. The ad would have had greater appeal with even a few words in Chinese. But the paper was ready to roll.

"Holy cats," said Billie Reese, "we have enough trouble around here with English, and we're late now."

'No problem," said George. "Ask Aunt Nan for a couple of good big Ashcroft potatoes."

As skeptical eyes looked on, he cut the tubers in half. The letters, torn out of the Chinese *Times,* were traced onto the smooth white surface of the vegetable which was then measured to be type high. When the sculpting was completed, plaster of Paris held it solid in the form, and *that* week, the Chinese raised $25,000 in Lillooet.

The family star was in the ascendancy right through to the summer of 1939. George was a much-sought-after speaker on trade matters in the Pacific. "Extend our shipping to the southern coast of Asia, provide airmail services at reasonable cost, encourage settlement from the Pacific colonies of Great Britain, exchange teachers, give us a Canadian Embassy in China, extend the PGE to the Peace River, and bring some of that golden wheat through the port of Vancouver."

A Highway to Alaska took on a new significance for him after getting mixed up in the Sino-Japanese hostilities in 1937. "There could be but one major objection to the project, and that would come from the high command of the Japanese Empire," he said in Seattle to the Chamber of Commerce.

"Those of you who laugh forget that our neighbouring Province of Alberta has brought in a crude-oil field in the past year which, with oil discovery in our own Northern B.C., will make Canada independent of outside distributors and possibly a valuable source of fuel to allies of the future."

"Western industry can be trampled into dust by an Asiatic economy established upon a system of peonage in field and factory. In the steel, mining, and shipping industries of Japan, men and women receive less than one-tenth the wages paid here. Conquest of China by Japan will give that country unlimited raw materials and manpower with which she could easily dominate the Pacific and perhaps the whole world. We have nine thousand miles of Pacific seaboard in B.C. and we don't own one deepsea freighter. We buy one and a half million dollars worth of rubber from the Straights settlements, and haven't the gumption to provide them with box materials to ship it in. They get their boxes in Japan!"

Articles, press handouts, editorials — all came billowing over the platen of his typewriter.

"For God's sake, write a book, and get it off your chest that way," said Margaret.

He wrote the book and poured over it for months. It was going to be a great success.

The trip to the Pacific had given my parents a new dimension in selling a totally rural area to the rest of the Province. Lillooet's almost tropical climate nurtured glorious fruit of field and tree.

"TOMATO WEEK," clarioned the front-page banner, while a rousing editorial outlined with what little effort a local co-op could establish a cannery and *make jobs*.

"CANTALOUP FESTIVAL FOR NEXT YEAR," projected the front-page of the week following, accompanied by an imagined eye-witness story of Water Street in the Vancouver wholesale district receiving its first carload of the luscious Lillooet fruit.

"Fer Chrissakes, Aunt Nan," confided Dusty one hot June day, "they've all pulled out and forgot to leave me a headline. Call it and you got it. Shall we push the PGE on to the Peace?"

"Yes, sure. And arm every post-office striker with a pick axe to build it. Aren't you saying anything about the new paper at Squamish?"

Dusty did run something on the new Howe Sound *News*. Reading it thirty years later is a little unsettling. In a declaration of faith concerning the future of the little port on Howe Sound, George had foretold some wonders that must surely have made him look foolish in 1938 — electric locomotives whistling through the Peace Pass in the Rockies; oil tankers on the track at Squamish from Peace River oil wells; grain ships in the harbour for China; glistening beacons on the mountain sides to guide the trains, and the planes; and a paved boulevard along Howe Sound to the city of Vancouver. All this was to happen by 1963, he said, and they laughed. But it all happened.

And what was Margaret doing that week? Oscar Carlson. The unfortunate man came within a shade of drowning in his soup at See Hing Lung's restaurant. He got drunk and fell asleep, dropping his head into the juicy gargle.

"My my," said Aunt Nan. "This week's paper I'll have to send to them down East. They wouldn't believe me if I told them."

Every issue, the paper banged away at the Japanese menace in the Pacific. Meanwhile, encouraged by Dad, old men set down bits of history, learned at the knees of their gold-seeking fathers, and submitted them for safe-keeping to the columns of the paper. A Lillooet woman, a life-long cripple following the Lusitania disaster, leaving on a journey to the hospital, wrote her good-byes in eight lines of poignant verse for the editorial page.

"Of course use it. You never can tell what encouragement it will give people," said my father. So Hazel got her poems into daily editorial pages and eventually into a book. Nina went on to a career in radio. Ralph became so well known he went in for politics and eventually became a Cabinet Minister. H.E. Taylor took on a *nom de plume* and is temporarily lost in the shuffle. But he was probably the cleverest of all. He applied a gift of meter and rhyme effortlessly to the daily grind at Williams Lake where he was, in fact, Indian agent. Each week the *News* at Williams Lake had a neat little two-inch bundle of Taylor's wit on the editorial page, just big enough to slide over the stone to the Lillooet editorial page. Mother once sent H.E. some luscious snow apples which each fall would colour the news-office yard a rich rosy red. Wrote Taylor in a "Letter to the Editor":

"Some people get all hot and drippin', in praising up the Ribstone Pippin.
But the Snows get you hot and het, the Snows that grow at Lillooet.
The Snows that soothe your mental flurry, the apples grown by Mrs. Murray.
They're better far than Scotch or beer.
They're better far than wretched pelf.
In fact they're — well — they're life itself."

News was often spotty, therefore anything important got a wide play. In January of 1938, there was the election fight in which a bystander received a fractured skull, and the whole thing was in and out of the courts and newspaper for a year before settlement. In May, a drama of the last great West took place — a cattle rustling trial which took up columns, half in the "you-all" dialect of the crafty old defendant, aged seventy-six. This was the year of the first mail plane to the Peace River, in which the mail in a brand-new canvas sack didn't weigh as much as the lock on the sack. M.L.A.s in the electoral district which the mail flight would serve were invited aboard for the inaugural trip. Sheldon Luck and Ginger Coote were at the controls. Passenger flying was so new in the hinterland at this time that the four-place Fairchild's weight capacity was decided only after one or two tries at getting airborne.

"What's the matter?" asked Margaret, as Luck taxied the Fairchild up from the end of the lake to the waiting bystanders.

"Nothing. Can't get it off the ice, is all. We'll have to lighten her." Ginger was disembarking the passengers.

"God, George," he said to my father. "I know how much this means to you, but you're the heaviest."

Still, George got as good a story out of it as if he had gone.

And there were obituaries. "As life slipped from him, the old lady bent over her husband, and wiped the old chief's forehead gently. Remember God," she said to him. "Now is the time, Joe, to remember God."

Old Chief Sundown, otherwise Joe DeShields, whose little hand-hewn cottage and riotous garden nestled next to the bank on the Main Street, had collapsed on one of the sunny benches. George had helped carry him home and had heard the words.

"At the end," the story continued, "stolid Indian women came and sat near the house, and white people of all classes came to express their sympathy."

There was hometown tragedy too. When a neighbour's eight-year-old boy had his skull punctured in a sleighing accident, Margaret first gathered up a feather tick off her own bed to improvise a flat surface in the back seat of a sedan for the child. Then she hurried to her typewriter to say, "Last night in Egan's Alley, tragedy raced and overtook an eight-year-old sleighrider . . ."

At least a dozen youngsters learned the business of

writing or producing news in these years. And the bundle of clips each January from the Dominion Clipping Service in Toronto was a two-arm load from the post-office. In fifty years of newspapering, however, George and Margaret won not so much as a single award of any kind, save a twenty-five dollar war bond for one of Margaret's World War Two editorials called "Hold that Line". The staff, as a matter of fact, considered it ordinary.

General Sir Henry Paige Croft, Bart., C.M.G., M.P., arrived in September from England. War clouds were hanging over Europe. That master public-relations stroke, the Royal Visit to the Dominion of Canada, was already on the drawing boards at Whitehall. Country after country was being gobbled up by the paper-hanger Hitler. The Sudetan take-over had just been accomplished in Europe. And here, in British Columbia, adjacent to railways, roads, telephone and telegraph, schools and churches, were 3,915,000 acres of vacant land.

"Prayer is not enough," wrote George in September. "There must also be works. Settle the vacant land. Let us bring in Sir Henry's ten thousand settlers."

"And have them starve to death?" jeered the outspoken editor of the neighbouring Ashcroft *Journal*.

Back shot the editorial reply from Lillooet. "You were a Scottish immigrant fifty years ago. Did you starve, Bob?"

Sir Henry, his son, his secretary, the shipping master at Newcastle-on-Tyne, were met at Kamloops by Cabinet Ministers from Ottawa, M.P.s and M.L.A.s, and together the party tramped the open fields and drove the gravel roads, tea-ed with Women's Institutes, banqueted with their farmer-husbands and with boards of trade from there to Prince George and Prince Rupert.

George travelled with the Crofts all the way, working out with them a simple enough scheme to provide for the new settlers. But by the time the governments of the two countries got around to investigating the treasury possibilities of establishing these settlers, the world had its mind on tanks and bombers, and the emigrating settlers were being fitted out in khaki.

As 1939 wore on, the war momentum built up. Communiques from London on the settlement scheme grew vague and finally stopped altogether, Paige-Croft was suddenly

Undersecretary for War in the British Cabinet. The editorials begged for the Alaska road, feared for the Japanese fishing fleet at Steveston, and warned that if business was bad it was going to get worse. Margaret anguished through columns of reminiscence of the 1914 conflagration. The paper suddenly filled up with accidents, suicides, and murders. The only real diversion that spring was provided by a miner at Bralorne who got grinding up highgrade, sifted and peddled it to Jim Brothers in Lillooet. Even Steve, the office cat, went to pieces and took to massacring birds so that the editor was forced to advertise for a bell small enough to collar him with.

And suddenly there arrived the invitation to meet the King and Queen. Mother discussed it with readers. What would she wear? And what a time she was having practising the curtsy with the aid of one of her husband's walking sticks! As some ladies consulted with *couturieres* on fox-edged georgettes — which had commentators and reporters cross-eyed for the entire visit, mixing up plump dark Canadian matrons with the Queen of England — Margaret went down to Parks Store and bought two boxes of hyacinth blue, three-ply fingering, and knitted her own. Then she and George whipped off to Vancouver over the twisting canyon roads to have their first glimpse of the Royal Pair outside the old *Chinook* office on Main Street, and later they were presented at Victoria.

Dad said the presentation aged him twenty years, fearing how Mother was going to act — or react, he wasn't sure which. And the two-hour wait in a stuffy anteroom to the blue-carpeted Legislative Chamber as the Royal Couple caught up with their schedule did not help. The emotional Margaret thought first of her Irish father, Pat Lally, and wondered if she might do something awful like pull the Royal Personage off the dais and kick him. Then she thought of the battleship out of Shanghai and wondered if she might pull him off the dais and kiss him. George, who read her like a book, administered a smart jab to the ribs as the line started to move, advising her sharply to pull herself together. And the battleship won.

"I didn't kiss him," said Margaret in her column the next week. "But I shook hands till his poor little sword rattled."

When war came in September, it was a relief to know where you stood.

"Wait, Dan, a little. We have three papers to get out here. I just cannot let you go, that's all. All these bills. The business will collapse." As Margaret pleaded with her son, she was aware that she had said these words before — twenty-five years before.

"The hell with it," said Dan. "I'm going."

Margaret wrote about it the next week. "With a stroke of pen, the simple oath of allegiance, the return of a few personal trinkets that find no place in a soldier's kit, the future has been swept away, leaving us momentarily very very old and bewildered. The warmth has gone out of the Lillooet sunshine."

Margaret could turn her emotions to copy. But a little bit of George died that day, and he didn't set it in type.

Pioneer Mine went out on strike in October, only to find that any strike was illegal for the duration of the war. Some 550 men were out of work for months. The loss in new wealth from the bowels of the earth was counted in the hundreds of thousands of dollars. *News* readers at the mines drifted away to be replaced by a new and older crop. In previous wage disputes, the paper had supported the miners. This time it supported the law, and the disgruntled miners retaliated by cancelling subscriptions and getting out a sheet of their own.

"Your diatribes," wrote Angus McIsaac of Spence's Bridge, old friend and reader, "against the CIO leaders have been applied before to others who fought for real democracy. Cancel my paper."

"Easy for you, McIsaac, powerful official of a great union, well-paid employee of a great railroad, to talk. But why violate the law and cause misery and distress in an issue that can only come second to the terrible war which engulfs us?" This the paper answered back.

But there were plenty like McIsaac around who took a dim view of the editorial stand. Supporters among the miners joined the army, went into defence work, and drifted away. Never again was it quite the same at the mines.

Being a Liberal paper didn't mean always that editorial policy hewed to the party line. Radio had ended an era in which newspapers had direct effect on the way people voted, but the Murrays had not got the message. George made no bones about making the newspaper a sounding box for the "hinterland," as he called it, and at the same time for himself. And as the war got into its stride and it became increasingly evident that the light he had caused to flicker momentarily across the northern part of the province was going out, both he and Margaret doubled their efforts.

Margaret let go a blast at the Premier, her husband's chief. He had been quoted in the daily press as agreeing with certain troops, stationed at Nanaimo, when they complained about being tired of apples. He, Mr. Pattullo said, had tired of porridge as a child.

"What are we coming to?" editorialized Margaret. "It smacks of senile decay on the part of the Premier, panty-waist fortitude on the part of the soldiers, meddlesome mischievous effort by the publisher to stir up such silly controversy. Pattullo can thank the goodly porridge of his Zorra, Ontario, breeding for his long hold on the Liberals of this province."

This kind of writing could not be expected to endear her husband to the Premier. In the same issue, she flayed the cost of British Columbia education and pointed up the fact that Johnny couldn't read in 1940, either. She had forecast the yearly Legislative session in Victoria: "The reformists will fold their soft hands over their contented breasts and feel satisfied. The columnists who poke fun at yokel members whose wispy hair and table manners are the twisted delight of today's public, will go back and polish the seat of a chair. The Cabinet will heave a sigh of relief. Only the private members, the back-benchers, will know what the country needs. The city men take a streetcar. But the country members come back and stare the roads in the face, to contemplate how much better or worse they will be in another year, with its new grants and provisions." In very truth, elections were won or lost on roads in the Cariboo.

Not even Margaret's wind up "par" — "No one else in the family or on the staff should be held responsible for this week's opinion. It's all mine. M.L.M." — mollified her husband.

"Margaret," wrote George from Victoria, "in the name of reason, what are you trying to do to me?"

At Victoria where another light was dimming for George, 1940 caught him and other country members in the bewildering maze of changing days. He was driven back in upon himself thinking. He and his up-country colleagues came forward here and there, with soft but considered voices, warning: "If you cut down 75,000 acres of trees yearly and replace them with 10,000 acres of seedlings, you will one day want for trees; if you exhaust your own ores and neglect finding new deposits, you will one day whistle for a mining industry; if you gamble with tax money, you may not win the lottery. Fish may be over-caught, game slowly extinguished. Writing letters does not till the soil or fertilize it. In the end, human wants can be filled only by human effort."

To this, George added a further reflective note. "Lack of action to thrust the Pacific Great Eastern Railway north by great and responsible business executives in this province will force the political setup in B.C. into the most radical lines yet introduced into the affairs of this province," he said quietly. "This complacency may mean the end of the great parties who face each other on either side of this House. The Liberal Party may never return in our time, nor in the time of our children."

"Ha, ha, ha," came the reply. "Good old dreamy George. Fine fellow, though. Can sure talk."

"Don't be too sure. Coalition *sounds* good, mind you." Coalition in British Columbia was the coming together of the two old-line parties in an effort to efficiently prosecute the war. Had it included the third party, the C.C.F., George might have been for it. It did not.

And so they talked and tossed it off. But an expert Press Gallery correspondent, Sandham Graves of the Victoria *Colonist,* was moved to write this: "Often it is the real voice of Canada that speaks from a rural riding where men fish or plough or chop wood for a living. There is something infinitely attractive in the real voice of Canada. There is a basic optimism borne of many conquests on the edge of the wilderness. It is friendly; human beings themselves being among the scarcest evidences in a great, empty land. It is a voice that speaks from a real and timeless set of values. Man is judged by what he does, the surest test of all . . . it may not be fashionable to say so, but the saving grace of your present-day Parliament is the country member."

The Empress Hotel in Victoria is a twin sister to the old Vancouver Hotel as it used to be. Both main dining rooms glistened with polished mahogany, dark burlapped walls, Edwardian royalty framed in pompadour, lace and orders, tiaras and court dress. Clusters of lamps burned yellow in the dim interior, casting stars around the room on the table silver and service implements. And there were potted palms.

"We really should have walked uptown and saved the money," said Margaret, as she shook out her table napkin. She was down for just a couple of days of the session this time, just long enough to hear her husband speak in reply to the speech from the throne. "Besides, we need the walk."

"Before this war is over, we'll have plenty of walking," he answered. "How about a small steak?" He looked at her over the years, twenty-seven of them. He was grey but dashing as is the way with dark-skinned people with black eyes and brows. Nature had not been so kind to Margaret whose fair skin was faded against the short hair which was merely pepper and salt. But her hands were small and attractive still, her ankles well-turned, and the classic little round Dobbs hat she usually wore did its best. "You look rather well tonight, my dear," he said.

"And you look tired. Maybe depressed is a better word."

"Maybe it is. Hart is cutting out statute labour. No more road work for farmers paying taxes. Everything is main highways. Grubstakes and mining trails are out for the duration. Truthfully, it would be better to be defeated and be quit of it all."

"Resign then. We'll just sit out the war with the paper."

"I can't do it. I can't agree with coalition. Coalition could well be the end of the Liberals in this province, but I'll be defeated as a Liberal, not a Coalitionist."

"Well, that seems to settle that," said Margaret. "And here is the soup."

The edge of bitterness showed now with George. Failure consumed him and drove him to all sorts of extremes as he thrashed around seeking an escape for himself. His extrovert wife, watching him withdraw from the scene at times like this could not understand the suffering that went with it.

With an election coming up, would he make it? And how could he unless he bent to the task of getting out literature, working on voters' lists, finding the necessary money.

"I could fairly explode," wrote Margaret to her daughter, "shower brimstone and lava over a large area, burn some and scare hell out of others. Your father takes so much time and management with his temperamental whims that this place has been disorganized since May 1. If he's licked in this election, he'll be like the peacock. And he will be licked unless he gums his hands to the task. The mining bug has bit him. He spent three hundred dollars on a cinnabar prospect, and this is what he got: one partner steals powder from the railroad, and the attorney-general threatens to expose. The lawyer fails to register the claims. Another partner double-crosses on the bill of sale and he can't restake. Am I supposed to clap hands that now *you* are looking for diversion in England?"

George retreated into old Number Five upstairs and took it out on the typewriter keys. In editorials, news stories, faked "Letters to the Editor," fillers, even classified ads, he fought to stand on his record, and the record of his party. He projected, sermonized and reasoned, and started his campaign with a good row with Bruce Hutchison, even then an important voice among western journalists. Bruce had criticized the roads in the Lillooet riding. The fact that he was intimate with the opposition candidate only poured salt in the wound.

"Verbose cynic," said the paper, thus taking on every city newspaper in the province. "Bruce counted his political chickens eight years ago and they turned out to be ducklings. He hasn't set foot in the place since," it sniffed.

The letters column raged. "This rag of a paper with its Liberal editor has the nerve to speak as though it represents the entire district," wrote R.H.E. Taylor of Pemberton.

"One way to save a dollar for war expenditure seems to have escaped your notice," wrote another citizen. "This is by *not* subscribing to your paper. Another way is for the government to stop wasting money. And a third is for Murray to stop agitating about big schemes which mean nothing."

Even town children took sides in the election. One of them stuck a ball bearing into the plumbing on the Mile

Zero cairn, a stone monument built under the paper's leadership, to mark the beginning of the Cariboo Road. The cairn trustees — mostly Murray supporters — had just antied up almost four dollars apiece to finally get it paid for. "A Drink in Thy Name" engraved on a brass plaque above the fountain had been his idea. So well was the sabotage accomplished during that election campaign that the fountain has never dispensed a drink since — in anyone's name. And election night, a neatly aimed rock dispatched the light which crowned it — the only street light in town.

George and Margaret were alone the night the election returns came in. There did not seem to be another Liberal in the town. Even Joe Russell was chomping his cigarette-holder in someone else's living-room that night. The children were off to the wars. Aunt Nan was in the south, the remaining staff preparing to join up.

"I told you, dear, that you'd have to stir yourself more." Margaret said it gently to measure his disappointment as the returns got worse and worse.

"Margaret," he turned to her, "I've done my utmost for Lillooet. No man could have tried harder. This was bound to happen."

"Are you sure you feel that way about it?"

"Look, I'm free again. I've wiped the slate. I did what I thought was right and was turned down. Now we must see what great adventure is still before us." He took her in his arms.

"First, we'll get at that book," said Margaret, after a long moment and a quick dab at her eyes. "I'll call Hilda Haylmore first thing in the morning. She said she'd type it for seventy-five cents an hour. I wonder how she voted. You just don't know any more."

By the time they got to Idaho with the book for publishing, Pearl Harbor was news several months old, the Pacific coast was blacked out, "A" is for Apples and other mysterious code messages were being broadcast several times a day, and the newspapers were filled with the news of uprooting Japanese aliens and re-establishing them in the interior. Trade in the Pacific was dead, for even with Americans in the war, the contest looked like it could go on and on.

It was May and their spirits were infected with the promise of a new season as they discussed it, hurtling into the sagebrush beyond Lytton on the way home. The big slide was presently behind them and they were levelling out on the straight stretch to East Lillooet.

Suddenly up front, the Lytton stage had stopped in the middle of the road, with people standing around it. The driver was boarding passengers.

"Will you look at that," said George, stopping the car.

Two elderly Japanese were bidding each other good-bye. They held their palms together against their diaphragms and bowed — once, twice, three times. The driver was giving careful attention. His Lytton stage hadn't been so filled up in a year. Couple number one dissolved and was replaced by couple number two. George walked up ahead and the driver, noticing him, came to meet him.

"When did this happen?" asked George.

"Yesterday morning. Where were you?"

"Many?" asked George.

"Altogether, 3,800," said the driver.

"I don't know how we worried out the year, but we did," recalled Margaret later. "It was pretty bad. We had never minced words concerning our fear of the Japanese Empire or their people in Vancouver. People soon forget, but we were not alone in this fear. We had Japanese submarines off the coast and could not reasonably be expected to feel otherwise. Steveston, near Vancouver, was a thriving fishing community with a harbour full of small craft and knowledgeable mariners. Wharves loaded with fuel and a fleet of Japanese-owned trucks standing. Everyone was scared and made no bones about it.

The Japanese had been sent to Lillooet at the command of the Federal Government, practically overnight, to the relatively remote and bottle-necked benches, there quietly to wait out the war. There had been rumors, but destinations were a well-kept secret until presently, filling Pullman after Pullman, there they sat on the siding at Lillooet. Quickly they filled in for the population away on the various fronts of World War II. Gratefully accepted was their trade in stores where the cash register bells were gathering rust. Gradually they were made to feel at home, since they are likeable and industrious people. Even the Chinese community softened and accepted them.

It appeared there were two outfits in town who found it a bitter potion. Margaret had kept up her running fight to the very end, with a sizzling editorial on the hook for the operator to set the week they were in Idaho. And Jack Wright, hotel owner, died hard too — perhaps being just a touch influenced by the fact that the Japanese did not enjoy Canadian beer.

"You better look out, Margaret Murray, or the people around here will tar and feather you. And don't laugh. You hear some pretty heated talk standing behind those barroom taps..."

"Ah, the hell with them," said Margaret. "At least I'm honest and say what I think out in the open."

"That's all very well," said Jack. "But as a friend I'm warning you. Shut your mouth down there at that paper or — leave town. Get out. What is there to stay for? What justice is left? What is the use of anything?"

Margaret went home and put her mind on writing her next travelogue, which she hoped would be up where the Americans were just barely starting on George's road — the great defence project now, to Alaska. *Their* road, she told people, even if it was starting from Edmonton instead of Vancouver.

But Jack Wright put in a troubled night. And next morning while driving to his summer place across the river, he went over the bank in his dashing sports car and died underneath it.

Stars and Stripes

The first regiment of troops on the project walked their heavy equipment — tractors, trucks, scrapers, and shovels — overland for 325 miles in winter weather, thirty-five degrees below zero, to get it to an inland point before a frozen winter trail broke up behind them.

—Official History of the
Alcan Military Highway

Margaret Murray's next travelogue would never have been written at all had it not been for Andy Johnson, linotype operator. His predecessor had joined the air force, but in the nick of time George had found Andy via a classified advertisement in the Victoria *Times*. He was beachcombing on the West Coast of Vancouver Island, a reject from the services, and a dropout from a print shop, thanks to a recurring asthma. After a scholarly discussion on the treasures to be found on a pounding but neglected North Pacific beach, Andy sat for a moment on his drift log looking out to sea. "I'll come," he said suddenly. "I hear there's jade along the Fraser."

Andy was an op who could set up a message in the shape of a Christmas tree, a Hallowe'en witch or an Easter bunny. With odds and ends of matts, he could turn out a strip of magnificent border for an ad. He could set eight or nine galleys in a shift, particularly at those times when he was whipping himself with remorse and good resolutions following a prolonged series of libations. And all this without the mechanical devices that later lined up slugs and counted spaces automatically. He was greased lightning with a comp stick as well.

"No continued stuff for me, though," declared Andy,

with a quick nervous grin. "Bores me to death. Give me lotsa short stories and lots of coffee for my bowels and I'm away."

Mrs. Grant White of the Bride River, at this point gave Margaret a parlour organ. The E above middle C wouldn't work, which George pointed out to the new man as they inspected the little old antique the day it arrived.

"Okay," said Andy, "I'll get a screwdriver . . ."

That was at two in the afternoon. At two the next morning, Andy was still at the organ with the hammers, shafts, bellows, reeds, ivories, pedals and hardware scattered from one end of the living room to the other. Andy not only had the organ to pieces but went to pieces himself. He sought the only cure he knew for his frustration. None of this might have been permitted had Mother been home. But she was off to a Women's Institute convention in Regina and there was no one to say them nay. The day before she was due back, George gathered the organ into gunnysacks and shipped it off to Vancouver for repairs. In the excitement of the following weeks, he forgot all about it and it was finally sold to an evangelical group with whom it did well on street corners for years.

Old Instituters never die and forget each other. And Margaret, who had once salvaged the family fortunes demonstrating hooked rugs under W.I. auspices, had again been on the receiving end of a lifeline in the form of a pass and expenses to the prairie convention. One look at the booming railroad yards in Edmonton on the way had infected her with the excitement which was attending the building of the highway to Alaska. And after all, wasn't it *their* highway?

"George," she said, barely in the door on her return to Lillooet, "I did a terrible thing. I checked into the hotel at Regina, attended the opening banquet, checked out again, and took the next train back to Edmonton."

"What did you use for money?" asked her husband, good-humouredly. It was Sunday and the only sound was the August heat, which fairly sizzled the drops of water idly swirling out from the tired lawn sprinkler under the apple trees. Margaret returning from a journey was always an invigorating experience. This time she was like a fresh and sparkling breeze.

"I didn't need much money," answered Mother. "I talked the Northern Alberta Railways out of a pass to Dawson Creek. Sit down and I'll give you a quick rundown and you can ask questions later."

There had been seventeen sleeper coaches packed to the doors on the Northern Alberta train she caught in Edmonton. Four hundred and eighty aboard. One of seven trains that day. People everywhere. Four to a section, two to a berth, the corridors and smoking rooms full, also the platforms. There were army brass, enlisted men, Canadian Air Force boys, straw bosses in civilian clothes, hob-nailed cat-skinners, buckskin-jacketed packers, shirt-sleeved labourers, and a few women. She had to sit with someone so she shared a seat with a young woman from Fort St. John who promptly confessed she was glad to have the company.

Fifteen miles down the line from Dawson Creek, lined along both sides of the tracks, stood solid stacks of lumber, roofing, dismantled CCC buildings in ten-foot lengths, door frames, windows, bricks, blocks, and beaverboard.

The engines — one pulling, one shoving — chugged into a tiny station, alive with uniforms and trucks and loading ramps and bales and boxes, busses, lorries — a seething mass of men and machines. This was Dawson Creek. Mother had wired the Bradens — Glen Braden had been on the inaugural mail flight to the Peace from Ashcroft — and they were down to the train to meet her. Louisa had potato vines five feet high and the sweet peas were climbing over her roof. Beautiful day. Lovely blue sky. Crops getting ripe. Seventy bushel wheat, a hundred bushel oats. They introduced Margaret to a fellow named Spinney. He'd started with two little trucks hauling freight around the Peace Block. The Americans came. "And how many trucks do you suppose Spinney has in his pool this week? Seven thousand! Think of it!" The Yanks were so happy to find this self-educated little Irishman who understood organization that he fitted in beautifully.

The Bradens had company, and besides Mother wanted to see all she could, so Glen took her to a hotel, the Michaud's Dew Drop Inn, where they said she could have the next bed to come vacant. They had twenty-five rooms and people were even sleeping on the floor. Finally she got tired and sat on the stairs with about thirty other people. Still no room. There were no chairs in the lobby and she took a place at the top of the first flight. By about eleven at night she had worked down the stairs until she was on eye-level with the beer parlour. She had a bottle of Flytox to keep the bugs and mosquitoes away. It didn't get dark until almost midnight, and was light again by three in the morning.

There were two big holes in the street walls where they were going to put in windows so there were plenty of bugs and plenty to see.

"Seeing into the beer parlour was best of all," Margaret went on, still imbued with the excitement of the moment. "The noise was awful and about eleven o'clock a big fight breaks out in the pub. I'm up high and could see it all. They were throwing beer bottles around, knocking over tables, and the bouncers were tossing the men out of the window holes right and left. All you could see was arms and legs. Next morning I went to eight o'clock Mass and counted about sixteen men with plaster on face or hands, blood on tunics, or something to indicate where they'd been the night before.

She spent the whole night on the stairs, but the second night she got a bed, sharing with another woman and her small daughter. Mrs. Michaud said she was sorry about how crowded it was, but Margaret should see how it was in Fort St. John.

The Dew Drop had a weird system of plumbing. The building went two stories above the street, and the toilet on the third floor was arranged so that the effluvia dropped straight down to the ground through a casing arrangement that picked up the first and main floor contributions as well. This was so upsetting to Mother, thinking some of it might hit her, that her internal arrangement ceased to function altogether for several days.

Mother wanted to ride the Highway with one of Spinney's trucks, but he said it would be too rough for a woman, so she had to go to Frank Clarke, Dad's old friend, the road engineer. Food was a problem *en route*. You might get a sandwich right away, then again you might wait an hour and a half for them to cook some more meat or grind some more hamburger. By the time Frank and Margaret got to Fort St. John, she was weak with hunger.

They left Dawson at five in the morning, two hours to drive to the Peace River, then a three-hour wait for the ferry because there were so many trucks ahead of them waiting, too. They sat there and looked across the river where the bulldozers were crawling around like caterpillars, getting ready to put the anchorage in on the north side of the big Peace bridge.

"As sure as I sit here, while we watched, one of those dozers gets too far over, and the whole shooting match tumbles over the edge. The driver is thrown out. And everything lands on the river bank, hundreds of feet below. I said to Frank, 'In the name of God will you look at that.' And he says, 'Margaret, you haven't seen anything yet. They poured a fellow into one of those piers along with the cement, day before yesterday.'"

At Fort St. John, they got on the main street and lined up in front of a cafe called 'Pops.' There were at least two dozen in the queue and every once in a while a great big lorry came by raising a dust that choked everyone within shouting distance, it was that fine. They stood in dust over their shoe tops. No sidewalks. Just a little step outside Pops.

"So Frank and I are finally within spittin' distance of a cup of coffee. It's past noon. I was famished. And what happens? They lock the door. 'Nothin' more to eat till the truck comes in,' says the waitress. Bang! So Frank finally took me to a U.S. Army camp a little ways out of town. We explained to them and they gave us a good meal."

About three blocks west of town, a huge headquarters camp, Fort Alcan, seemed to stretch up a rolling field as far as the eye could see. Hundreds of oblong barracks buildings, a field hospital, administration offices. From here General James A. O'Connor, a nuggety little man, no side at all to him, commanded the southern sector of the road. And there was Old Glory waving in the breeze, about eighteen inches higher than the Canadian Ensign.

"I know it's thirty years since I lived under it, but the sight of the Stars and Stripes thrills me terribly still."

The general's car was outside, with the driver napping at the wheel, the flag on the radiator lifting and dropping with the breeze. Three official cars were parked nearby and jeeps were coming and going with their various cargoes of military police, supplies, work parties. Inside, the office was alive with coffee trousers and chocolate tunics. Richard Neuberger, later to be a U.S. Senator from the state of Oregon, was the general's aide. O'Connor said 'There's nothing we can tell you — we're just doing the best we can as fast as we can.' Mother said, "God be praised you're here."

"Yes, Mrs. Murray," the general replied, "God be praised Uncle Sam has a place to defend himself."

Later Margaret stood in the village and took in the street scene. The place was solid with lorries and jeeps and turnapulls and tractors pulling big fat decks loaded with rooter ploughs and scrapers. There were dump trucks, half yard shovels and one command car. All were parked with motors running so that it seemed the road vibrated under your feet. One tractor had twenty-two tires on it. Right behind where she stood was a two-story Euclid. The air was blue with sunshine filtering through exhaust and dust. She felt a motion behind her, and this young truck driver was scrambling up to his cab. One tire on that machine weighed 2300 pounds. The hub hit her just about at the shoulder.

"What's in there?" she shouted at him, pointing to a tin-covered building where people queued up outside.

"Ma'am?" he hollered down, not having heard.

"I repeat, what's in there?"

"That there," he says, "is the First National Bank." And he grins.

But sure enough, it's the Canadian Bank of Commerce, occupying the front of the Pomeroy Garage. Two tellers, an accountant, one girl, a counter and a small safe — these had pushed back a rack of parts bins and banking is as usual with the noise of anvils, welding torches and revving motors adding to the confusion.

Mother carried on down the uneven dirt road. Next to the 'First National' was a building going up inside an elaborate scaffolding that she didn't bother stepping over and under to ask any questions. But people slept there, among the partitions, six to a room on the floor in sleeping bags. It was going to be a hotel. And next to that was going to be a theatre and dance hall. Across the street they were building a bakery and next they were putting in a building for a furniture store.

She went to see Dad's old friend, Mrs. Carmichael. But

the old log hotel parlour was now the Public Roads Administration Office, and a handsome big Virginian by the name of Clark Morrison rolled his cigar around in his mouth and asked what he could do for 'y'all.' Margaret never did see the proprietress. All the rooms were for PRA personnal and Mrs. Carmichael just ran the dining room and beer parlour. She wasn't around because they had just got a load of beer in the night before. It had all been drunk by closing time. Never did last more than a couple of hours, apparently, and afterwards there was lots of cleaning up to do. Across the street south and east were the police barracks on one corner and Finch's store on the other as Dad remembered them. And kitty-cornered, a trapper named Brandt was building a new bank premises. Not before time.

Mother stepped over a crap game on the wooden platform outside the hotel. Two Negroes and two white men were galloping those bones like papa never 'shoed' mama never in her life. They called the Canadian bills 'blankets' on account of their size. They had spread a tunic and held the blankets down against the wind with pebbles. The law said they had to have twenty-five dollars Canadian off every cheque, and they figured it was like play money.

She crossed the street, passed a jeep with four military police in white helmets and webbing and pistol holders. They were just parked, watching the street. And she went in to see the telegrapher, who had a little office a ways up. "I'd be too busy to read it," was all he said.

She walked on and came to a garage and taxi office. Someone told her a man named Bowes would be a good one to see. So she said to this tall, rangy, blue-eyed Irishman, "What would you think of a newspaper in Fort St. John?"

"A damned good idea," he said, but she would have to excuse him a minute. He was wanted in the shop but would be right back. He never came back at all.

"So I carried on up to the hospital, just up the street. The Sister Superior in starched whites was fondling a clump of the biggest blue pansies I have ever seen in all my life. 'We are busy. We do not read or sew at all,' she said in her French accent. 'Maybe later. But yes, Madame, in the future. Forsanjin will grow and grow how beeg?' "

Margaret moved on. She asked one fellow who ran a variety store what he thought about a paper, and he said,

"Yes, if you print it here." Another storekeeper said, "Paper? Christ, yes! Bring me all ya got. I been out of wrapping paper for three weeks!"

Mother's eyes were wide with memory's excitement.

"Darling, it's wonderful country. Everything you've said and written and more. It will open up a vast empire. It's going to be a beautiful wide smooth highway. This muskeg talk in the papers is overdone . . ."

As Margaret talked, the metal pot on the linotype had pinged twice, and the gloom of evening was setting in over the heat. The metal was molten because Andy was coming back to set some type. And presently a chair scraped on the floor below and the old, familiar lick-lack-clickety-ack-ack-wham of the machine broke the quiet.

"I'll just go down and see if he needs anything down there," said George, and left the room. He seemed deeply lost in thought, far away from this place.

A long cord dropped from the ceiling over the linotype, and this was caught and fastened to the copy rack, with a metal half-shade affixed to cast light on the keyboard. It just caught Andy's rather definite chin.

"Got plenty of copy there, boy?" Father asked. "I have a crop story over here on the stone if you need it . . . Mrs. Murray is back. Did you have a nice afternoon?"

George paused by the big, black, pot-bellied stove. Even in summer, the large iron kettle of water sat there, filled every other day, in a completely vain attempt to beat the dry air and the electricity in paper that plagued the up-country print shops.

"Nice afternoon? I'll say. I'll bet we walked forty miles. My dogs are really yappin'. Those Dillon boys know all the old river workings, all the old cemeteries, all the old every-thin'."

"Did you find any jade?"

"Well, I think we did but it weighed ten ton. But what we did find — see what you make of it — is right in that stew pot beside you. I thought I'd take it out in the kitchen and give it a boil up later, and see what I could do with it."

George took a poker down off the dark wall and dipped it into the water. Gently the poker lifted its burden from the pot.

"Well, go ahead," said Andy, impatiently watching. "Lift

it out, for crying out loud. It won't bitecha, gawdammit."

Slowly the poker hauled up its dripping prize, to which long, black strings of hair were still affixed.

"Ain't that a jim-dandy? Whaddya say I polish it and make a nice lamp shade out of him, hey?"

"Yes, indeed," said George, weakly. "A very sound idea . . ." He let the skull plop back into its aromatic bath, dropped the poker and fled.

As he passed the open front office door on his way upstairs, his nostrils were assailed with the heavy, sweetish scent of rotting fruit, for which the harvesters were long gone. Outside, not a light, not a sound. Not a movement, unless you counted the million little night insects battling against the window panes to gain the light within.

He hurried up the stairs and into the living room, and stood in the threshold.

"Margaret," he said, "we're going to Fort St. John."

"Dozers North"

Fort St. John was originally a fur-trading post, and for many years it was nestled on the banks of the Peace River directly south of its present location. Early explorers commented on the lush growth that distinguished the flats extending for miles above the velvety coulees which back-dropped the Hudson's Bay compound on the river. When fur became a less lucrative crop, trappers took notice of the soil and extended their clearing and gardens. Gradually the economy turned from fur to farm, mixing the two. In the thirties, a railroad from Edmonton came into the southern part of this British Columbia Peace River Block and brought homesteaders. But the little Fort was still fifty miles away from the railroad and across the wide and languid Peace River. The soil which held the moisture and grew the beautiful wheat stuck firmly to the wagon wheels when wet, making travel impossible at break-up and freeze-up and whenever the rain fell. Still, the land produced in abundance, game and fish were plentiful, and the homesteaders continued to trickle in and settle the areas adjacent to the river which provided transportation.

Every provincial government from Sir Richard McBride's on down had promised an extension of the provincial north-south railway to the Peace. Millions of dollars of surveys had been carried out and demonstrated it an area rich in resources. Oil was what turned up in water wells. Gas seeped through fissures in the ground and could be lit and used to boil a mulligan. Two billion tons of fine anthracite coal at Hudson's Hope was just lying there. And the grain!

"When I got off my saddle horse to stretch my legs and walk a bit, I became lost," wrote George Murray in 1931, then on assignment for Southam's. "I couldn't see the settlement for the wheat, which was over my head." By this time, in order to be nearer the settlers, the little Fort had moved back from the river, up the coulee, and over the flat to Fish Creek.

This inland empire was an integral part of British Columbia, though seven hundred miles and a couple of mountain ranges from the Pacific shore where most of the people in the province resided. That southern population was swollen and festering in the thirties, as its relief rolls mushroomed with Canadians from all over the Dominion seeking a mild climate and a cheaper way of life while they sat out the Depression.

Who reads government surveys? Evidently not British Columbia politicians of days gone by. "Put relief dollars to work extending the railway," said backbencher Murray in the 1933 Legislature at Victoria, striving to impress the government with the stake they were neglecting in the Peace. "Our elevators are empty. Our ships are idle. Our freight cars are running empty. Yet riches beyond the dreams of Midas lie at our back door."

But no one listened.

It took a war to advance the country fifty years. It took one hundred and thirty-five million American dollars to provide a defence road to Alaska, and waken Canada's Pacific province to its own wealth. It took war correspondents and magazine writers from the United States to convince British Columbians that here indeed was a magnificent country, and it was theirs.

The 1930 wave of settlement had attracted almost exclusively dried-out Saskatchewan farmers who were looking for a place which might afford them a livelihood.

"Man, there's a living for you up there. The soil is rich and black and deep. Cabbages, seventeen pound, sound as a nut. The wheat would make you weep. Eighty bushel to the acre. And game and fish. For cash, go trapping."

So said the poolroom proprietor at Wynyard to a young mechanic out of work, ten years before the war. Instead of cutting the car down to a Bennett buggy, Les Bazeley cut his into a truck, piled his wife and baby and household effects aboard and started for the land of promise. There was nothing to lose.

The fabric of the settlement was woven around farm people. Although a telegraph office, a store, a fur-trading post, a log hotel, and a hospital had combined in the twenties to pinpoint the town, all these people relied directly on the land during the thread-bare years. With the possible exception of later Hudson's Bay managers, there was not a family which did not put in some sort of a crop to feed a cow, horses, and provide a little bacon for themselves. Even the Sisters of Providence at the hospital farmed a five-acre garden, milked cows, raised pigs and chickens. Babies were paid for in onions and turnips and quarters of beef. Sister Superior herself, bundled in a huge fur coat, climbed on the seat of the democrat each fall and drove out to the farms in search of payments on bills. She took cordwood, potatoes, fat cockerels, sauerkraut, or whatever was available, and on the return journey kept her feet warm by tucking them under the livestock!

There was the family from Saskatchewan which faced the winter of 1931 with six of them in a log cabin with sod roof and dirt floor spread with evergreens. They had exactly five dollars cash to see them through the winter — for shells for the shotgun. The Brussels carpets left over from the two-dollar wheat era on the Canadian prairies were strung on wires to make partitions. If, like Mrs. Clark of Pineview, you remember ten years later only that your house smelled lovely with those boughs on the floor, the Depression had not existed for you at all. It was all in the mind. And if like her husband Ed, you hung on for twelve years, you sold the gasping old steam engine you brought into the country for a mighty fine profit. For around it you had built a sawmill during those lean times and you were set. So was the fellow who bought it, for in the next few years he parlayed it up to a million-dollar empire of timber, sawmills, and lumber yards. He was Gordon G. Moore of the Fort St. John Lumber Company.

Or take John Grossman, who speaks for the new Canadians of the thirties. "I shoot rabbits in the head, pull the hide off and clean them. Then I hang them in flour sack on the north side of my shack. After cooking for half an hour, all disease germs are dead. But to handle and cook is repulsive to the mind. I consider it a last resort. Of course, everyone does the same. Times are hard . . ."

Thus a German immigrant comforts himself in the solitude of his homestead cabin at Rose Prairie and writes in his diary in laboured English to more quickly learn the language of his adopted land.

A man who rushed into town in 1942 from his North Pine homestead to keep books and sell men's suits puts it this way:

"Hard times," says Bob Curiston, "was a log cabin, dirt floor, sod roof which the wind had lifted around the edges, stovepipe through window, tin stove, rope bed. I put a shell into my .22 before we piled into the sack. In the middle of the night, I came awake. Two fiery eyes were regarding me in the middle of the cabin. I groped for my rifle. What was this monster with the red eyes? Books mentioned mountain lions being native to B.C. No sense taking chances. I aimed a bullet right between the glowing eyes and fired."

Someone lit the coal oil lamp.

As the glow filtered through the sooty chimney, there on the cabin floor lay Bob Curiston's 'trophy,' a foot-long packrat, with a mighty tail, obviously the chairman of a scuffling, whiffy delegation.

The keynote of life was simplicity. There was no money, no traffic, few women and little temptation. Liquor Act infringement was the only serious crime. Many homesteaders ran off a batch of moonshine now and again to relieve the monotony. Had they had the money to pay for it at a government liquor store, the source of supply was, depending on the weather, two days to several lightyears away at Pouce Coupe, beyond Dawson Creek to the south.

The local police had heard many cases involving liquor. The beloved old judge from Prince George, Harold A. Robertson, was occupying the bench one time and the town prosecutor was quizzing a rancher closely.

"Do you admit to buying five pounds of raisins from Finch?" asked the prosecution, waving a counter checkbook aloft. "Is this your signature?"

At this precise moment, from back in the living quarters of the local constable, the sharp report of a gun was heard. Or was it a gun? The judge had hardly raised his head before another of the same occurred, followed by a barrage of shots and ricocheting projectiles. Had the moonshiner's neighbours come looking for retribution, shooting their way through the house?

Judge Robertson looked at Constable Sandy and slowly became aware of the truth. The latest batch of Sandy's vintage had just hit the ceiling, all twenty-four bottles of it, corked and tied down and set carefully to settle behind the heater in the living room. The case was quickly concluded and all hands retired to the scene of the barrage for a drink.

This was the improvised courtroom in which E.J. Paling, the JP, once held forth with a drunk before him for sentence. Paling recognized the man as an old rancher like himself.

"What the hell are you here for?" he asked, unceremoniously.

"Well," said Hansen, "I guess I got drunk."

"You guess you got drunk," thundered the bench. "You did get drunk. You're here, aren't you? It'll cost you ten dollars."

Hansen stood there.

"Haven't got the ten dollars, hey?" asked the magistrate fiercely. "Well, here . . ." Paling dug into his hip pocket. "I have it. And for God's sake, behave yourself after this."

The only real excitement provided in the North Peace in the thirties was that surrounding a little bush-flying outfit called United Air Transport. Its pilot-president called in one day for an injured logger, landed on the main street of Fort St. John in break-up, and had to find some solid footing before he could take off with the extra-patient load. One of the settlers standing by suggested his place.

"She's froze solid," said W.J. "Red" Powell, who lived on the shores of Charlie Lake. "We can drive old Roy out and meet you there."

And before he left that day, flyer Grant McConachie had himself a base in Fort St. John. Mrs. Powell set the radio equipment up in her front room until a shack could be built on the back for the noisy, squealing outfit. U.A.T. continued to fly dogs to trappers, and groceries to survey parties, but when a mail contract came along in 1937, the Fort St. John base was joined by weather stations along the newly blazed flying trail to Whitehorse. Pilots and machines were added to the fleet, and suddenly McConachie's tiny outfit blossomed out with a new name, Yukon Southern. "John" was on the aerial map of Western Canada to stay. And although pilots flew by contact, and aircraft were still on pontoons and skis, Fort St. John remained operations base for McConachie, and the haven to which all his craft flew home before dark.

The Dominion government had not encouraged McConachie with mail contracts for nothing. In 1940, this body suddenly released the money that would build a chain of fully equipped airports extending from Edmonton to Whitehorse, following Yukon Southern's weather stations. It all added up when, later, the new airfields supplied the builders of the Alaska Highway and facilitated the flying of supplies to Russia over the top of the world. The little bush airline switched from floats to wheels, and McConachie left his original base of operations at Powells' house on Charlie Lake to land passengers on a field a mile west of town on Chiulli's farm.

The trappers and surveyors who had been his passengers were now swelled with Canadian and American officials, army officers, and engineers. No longer did the mail sack rest overnight on Ev Powell's kitchen table, with a sixty-thousand dollar gold brick on the floor beside it. All was now locked in a neat white- and red-trimmed office, while passengers and pilot jolted over the newly made road through the willows to little Fort St. John.

To accommodate the Tomlinson Construction people who were at work on the airport for the Department of Transport, a beer licence had been acquired by the log hotel. Mark Wah continued his independent restaurant, and a middle-aged settler named Carl Hanke got a hunch that an auto court might be a good idea. This he built opposite the hospital. His wife put a wood stove in one of the units and opened a restaurant which served an unvarying menu of roast beef, roast pork, and ground round steak. A baker from Dawson Creek decided to put up a building. The telegrapher got help in the office. Bowes and Herron added a few more services to their Delco lighting plant. The police-blotter entries increased from one or two notations a week to one or two a day. But the winter passed uneventfully enough. With the mercury at fifty below, it does. The odd frozen trapper had to be buried decently, a welfare case here or there to be investigated, cruelty to livestock reported, and the Pound Act enforced, an old Indian to hospital — these comprised a policeman's work in Fort St. John that winter. After break-up, work started in earnest on the airport, and the construction people's payroll boosted the economy of the town.

The airline was growing too. The passengers who came into town to take meals were now accompanied by crews in navy blue uniforms and gold braid. The trip from Prince George still sometimes took five days. Not all flying time, but the time required to change planes over at Abbott's gravelly field across the Peace to a smaller, higher, lighter, bigger-wheeled craft that could negotiate the soft earth of Chiulli's farm. Once started, McConachie couldn't lose. He was assisted greatly about this time by an accident at the Vancouver airport in which a Spitfire on the tarmac ran into a tri-motored Ford of his and chewed it up. The insurance money bought three new aircraft whose commodious interiors and smashing stewardesses were unbelievably smart and modern.

Fort St. John was certainly ready for a boost.

Then March 9, 1942, a week of bitter thirty-below weather. A farmer slowed his team in front of the Finch General store and peered from his caboose, a covered-in sleigh with stove and chimney and back door, and just enough opening

GOVERNOR GENERAL Roland P. Michener pins the Order of Canada Service Medal on Dr. Margaret Lally Murray at Government House, Ottawa, March, 1971.

GEORGE, the young publisher of the South Vancouver Chinook, in 1912.

THE GIRL THAT HE married was his bookkeeper, Margaret Lally, newly arrived in 'redcoat country' from Western Kansas.

30TH & MAIN STREET, South Vancouver, in 1912. Beyond this point were stumps and bracken but a wooden sidewalk ran to 33rd, where stood the building which housed the Chinook & Peach's Plumbing.

THE CHINOOK STAFF. Left to right, John Jackson, E. M. Young, John Rankin, Eddie Caldwell, Lorne McCullough and Gales Johnson.

THE MURRAYS always had a thing about 'the land'. This was what they could afford in 1916. This property is behind the Imperial Oil plant at Ioco. It had been naval reserve, and the land clearers often found iron round shot from the warships anchored in Burrard Inlet for gunnery practice. The entire area had been logged off at the turn of the century, and forest fires did the rest.

LAND WAS CLEARED around Burrard Inlet with stumping powder, stump pullers, horse-drawn fresnos and a powerful amount of blood, sweat and tears. George figured it cost a thousand dollars an acre when wages for a labourer were $1 a day and board. There were no roads. The little homestead was reached by boat.

AND HERE'S MARGARET and the two children, Georgina and Daniel, waiting for the street car to take them to Columbia and Hastings, where they walked down to the oily wharves of the Union Steamships and caught The Scenic (paddle wheel) or The Delta (motor ship) every Saturday afternoon. On arrival, they walked the two mile hill, to spend an exciting 36 hours watching their father cope with the stuff you see in the top picture.

VISITORS ENJOYED the week-end shows at Ioco as much as the family did. Here is a sample. The group is waiting for the boat. They are as interesting a lot as you'd find among Vancouver newspapermen of the day. Left to right; Sir St.Jean Mildmay, James Fitzmaurice, famous cartoonist, Noel Robinson, J. Francis Bursill, all journalists and their hosts.
Mildmay was the father of Audrey, the singer, Glynebourne and all that.

THIS IS LILLOOET 50 years ago from the bench behind the town. Here, in the thirties, George won a seat in the provincial legislature and served two terms. He and Margaret started the Bridge River-Lillooet News, and eventually bought the Phair ranch which is now part of the town.

THE CHILDREN were no longer children and were learning the newspaper business in Lillooet. Margaret was showing signs of wear. Family staffers were not paid, but non-family got $10 a month, board and a horse to ride.

WHEN THEY dismantled the old 14 Mile Bridge on the PGE, Lillooet went into a building boom. Some of the lumber landed at the Murrays, and presently the old horse barn was a little theatre. It still is.

MARGARET with Ken White and Grayden Styles — two of the $10-a-month staff. The News Office had been a boarding house for railway builders in 1912. It was a great day when the sign went up.

THE NEXT OUTPOST of empire was the Peace River. George and Margaret went up there to have a look at the Alaska Highway. This is what they saw. So they stayed and started a newspaper to tell the world about it.

GEORGE HAD PASS NUMBER 38 to travel the Alaska Highway. No wonder Uncle Sam's boys got foreign ribbons for this job. The world, however, never saw this picture. It was classified until after VJ Day.

JOHNNY BEATONS Bennett buggy shared the broad Fort St John main street with the latest and best motorized army equipment. You're looking, then as now, at the main intersection of the town. The Pomeroy (now the Fort) Hotel, and the Co-op beyond.

THE ALASKA HIGHWAY News Office, to which John Quelle came in 1951. When he saw it, he thought it must be a shack for news boys. Margaret recalls that he stood there twisting his ring, while tears welled up in his eyes.

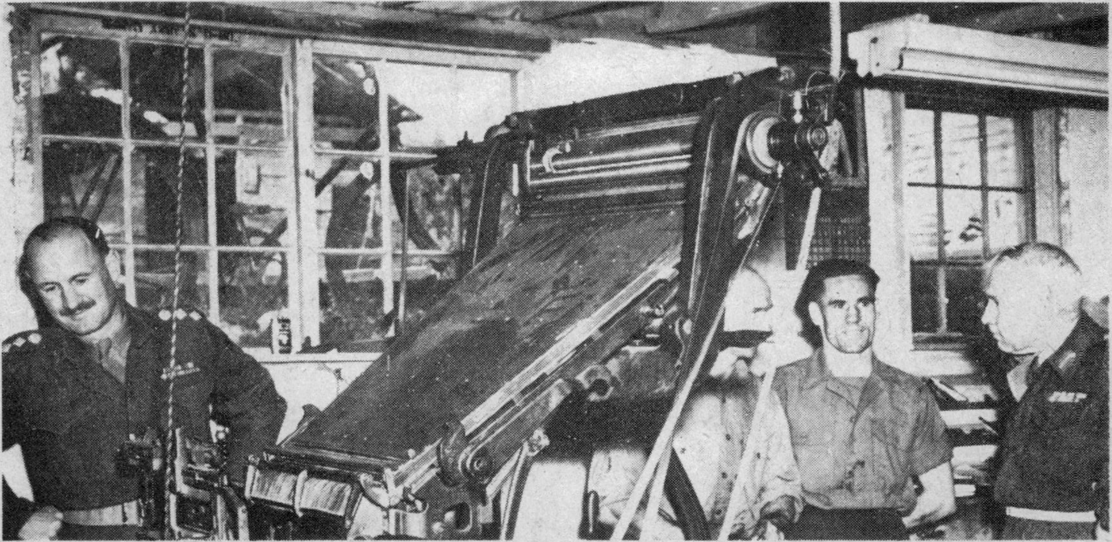

TONY AND GEORGE discuss the fine points of a linotype with General Worthington, right, and an aide left. John said that when he saw this job plant, he wanted to head out to Vancouver. But he didn't have the money.

IN THE 1949 federal election, Margaret left George to it, and got out of town. Here she is climbing into a plane at Whitehorse to help the Yukon candidate, Aubrey Simmons. "That way," she said later, "I got both my men in."

MARGARET'S WRITING was always something else. To the printers, a curse. To her fans, a delight. For years, she ran a cartoon on the editorial page, advising readers who demanded more punctuation, better spelling, etc to help themselves.

THE BEGINNING OF FAME came to Margaret following a water crisis in Fort St. John. She advised her readers editorially to only flush for No. 2, and to get out the old wash rag to save water. The flushes were heard all the way to Time Magazine's Montreal office. The news magazine flew in and took this picture of her, and ran it.

5,000 PEOPLE crowded into Lillooet to celebrate Margaret's eightieth birthday. There were tears all around. "Goodbye — I love you all," she said. Son Dan, right, and old friend Gordon Fox.

at the front to guide the horses.

"Them Bible fellers are arriving a mite early this year," observed the old man. "Look over there."

"Hell, them's sojers, Pa," says junior, rubbing the fog off the window with his parka sleeve. "Them's army tents. I seen 'em in the moom pitchas."

"G'way . . . leave me have a look. By gad, you're right!"

The great defence project, the Alcan, had started.

The quartermaster outfit, the United States Army's Thirty-fifth, had barely got tent pegs down in the frozen ground among the willows on Fort St. John's main street when the equipment that was its special charge formed up. Snorting, wallowing monsters in a parade scared horses, blanched the leathery old faces of the Indians who watched from behind the roadside bush, and stunned the settlers who couldn't believe their own eyes. This antediluvian procession started on the improvised ramps of the sleepy little Northern Alberta Railroad at Dawson Creek, and almost literally never stopped until it got to Fairbanks, Alaska.

A pause, and there — seemingly all at once — there it was, Fort Alcan, waving the Stars and Stripes and housing ten thousand troops, half a mile west of the Fort St. John crossroads. Another pause, and there was the big Public Roads Administration base just this side of Mile 0, which marked the end of the existing wagon road from Dawson Creek. Even as an Engineer officer climbed on the lead bulldozer to direct the vanguard into the bush, the concrete pilings were going in for a laundry on the shores of Charlie Lake that would wash and iron for every American soldier between Fort St. John and Whitehorse. The command "Dozers North" had replaced the familiar and colourful "Wagons West" as in the early expeditions to the Pacific coast, but it was the same wilderness, still untouched, a couple of centuries later.

Not a word had leaked on the giant plan. Settlers had heard about McCusker's call to the Metis packers and dog drivers. Knox McCusker was a Dominion Land Surveyor whose business seemed to embrace everything north of the Fifty-fourth Parallel. When he was at home, he was in Fort St. John. He was the only Canadian on the Alcan project directly employed by Washington and paid by Washington. And it was he who led Brigadier General William M. Hoge up the first four hundred and fifty miles of country that would eventually become Highway.

McCusker's message had come over Cece Berry's wonderful little radio station at Grande Prairie. But all sorts of frontier messages came over every day. "Keep Freddy as still as you can, and only two bundles each for the horses. We'll bring the doctor when the storm is over. Signed Dad." Now this was a message to understand and think about.

McCusker promptly sent word to the Napoleons, Calliouxs, Beatons, Belcourts, LaTendres, Campbells, and Camerons, who, complete with Shaganapis, from hilltop to valley, answered on the run. They knew the surveyor. He paid well. He fed well. What he wanted with dog teams so near break-up was his business. No one knew or cared that he had received his orders from Washington by runner from the Fort St. John telegraph office. He read by the flickering light of a campfire at the Horse Track, a camp spot on the winter Nelson trail, a message which contained four words: "Hire the dog teams," it said.

While these same dog-team parties went off in two columns, north to Fort Nelson, west to the Minaker River, to cover four hundred and fifty miles of possible highway within the month, the builders were furiously attaching the first miles of road. First the slashers, then the survey crew running a preliminary stadia line, then a heavy dozer following the line and opening a path for fleets of smaller dozers to widen it, clean up the debris, and make way for root ploughs, graders, scrapers, dump trucks, picks, shovels, saws, axes, and hundreds of Uncle Sam's boys to wield and operate them.

"An Indian coming down his dim old pack trail met a cat coming up," records McCusker in one of the early copies of our new paper. "Just as he came into view, the Negro operator shoved in the clutch and three jack pines flew into the air and rolled over the bank. The savage left and tarried not in the leaving. When he finally reached the trading post, he was only able to gasp, 'Big Black Devil, he come!' "

Back where grades became sufficiently good for truck use was located the truck head. All along above it, pack trains wound through the mud past cats, soldiers, graders, and you name it. Radios in car or house outfits kept everyone in touch with development all along the line.

By the end of August, the Fort St. John boys broke through the Nelson trail, and the Nelson outfit got through to the Whitehorse crews working south. The trail was cut. It remained only to get sawmills going for winter camps and bridges, and the civilians moved in to finish the job.

Meanwhile back in Fort St. John, everything had changed. From a one restaurant town where the proprietor was his own best customer, the place supported seven eating houses unable to handle the business. Sleeping places were impossible to get, with parking space in feed barn lofts selling at a dollar per body per night. The neighbour's field was an army camp. His hogs wore a bilious look, presumably from imbibing too freely of army swill.

"It took us more than a year to get up there," recalls Margaret. "During that year, we brought out a meagre paper, lived for overseas mail, and made our plans." Son Dan had by this time been four years in England in the ranks of the Canadian Army and was momentarily expected back in Canada to swap his sergeant's stripes for officer's pips. Georgina had left the publicity department of the Canadian Broadcasting Corporation in Vancouver to be a Wren (S.D. for special duties) Writer with the women's branch of the Royal Canadian Navy.

"In the name of God," wrote her mother by way of encouragement at her announcement, "what special duties are more important than this family's? The grapes of wrath will pucker and bitter the lives of those who have a duty, who fail to ask God to aware them of it, who let someone else be an unworthy substitute."

But I went anyway.

At Lillooet, trains on the PGE had dropped down to two a week, carrying mostly soldiers. This complicated things for the Murrays, who had made up their minds to have the Lillooet paper printed in Vancouver for the duration and required a direct route for getting copy down and printed issues back from the city printery. But worse, the restricted train schedule was squeezing the very life out of the Howe Sound *News* in Squamish for the same reasons. Undaunted, George wangled himself Civilian Pass Number 46 on the Alaska Highway, and pushed on to the north to line up their future, while Margaret spread herself over the southern end of the map, covering weekly operations at Lillooet, Squamish, and Vancouver. They were fifty-five and fifty-six years of age. No matter. Fort St. John was now the frontier, and that's where they had to be.

As usual, when any great turning point arrived for the Murrays, the answer was a special edition. The mere sound of the words seemed to tap unplumbed depths of enthusiasm and ambition. A beautiful spread of type and pictures and art work lifted them, inspired them, drove them forward.

"We'll have it ready for the Armistice. We'll have the first concrete, informative, comprehensive piece of literature on the country — and it will be a fifty-page newspaper," said George, his first trip back from the Peace, already at work on a wonderful dummy of the edition.

"The change in your father is wonderful," wrote Margaret to the children. "He has been making speeches about it for so many years, all those newspaper articles on "the Promised Land" in the thirties refreshing his memory, that he has all the necessary research in his head."

Besides, they had credit at the engravers, and friends in all the morgues on the city dailies. George got a few features into type and proofs pasted in. The same with pictures. You had to watch him, though. He ordered one full page, hand-lettered in Old English, as if the great railroad builder, Van Horne of the CPR, were speaking across the century to Canadians. It was lovely writing, but artwork cost money, and how badly the Murrays needed that money! They were just barely able to get the Lillooet paper paid for each week in Vancouver.

"And by now," says Margaret, "I had it all figured out — what we were going to do with the Howe Sound *News*. We were going to change its name to the Alaska Highway *News* and publish it in Fort St. John."

"How do you figure we can do that, Marg?" said George, the cautious one, questioning the ethics involved.

"Who cares whether we get the Howe Sound *News* out at Squamish or at Fort St. John?"

"The Wartime Prices and Trade Board, for instance."

"Well, we're not asking for anything more than the paper quota we already have. Howe Sound is through. The North End of the province is just starting, and they need a paper. Morally, it's right. And you know it's right. Leave it to God. Argue later."

"There you go again, Margaret. Why involve the Deity in a sharp piece of manipulation like this?"

"My dear husband, I don't think it's sharp. I think it just makes sense. Unravel the red tape later. Anyway, I leave everything to God. He hasn't complained yet."

George went back to the Peace to sell the special. Margaret, with mailing list, necessary cuts and files, got out the first issue for Lillooet from Vancouver. Someone else could worry about machines and printers and the state of the wartime employment situation. Until the war was over, the Murrays commuted between the Peace River and Vancouver, alternating positions regularly.

Mother travelled by CNR to Edmonton. She threw a few things in two old trunks — a couple of good knives, a double boiler, iron skillet, shears, yardstick, envelopes, and letter-head, five pounds of paste flour, a roll of mailing-list paper, copy paper for a year, and string. She put pillows and blankets and other linen on top of one trunk, and a feather tick on top of the other.

Thus outfitted, the Murrays rode into still another colourful era of journalism, the like of which will never be duplicated in the Northwest. On the way to Fort St. John, they were almost knocked off the NAR railway platform by the first wave of American Army on the way out. The American Engineers, who had climbed aboard the first bulldozers to lead and direct an army of road-builders through the muskeg to Alaska, had completed the pilot job and were off to Burma or Europe or the South Pacific. Civilian contractors would surface and bridge, lay pipeline, and mop up.

Fort St. John

The truth was that the little settlement of Fort St. John, remote, neglected, slumbering out the war without so much as a gravel road on which to haul its fabulous grain to market, had suddenly been catapulted into chaos. From a population of some hundred-odd people, it soared to a rip-roaring town of ten thousand. From a sleepy little crossroads community, it became, in ten days time, the jumping-off place for thousands of troops, contractors, pilots, surveyors, mechanics, guides, catskinners and truck drivers. So fast did the United States Army lead the builders that, before break-up, April 10, 1942, scarcely six weeks from their arrival at Dawson Creek, the American Engineers were established in a camp site two hundred and fifty miles more or less north of Fort St. John, at the lonely fur-trading post of Fort Nelson.

The sudden prosperity was unbelievable. But as soon as the citizens of the district realized what was happening to them, they performed miracles in exerting their ability to adjust. Some moved out of their houses and rented them. Some simply moved out the front-room furniture and started a cafe. The odd bored female chucked out the whole family and sold her personal attentions to the boys. Women with native skills made and sold moccasins and mukluks. An enterprising daughter of a nearby farm sewed pretty bright parkas with wolverine fur and rick-rack trim, fifty fifty dollars each. Elsie Stuby and Lucy Scheck made pie. Elsie sold fifty a day to the Public Roads Administration camp, delivering them by team and democrat, and bought the homestead with the proceeds. Old Mrs. Parsons, who had been waiting a quarter of a century for her luck to change, got an ice-cream freezer rigged up to a gas engine, froze cream, sugar and vanilla, and sold it out the front door of her farm house as the highway literally pushed through the yard. So popular was her product that she had difficulty keeping it for sale by the dish.

"The Matron's respects m'am and can the army hospital have a gallon?"

"Land sakes, boy, it's only half froze!"

Anyone who wanted to work did so at current city wages. The United States Equipment Depot, Public Roads Administration, Department of Transport, Canadian Pacific Airlines, both armies, both air forces, and umpteen construction companies bid for services offered.

"Wanted: Typist, clerical," read one of the early advertisements in the classified column of the new paper. "You have to type a little, write a little, sit at a desk. Think a little, try a little, we'll show you the rest." Little wonder if typist-clerical was a little stupid by day. She had probably danced all night in the dust and debris down at the American Red Cross, considering it to be her patriotic duty.

The hospital lost some of its best staff to the laundry. Business people who had once fed the help in lieu of wages lost hired girls to the hotels, where tips were good and everything exciting.

The one barber in town solved his predicament by giving out chits for haircuts. He issued twenty-five numbered tickets for the morning, thirty-five for the afternoon, and fifteen for the evening. The biggest news this side of the Atlantic was whose number was presently up at the poolroom barber shop. This arrangement also put the poolroom on its feet, catering to the longhairs.

The Canadian Bank of Commerce moved into its new quarters with a staff of fourteen, mostly girls. Rose DeTonnancourt, a senior clerk at the time, recalls that they handled a payroll of two anda half million dollars a month, most of it stacked at the tellers' feet in cardboard boxes. In two years of operation, they made one mistake. They underpaid a customer three hundred dollars, and it took them eighteen months to trace him down to Minneapolis and return it. He had never even mssed it.

If you had any strength left after cashing your cheque, getting your hair cut, queueing for your supper, and battling your way into the beer parlour for a drink, you could dine and dance at three places in town. Little Heaven, of doubtful character, was the old community hall where everything went on except opium-smoking under the back stoop; or Black Betty's place, which smelled of new lumber and grease; or the White Spot. This last place was the most colourful, since it was run by a carny named Leo who stocked punch boards, bootleg whisky at forty dollars a bottle, a twenty-five cent picture-taking machine, lots of mixer, and a juke box. Leo had enough of the sawdust trail in him to serve a little colour along with the coffee, and his girl friend, Kathleen, was pretty and chatty.

Kathleen often drank too much and once cut her hand in the line of duty and was taken to the hospital. The Doctor stitched her up without anaesthetic, having a thing about alcohol not mixing with ether. Kathleen said Hail Mary's all through the process, intoning the proper name with such force and fury as to bring all the nuns running from the chapel to hush her.

". . . blessed art thou . . . . thy womb, JESUS!" yelled Kathleen. The nuns retired, palming their temples, unmindful of the patient's invitation to remain.

"Ya'll be joinin' me now, Sisters, for the next decade, so ya will."

While the town coped with knifings, fights over women, accidents, crazy people, rape, and murder, the farm people quietly filled their granaries against the day, fast approaching, when they could economically and quickly transport their beautiful grain by truck to the big elevators at Dawson Creek. Those landowners adjacent to the highway survey were too surprised to be either happy or unhappy with the fifteen dollars an acre the Government had offered in the spring of 1942 for right-of-way land. But by harvest time, the disfigured grain fields had a graded, ditched, and gravelled road running through them — going fifty miles to a market. Farm women worked if they wanted to. A staff of seventy washed and ironed for the troops at Charlie Lake, with a starting wage of a hundred and twenty-five a month and board. Youngsters of fifteen could hire on as water boys and earn seventy-five a month and board.

The waterline zipped through town from Charlie Lake to supply the great Fort St. John airport one afternoon, when everyone was too busy to notice. But it did not get by the Omer Bougie farm. Omer's wife, Marie, was out there waving her apron, armed with a devil's food cake, and sweet-talked the engineer major into a service connection, whether he liked it or not. "It's our land, and I won't let you over," said Marie stoutly, "but have a piece of cake." With the waterline due for completion "yesterday," and faced with an offensive like Marie's, flying an apron and armed with a cake plate, what could a beleaguered pipeline platoon major do? The Bougies got the water.

In such a way did the town get sidewalks. Zac Ericsson was the manager of the beer parlour in the old log hotel. He had come from a Grande Prairie homestead and could stand everything about Fort St. John but the mud. When it rained hard, little rivers ran all over town. The heavy equipment passing through in wet weather pressed the gravel into the bottomless roads as fast as it was dumped. Fort St. John needed sidewalks, and Zac would see that they were provided.

Big contractors and important army officers constantly imposed upon him for refreshments when the legal limits had been reached, or when the clock indicated that officially there was no more beer that day. "I need two barrels and I can't get back for a week. Here's the cash," said the Kansas City Bridge executive, storming in two minutes before closing time.

"All right," said Zac, "the beer you shall have. But I need ten kegs of six-inch nails, and unless they're outside the back door by tomorrow morning, you will get no more beer here." Ten kegs of spikes were on the desired spot by morning.

A Public Roads Administration chief was the next to ask a favour. The American sought help from Zac in assuaging the thirsts of numerous Texas and Oklahoma bulldozer engineers. "Drop me off a thousand feet of two-by-twelves today, another tomorrow, and so on until I have enough to build a sidewalk from Gus Halversen's livery stable to Mark Wah's cafe," suggested Zac.

And behold, the lumber appeared as by magic. A work force of a hundred men, lying around town *en route* north, was hypnotized into cutting the planks and the stringers and putting them on the ground.

For fifteen years the people of Fort St. John walked on those sidewalks. They zigged and they zagged, they lurched and they undulated. Frank Willis of the CBC has said that walking them was like nothing so much as the deck of the *Blue Nose* in a hurricane. Drunks smart enough to use them in an argument in court could well explain their classic arms-around-telephone-pole attitude, especially in wet weather. But in their day, they were a credit to the hardy old homesteader who knew a good trade when he saw one.

The cottage-roofed frame house George had acquired in which to locate the news office had been vacated earlier by Homer Keith, engineer in charge for the Department of Transport. It had been moved in from somewhere, and the only thing that recommended it was that is was available. A few things had been knocked together for the living quarters behind. A bed and stove had been borrowed. A forty-five gallon oil drum held water, purchased at the back door for seventy-five cents a fill.

"The cupboards," says Margaret, "were orange crates from the butcher shop next door. You get the general idea."

A folding army table was set up in the front room, which served as an office. A pie plate and chocolate box held the cash sales. Iron wall spikes and wall files held bills, receipts, and copy. A big cardboard carton held last week's deathless prose, rolled, tied with string, and dated for posterity. An oil can took care of waste paper. They put an ad in the paper asking for old kitchen chairs for the office, but furniture was so scarce that when a shipment did come in from Edmonton to the store downtown, it was snapped up right off the truck and never got into the store at all. Mother didn't know what they were going to do for a counter until someone volunteered a pair of saw horses, tall ones. Planks were laid across and that was the counter, chest-high! An oil drum turned on its side, with a door welded on one end and four feet fashioned out of two-inch pipe, was the stove. It took a four-foot log. Margaret put a green skirt of cardboard on the drop light over the table, set up her typewriter, and went to work, which meant covering the town for news and getting to know the people.

The *News* office was a block north of Fort St. John's main intersection. On the four main corners were a bank, a police barracks, a hotel, and a general store. A sign out in the dandelions near the sidewalk in front of the Provincial Police office lurched crazily and proclaimed the names of the two main streets — Glacier running east and west, and Arctic running north and south. The Americans named them. The

Alaska Highway was one mile to the west. Glacier Street, the main thoroughfare, was probably one of the ugliest streets in Canada, resembling the top line of a very old rusted crosscut saw, with half the teeth missing, and those remaining worn down or broken off. Unlike Lillooet, with its venerable balconies, hitching posts, aging "gingerbread" houses, and ancient leafy trees, Fort St. John was a raw western town with the hard-bitten look of the people who built it eighteen years before.

Every building was an unrelieved oblong. Not a tree softened the square hard corners. Not a blade of lawn grass showed except at the hospital at the eastern edge of the village, and that was grey with dust in summer and white with snow in winter. Granaries, machine sheds, old farm houses, barns — all these were hauled into town and pressed into service. A Public Roads Administration employee paid sixty dollars a month for a chicken house in which to install his wife. The proprietor of the Husky Cafe pinned up a snapshot that fall which was captioned, "The only empty premises in town." It was a tiny bird-house at the top of a long pole.

Paddy Carrol ran the Husky Cafe and Bowling Alley. His wife, Bea, tossed the hamburgers which were served with liberal dollops of philosophy from her spouse. Nor were hamburgers and conversation the only items tossed around the premises. Eggs and pies were other ammunition, hurled fore and aft by husband and wife when tempers frayed owing to such exigencies of war as the late arrival of the bread truck. Sometimes it never arrived at all. Carrol was a self styled Communist, a confusing thing to be in the early forties with aid to Russia filling the skies along the Northwest Staging Route. People figured he was kidding. He affected a maestro's hair style and summed up his feelings about the government in one sentence: "They'll get you in the fanals."

Tommy Hargreaves, a notary public, shared the marriage harvest when no recognized church authority was in the village, with Margaret McLeod, a government agent who handled land sales. Licences and vital statistics were in a dark, grey building just north of the *News* office. G.I. Joe and his tootsie would float around dreamily — Mother on several occasions obliged with the loan of her wedding ring, the only required prop — and the knot would be tied. Sometimes all the best trying didn't do any good, as when the groom was already married with a half dozen kids in the States. And sometimes the MP's would invade the nuptial chamber and haul Johnny Doughboy out by the ears in the middle of the night for a fast draft Stateside. More often, of course, the lass from the last frontier went back to the United States with her husband to enrich and strengthen his blood line, and live happily ever after.

Civil law was upheld, when possible, by Bill and Gordie Youngberg, B.C. Provincial Policemen, who took a philosophical view of their duties. They chewed cigars and played poker and were often broken down in their police car, to be ignominiously hauled back to town by some passing mammoth of construction.

The police barracks, which hadn't changed in a decade, combined an office, cell and living quarters. Before the war, the cell door had mostlv swung wide even when occupied, since most customers were moonshiners, drunks, or feuders. Most sentences were worked out on the woodpile.

"The MP's were real rough," recalls Lumsden. "All you had to do about a soldier was call the provosts and the next morning they'd take him clean to Fort Lewis, State of Washington. We had trouble with possession of firearms and drinking because laws covering these things differed in our two countries. We had conmen and prostitutes and daffy jokers flying airplanes under the Peace River bridge on a dare. One of our citizens started a little poker game up above his used furniture store and it was on for the duration. Could we catch them at it? Never! He had a built-in radar system and it wasn't the loose boards on the back steps, either. They couldn't possibly have time. But when we'd get in there, the booze was out of sight, the ashtrays emptied and a nice friendly little pinochle game going on."

It was best to take nothing for granted. Once a 'lady' asked politely if she could have the handcuffs loosened for a moment to allow her to pull down her dress. Lumden loosened them — whereupon the 'lady' knocked him colder than a mackeral.

"Oh, she was a rough town for a while," he recalls ruefully.

How did the Murrays, by now in their late fifties, get along in a thumping little crossroads that hadn't yet picked itself up after an army had marched through it? How did they cope with people so busy that they did not know whether you were offering them a paper to read or paper to wrap vegetables in?

"Well," says Margaret, "you can say we did the best we could with what was at hand."

At hand for her was Cuthill's Meat Market, right next door. Ed Cuthill was an old-country butcher of great skill. His steaks rode along with charts, maps, and manifests in a pilot's attaché case, and were delivered all over the Northwest. And he was all business, aided and abetted only occasionally by a nip out of a dark brown bottle kept handy in the corned-beef barrel. When Margaret called on Cuthill for advertising, the sausage machine was grinding, the saw was sawing, the live chickens in a case were yawking and fluttering.

"Why sure," said Ed, "I'd like to help you out. You can put me down for a two-by-three advert. I'd make it more but I can't get help and I'm doing all the business I can handle. Look at those birds. If I can't get them dressed tonight, they lose weight."

"Mr. Cuthill," said Margaret, "you make this ad two-by-five and I'll come over and dress those chickens myself."

"You're kiddin'," says Cuthill.

"I'll show you who's kidding. I'll want lots of boiling water, so get it on."

Mother axed, scalded, plucked, and drew twenty-nine chickens before going to bed. Dad, amused at her salesmanship tactics, did the other seven. His Ontario education had not been in vain, either. "What Cuthill couldn't get over was that we even did the gizzards," laughs Margaret.

George's bid for neighbourliness was cutting hair. Not for twenty years had he a comb and taper in his hands, but the tonsorial situation in Fort St. John was impossible. The ticket method used by D'Allaire at the poolroom sounded fine, but with time of the essence, ticket holder 31 and his crew of ten men embracing the decade to 41, might have to catch an early transport back up the road, so that the whole system was apt to fall apart shortly after lunch.

"What a wonderful barber your father was," Margaret

recalls. "Mind you, he used all my tea towels, sheets, and aprons. But what did it matter? We got to know the people fast." It was a fact. Between cutting hair, plucking chickens, understanding parliamentary procedure, being aware of current problems and full of sound advice, Mother, with her great energy and Dad with his broad experience, were part of the town in no time.

They went, as always, to their separate churches, Father to the Presbyterian with a tent camp in the front yard, and Mother to the Catholic, where Father Otterbach and the organist had not spoken to each other in three years and communicated, when they had to, with brisk notes. Dad once said, "Don't forget to get down some place about Francis Cardinal Spellman visiting your mother's church in 1942. There is a vignette that shouldn't be lost."

This is how he told it. "Spellman, the great prelate of the Catholic Church in New York City, is visiting the American troops, you see. He pays a courtesy call on the parish priest while in Fort St. John. It's the end of another long day and the poor, weary, little man is soaking his feet in a bucket in his very crude quarters at the back of the church. The knock comes to the door. It opens and there the Cardinal in his red hat stands with two or three very important officers. The priest is stunned. He stands in his bare, wet feet, deeply embarrassed. There is an awkward silence, broken by Spellman, who takes off his hat, extends his hand and says gently, 'How beautiful are the feet of they who preach the gospel! How do you do, Father? The name is Spellman.'"

"How else," ended my Dad, "do you explain the Catholics getting a new rectory the next year, gift of the Americans?"

The Glacier Drug Store was the most elegant shop in town, a genteel incongruity plunked in the middle of bedlam. Ray and Frances Sandy had contrived to fill their shop with a Fifth Avenue elegance in the face of mud, dust, hobnails and gumboots. The creamy inlaid floor was scrubbed each night. The gleaming plate glass counters held wonders in perfume and cosmetics, often unavailable in the cities. The gift department, displayed under white fluorescent light, sterling silver and Spode and Daulton. A valiant effort was made to staff the pharmacy, but most B.C. druggists were away at the wars and the most promising one they ever succeeded in luring up from the coast had such an affinity for beef, iron and wine that they had to let him go. The hospital then filled the prescriptions for the community.

One of the several girls who worked in the shop was on duty one night when a rough talking character came in and asked for a box of American flags.

Margaret, awaiting advertising copy, stood aside and took in the scene. The incongruity of it: this lovely store and outside a sea of mud and standing trucks; bartender across the street shovelling out the beer parlour entrance with customers standing in front of and behind him.

What on earth would this character want with flags on such a day?

"But I'm sure we have no American flags," the clerk was saying. "I'll get Mrs. Sandy."

"That's a good one all right. A box of American flags, eh? Well you go and do something else and I'll tend to him," said Frances Sandy.

One of the fastest moving items in the store were prophylactics, and the Americans had some amazing names for them. But this, indeed, was a new one. Frances went straight to the drawer in which this merchandise was kept.

"That'll be seventy five cents," she said as she handed the package to the customer.

"Jeez, how big are they?" asked the mountain of wet mackinaw, opening the package. "Why Christ Almighty, didn't I say flags? American flags? We're having a Red Cross dance tonight and they were going to decorate the . . ."

All types and all kinds were around Fort St. John.

News of the World

Copy for the newspaper went down to Vancouver on Saturdays, courtesy of Canadian Pacific Airline pilots, who were sweet-talked into dropping the bundle into a mail box when they got to Vancouver. For two years it was opened each Sunday night in the back shop of the S. & S. printers out in Burnaby, set into type, the ads changed, the mailing list corrected, and the whole bundle of newspapers shipped back air express the following Wednesday. Most weeks they arrived safely, but complete editions of the Alaska Highway *News* have been delivered to St. John's Newfoundland, and St. John, New Brunswick. Some have found their way to Fort St. James and some have been lost completely.

The air express on the newspapers from Vancouver amounted to fifteen dollars. Each week, CPA assistant, Rollie Tonnancourt, delivered the bundle. He was so much part of the firm, wrangling the Saturday copy into the care of pilots and stewardesses, that he felt sorry for the old girl in the *News* office and never collected until Saturday when she had the newsstand money gathered up, and enough in the chocolate box to pay the express.

Whole issues have been reprinted and some issues have arrived on time that would have saved heartache all around had they never arrived at all. Errors were numerous. Some ghastly, some merely funny.

It was easy to see with a glance at the paper which of the Murrays was in Fort St. John and which was in Vancouver. George's copy was formal: "Charlie Lee, late of the New Palace Cafe in Dawson Creek, has taken over management of the Pomeroy Cafe. 'The future of Fort St. John is assured,' said Mr. Lee. 'Restaurant investment here is attractive to enterprising business executives.' "

No offence to Charlie Lee, who even then could probably buy and sell the Murrays several times over, but it is extremely doubtful that this Chinese *restauranteur* even understood these words, let alone uttered them. Cafes in 1944 in Fort St. John did not attract a formally educated Chinese, though Lee's son in China may well have been a colonel in Chiang Kaishek's army. The poor man probably said nothing but "yes" while George asked appropriate questions.

Margaret, however, had no set mould into which to pour a story, an item, or a statement. She took off five spaces from the left, and fasten your seat belt! This was Margaret's idea of a "District Local": "What do passengers do while a CPA Lodestar wings its way through the blue? They shoot craps. Altitude six thousand feet, temperature fifty-five below, bright sun, speed two hundred miles an hour. The stewardess passed Spearmint gum. The 'Highwaymen' all have a carton of their favourite brand. Puff, chew, talk, laugh, seven-come-eleven. 'Be good to me, Baby . . .'

"I got out at Grande Prairie and a cadaverous Chinese took my seat. He had made a fortune at Dawson Creek and was on his way to do some shopping in Edmonton. Game resumed in the rotunda of the airport during the stop. Gentlemanly Canadian Air Force boys tiptoed gingerly across windows of folding money as the ivories galloped."

The paper encouraged readers, so that the district news came pouring in. There was Uncle Dudley, the correspondent at Hudson's Hope. Uncle is the only man in Canada who lived so frugally and so long that his savings account from old age pension cheques had to be investigated by the government. "Spend it, spend it! The economy of the country depends on this money getting into circulation," reasoned the pension inspector. But Uncle liked to see it there in the bank. He grew just enough garden, trapped just enough fur, wrote just enough news — for which Margaret sent him a bottle of "snakebite" at Christmas and Easter — to live on.

One of Uncle Dudley's typical wind-up items went like this: "Today the fifth is wet and as I write this a potential grubstake ambles past my window in the form of a fully grown lynx. May he prosper and have a large progeny. Cheerio. Uncle Dudley."

A mess hall philosopher from camp 49 said it for the road builders.

"We live thick," he wrote the paper, "Meeting at meals

three times a day to give each other a new taste of that old musty cheese that we are. We agree on rules called etiquette to make this meeting tolerable. Before a meal you guys remind me of a steam engine needing refuelling. It won't budge. But after the fuel the pressure becomes terrific. Likewise you. After satisfying your hunger in seven minutes flat, you dash out in a frenzied manner past the meal checker, mumbling your meal ticket number incoherently, to disappear into the thin atmosphere of the Alcan Highway. Remember the rules that help us to stand each other. You call it politeness. And for gawdsakes state your number clearly. *Then* you can roll along the highway to your heart's content. Or by jeez I get a turnpike gate and a three hundred pound traffic cop . . ."

A short order cook commented on news of the Highway truck stops. "To begin with," he wrote, "Lum 'n Abner is no longer at Mile 187J but at Mile 233 from Dawson Creek, much to the confusion of truckers who have spent most of their time up till now learning the mileages . . . No one has seen Oscar for two weeks. Oscar is a big black bear with yellow nose and quite fat. Anyone finding please boot it's behind back here to Lum 'n Abners."

The wild animals in these construction years were as confused as anybody. The Americans petted and fed the moose babies, the cubs, the fawns and the kits and found themselves with growing problems — and pets — as the bears returned to wreck the cookhouse or the moose to stove in a staff car.

"Bear Flat is well named," wrote George, "Bears are on the rampage at half a dozen ranches. Mrs. Barney Dopp heard a scratching at her kitchen screen door. A big brown bear was wanting in. Mrs. Dopp reached for her husband's big rifle, aimed point blank. The bullet, in some manner, hit the corner of an iron pot and missed. Mrs. Dopp fired again through an open but screened window. Again she missed. The bear slouched off. Commenting later on his wife's marksmanship, Barney said, "Sadie shouda used the shot gun." But Mrs. Dopp said it was no laughing matter. The Americans have made pets of the bears, she held, so now they're not afraid of anyone, including game wardens. Besides, the forest fires are driving them in from the bush. Woman and children have a right to be protected she said.

"Score for the week on bears along the Hudson's Hope road: Ardill ranch 1, Tompkins ranch 2, Bennett 1, Dopp 2, Game warden 2 . . ."

The Fort St. John Airport was classified news, but items like these got by: "Slim Brunner and his men closed the circuit at 6:00 P.M. Wednesday, which lit up two long lines of coloured lights on the northwest, southeast runway, which in fog and darkness will now guide the planes safely into port . . . first lights on the Northwest Staging Route.

"There were thirty Cobra fighters over town at 10:00 A.M. Saturday, lifting off ten at a time, from a batch of sixty sitting on the tarmac. Bound for Russia.

"The town-to-airport road is the heaviest travelled in B.C. Eighteen buses a day run between Camp 49, Charlie Lake and airport. The water bill to keep the dust down for June, July, and August amounted to twenty thousand dollars."

From Fort Nelson: "One of the greatest dog stories ever told concerns the trials now going on here of dogs dropped by parachute for rescue work. Each husky weighs a hundred pounds. They are dropped from a mile in the air into the bush, equipped with medical supplies and mushed a hundred miles. Wing Search and Rescue chief, Major Joseph Westover, says they will be used in Japan for rescue work. The dogs love it."

Farmers gave items over the counter on crops: "Marie Bougie said they hauled the carrots in by team, but it took a tractor to get the turnips under cover. If you don't believe the editor, drop in at the *News* office and see the turnip the Bougies brought in by dump truck Monday. Hundreds of ears of sweet corn of excellent quality from Dominic La Fleur's, a good paying cash crop when the market offers. Excellent tomatoes from ranches of Tompkins and Todd. Three tons of beautiful potatoes from a half acre plot in Baldonnel."

From the hospital came reports like this: "She was taken to Edmonton for further treatment. The airport woman said she drank the creolin, thinking it was whisky."

While helping with the soft water supply for the hospital, Mabel Gauthier slipped off the wagon and fell into the cistern along with a ton of snow. She was hauled out and put to bed.

The paper practically wrote itself that first year, with a minimum of pruning for clarity's sake. "A good weekly," repeated my father, "mirrors its community. This is a magnificent era of development. Let us not smooth and polish and ruin the picture. Rather let us strive to keep the colours on the receding frontier bright and true."

Thus the Moberly Lake news, the first week, read as follows: "Dear Sir: The mailman Mr. Bazeley told me you wanted news from Moberly. Here she am boy. Stampede. One hell of a big crowd. Everybody drunk. If we had a censored censored bridge on Moberly River, there would have been lots more people from everyplace. Fifty cars and trucks here. Dance hall too small, 60 x 90. Yours truly, H. Garbutt."

United States Army personnel and contractors building the Alaska Highway so occupied local citizens during these months that unless invited to a party on the base, or having business there, many were unaware of what was being accomplished at the airport only four miles east of town.

The east-west runway was completed in 1942. Nothing fancy. No gravel, but instead sheets of interlocking metal plates to keep the planes out of the mud. Aircraft at first landed in clouds of dust kicked up by Tomlinson's turnapulls, as these giant earthmovers cruised around the flat prairie, levelling the land. Three permanent residences, a men's bunkhouse, and a tiny administration office dotted one side of the field. No control tower. You checked the wind and picked your spot.

Were there any accidents?

"None serious," says Bud Woodruff, one of the originals from the Department of Transport. "No loss of life during the construction of the airport. I remember one fellow landing with his wheels up, out of fuel. He jumped out of his U.S. service plane and looked wildly about him. 'Where the hang am I?' he asked a shovel operator, hanging out of his cab window. 'Can I get a train out of here?' " But this guy was only lost. Plenty of them got lost.

McConachie's planes, now Boeing 10's with a dozen seats, shared the runway in those early days of American participation in the war with other passenger planes and freight planes airlifting material to Northern airports then in construction. And presently there were the Cobras, P30's, the fighter craft being sent over to Russia, manned by downy-cheeked young pilots barely out of a lecture room. They were cocky and, already in "foreign" country, either ill-mannered or engaging, depending on the personality of each.

The planes for Russia travelled in settings. The hen plane was usually a B25 medium bomber, a Mitchell, fully equipped, manned by an experienced crew which did the navigating for the nine or ten fledglings which flew at her tail. The Cobras were without instruments. There were only five radio and five weather personnel to man the airport through a twenty-four hour period — until the airlift started to Russia. Then the United States Army Air Force broke out all over, like the measles.

Dust, noise, and organized confusion accompanied the airlift to Russia, as carpenters banged away on six hundred barrack blocks and a hangar that would hold four flying forts at once, with two hundred officers, parts depots, radio rooms, workshops, bathrooms, watchmen's quarters stacked three stories high around the perimeter of the huge oblong building. A heating plant to service a city, a fire department to match, a system of roads, a network of water mains, a regiment of electricians, and another of carpenters, spilled over the Sperling farm at the edge of the field and never stopped until an air base suitable for the second largest refueling depot in North America was complete down to the last detail.

As the year 1944 ended, and the Royal Canadian Air Force prepared to take over from the Americans all the communications and transportation along the Highway, there had been completed to Fort St. John the most powerful network of radio telegraph and telephone communications ever installed, with so many separate circuits that only a major catastrophe like an earthquake could knock them all out. This installation had a military objective, of course, but the Government of Canada was farseeing enough to realize that one day, when the route would become a major arterial airway over the top of the world, the RCAF'S contribution to the Allies' war machine would go on providing security to civilian air transportation.

No formal announcement was made anywhere concerning the withdrawal of the American Army from the Alaska Highway in 1944. But the "Letters" column in the Alaska Highway *News* told the story clearly as soldiers wrote requesting the bouncy little weekly to be sent on to them, and bidding farewell through its columns to their friends. In Fort St. John, troops waiting to move had plenty of time for letters. They came down with the mumps and were quarantined. Business immediately fell off at the dance halls, pubs, movies, and drug stores, prompting the following tribute in type: "We're in love with all the Yanks / And their merry boyish pranks." It continued on and on.

The Public Roads Administration remained to continue administering the Highway to its completion, but the Army, responsible only for its construction, was required to face up to a tremendous logistical problem. Having gotten all this material up north, what were they to do with it now they were leaving?

The United States was only a few months at war when the Alcan was undertaken. Japanese were camped on the Aleutian Islands. The task was complicated by the fact that, in their zeal, American manufacturers had oversupplied the operation to a scandalous degree. Some 14,000 pieces of equipment of an estimated value of $10,000,000 disappeared entirely on the Highway between 1942 and 1945. This included every conceivable type of gear and equipment required for road and airport construction. Five hundred trucks and gasoline shovels and the like were unaccounted for. When irregularities at Camp 49 were investigated, a building containing a $100,000 layout of lathes, hammers, drills, and so on, burnt mysteriously overnight along with all records.

The point here is not the loss of this material — responsibility for which was never officially fixed anyway — but that it was hardly missed. This was merely a fraction of the numbers of machines on hand in equipment depots along the road. What was not big enough or important enough to ship back to the United States for regrouping was left by the side of the road to await the demolition crews. With wrecking bars and sledge-hammers, Army personnel attacked every equipment yard between Dawson Creek and Whitehorse, burning and burying. Stoves, refrigerators, and washing machines were pushed over coulees and covered up by bulldozers. The torch was put to bedding and blankets and clothing.

"Don't worry about the Russians ever getting to the States," one wag quipped in the *News*. "The Canadians will steal them blind before they get to Fort Nelson."

But the facts are that there were not a thousand settlers between the Peace River and the Yukon border in 1942. The Highway, a joint defense project, was policed by the Royal Canadian Mounted, with road blocks strictly enforced. Beside every American camp on the road, temporary dump piles grew alarmingly as surplus supplies were set aside — when they needed ten, what to do with the other ninety cast iron stoves? — or there was no time to carry out repairs on equipment that was expendable. The human equation cannot be denied. There was corruption among underlings. But the haves, generally speaking, looked sympathetically at the have-nots and ordered out the trucks and bulldozers. Only the ages will tell the true story of waste on the Alcan, and the story of waste during war. As the winds erode and the waters shrink, historians of some future era will write it.

"The FBI is checking possession of stolen goods up this highway," warned the Fort St. John paper. "Uncle Sam leaves a lot of plunder laying along by the road side to rust and ruin, thereby tempting thrifty Canadian homesteaders to take some away to the security of their acres . . ."

"Get a bill of sale," cautioned Margaret, reporting a Fridgidaire, confiscated by the U.S. Army while authorities thawed out old records and files to find out who sold it and what else went with it, all property of Uncle Sam.

But the same issue invited the folks down to help themselves to green stringed beans in cans, five tons of which were all over the road on the Peace River Hill where a big white truck had thrown a front wheel, climbed a bank, flipped over three times and spilled the beans.

These were barely cleared away, when eight hundred Canadian Air Force men came up the highway to take the place of their opposite American numbers. Civilians offering service to the troops, who had noticed what the mumps did to business in Fort St. John, were beginning to think the honeymoon was over. In fact, it was just starting. The replacements — both service and civilian — brought dependents with them. The little towns along the highway were jumping.

"While all this is happening," recalls Margaret, "there is suddenly a crisis at the Fort St. John hospital." The American army doctors were leaving, and our own Doctor Kearney was ill in Vancouver. Besides, the hospital was in debt sixteen thousand dollars. One day, a big American lorry pulled up at the back door. A load of pills, the driver told the nun who answered the door. He wasn't just whistling Dixie. There were enough pills to keep everybody from here to Alaska running for the next five years. There were physic pills in jeraboam bottles two feet high. Salts, cascara, bandages, sulfa, big brown bottles of belladonna plasters, antiphlogistine, medicated poulticing, bed pans, urinals, rubber goods — all supplies on hand at the base hospital which was moving. "Have it empty in twenty-four hours," said the soldier-driver. "We need the truck."

On the eve of the Army's departure, practically, the town had a bazaar, raffled Victory Bonds, and raised three thousand dollars, enough to pay twenty-five dollars a month increase to keep the nurses. Nurses earned ninety dollars a month — thirty more than the lowliest laundry hand at Charlie Lake. American rates of pay were at least one-third higher than Canadian, for both Army and civilians, plus a bonus for being on foreign soil. On the other hand, Dr. LeSage, the United States Army doctor, operated on Canadians, courtesy of his government. No charge. As if the situation was not confusing enough, along came the demolition crews.

Out at the dump, mattresses, sheets, pillows, blankets, quilts, rugs were all going up in smoke. You could see bales of sheets, with hems burnt down only to the hemstitch line where the fuel had missed them. Bales of Red Cross quilts were burned. Fort St. John and district, which raised thousands for the Red Cross during the war, just never got over the sight of those bales. The economics involved in moving the stuff meant nothing to them. They saw it as their hard-earned money going up in smoke. It got so bad with people needing and wanting the stuff, they had to arm guards to keep the public away.

One night, Mother drove out with Father Youngbluth to the dump beyond the Airport. She could not believe that all this useful material was being destroyed. The priest was pretty good with a fly fishing-rod. Carefully he lowered his hook, fashioned of haywire, over the side of the ridge running out between the coulees. His first catch was a pair of rubber boots. Then up came a bale of mackinaws, size thirty-four. The fishing was good. A bale of thirty-two's came next, and a bale of forty-four's. The Moberly Lake Indians would have been outfitted to a man, but suddenly the headlights of a car showed over the hill.

"They're coming!" Mother cried. "Quick, under the tarp with the loot." Ten American officers piled out of three cars, their headlights illuminating the day's accomplishments. Suddenly one of them picked out in the beam of his flashlight a group of bears eating pork chops down at the bottom of the side hill — barrels of beautiful loin on which the dry ice had given out. And the bears, happily munching chops, distracted the officers' attention so that Father Youngbluth got his pickup — and contraband — turned around and safely up the hill.

Wartime security was the only thing that ever sealed the lips of Margaret Murray and kept her from saying what she felt needed to be said. Newspapers, of course, were carefully censored, even a little weekly like the one in Fort St. John. Maybe even particularly the one in Fort St. John.

One night, at a dance in Taylor, Air Force blue and Army tan, copiously reinforced with bootleg whisky, had it out in the middle of the floor, where arms and legs were piled six feet high in a melee, and one man got his throat cut. Someone threw a tunic over him as they lifted him shoulder high and bore him from view.

Who was he?

"Who are you talking about?" asked the Army blandly. "What dance hall? Which town?" So it was with everything.

But if Margaret got a little crotchety with the red tape of censorship in matters such as these, she was absolutely fit to be tied over the appalling waste. She could not stand it. It kept her awake at night. Dad reasoned with her that this was war, and there had to be regulations. If all the war surplus materials were handed over to civilians, it would upset the economic balance of the country. But to Margaret it was waste and it was wrong. And she was going to do something about it!

She decided against taking on the whole American Army single-handed; instead she decided to let the Southam Newspapers do it for her. She got on the phone to Pinkie McKelvie at the *Province* in Vancouver. Would he like a story? He would, and he came.

They drove out to the dump with Cecil Warren, the furniture man. They parked the car and sat there — and watched hundreds of thousands of dollars of everything from refrigerators to Ford motors to sugar, knocked with a sledgehammer, being ploughed under the big dozers. What would burn was covered with oil and set alight. Huge oil drums, used by the settlers for water barrels, were picked with tiny holes. Food, sheep-lined leather flying suits, bales of Stanfields underwear — all were dispatched. They knew just where to strike to ruin a useful thing — the oven door of a stove, the lid of a heater, the handle of a refrigerator, the agitator on a washing machine.

Mother said to the officer standing by overseeing, "Why can't you store all this plunder against the day when people are hungry and cold?"

"Good hunch ya got there, ma'am," he replied. "But we couldn't do it. All this stuff is duty free. All under defence contract. The best has been hauled on flat cars to Minnesota, and orders are orders."

"The memory of it will never leave me," Mother said. "No wonder the Alaska Highway cost a hundred and thirty-five million dollars. It should have cost not a cent more than fifty million."

As the road-building Army moved out in a dust-covered olive drab procession including all manner of machines and pick-a-back trailers — an amazing sight — carrying stacked busloads of American troops, they could hardly anticipate that on the Northern Alberta Railroad platform at Dawson Creek they would jostle the vanguard of another sort of army on its way in, and that some of them would, indeed, be joining its ranks in years to come.

The oil scouts had arrived. There was no question about the petroleum resources in Northern British Columbia and the Yukon. For a hundred years men had known, around Hudson's Hope, that escaping gas at Link Creek could be lit to boil a trapper's billy-can of tea. For fifty years mineral surveys had noted more specifically the geological formation of the country and had made deductions concerning oil and gas that filled twenty of the books that my father stacked around him in the British Columbia Legislature in 1933. A war had merely advanced men's thinking half a century by opening the wilderness with a highway and communications that made these riches accessible.

There was nothing mechanized about the scouts for this oil army. They took to the hills, hacking their way into the ground they were to explore. Pack horses, grub, tents, and personnel were problems in 1943. However, the Peace country — though a war was on — was never short of men who loved to get out in the hills, and the average ages of the first Phillips Petroleum exploration parties were well above the enlistment bracket.

The government reserve on land wasn't lifted until 1947, and beyond calling at the Alaska Highway *News* office for old newspapers in which to wrap drill cores for shipment to labs in Calgary, the key men for Phillips, Socony Vacuum, Imperial Oil, and Economy Corporation had nothing to report on petroleum, but lots to say on the agricultural possibilities of the unexplored fringes of the district.

The Murrays got the story anyway. Down at Pouce Coupe, while drilling for water in the Public Works yard, the district engineer got a wet gas-well instead. It blew and had to be cemented in. And obligingly it occurred on the twentieth anniversary of the sealing off of the first Peace River petroleum find at Commotion Creek near Pouce. The paper had a peg on which to hang a fine petroleum story, calling on various incidents of water wells from Fort Nelson to the Alberta border crashing in with oil and gas. Dr. Williams, who had even supervised the government drilling project at Commotion Creek in the twenties, was available for comment. The story was headlined "Dame Nature Kicks Over the Traces — Puts Her Foot in Oil." It was important because it was the first indication that the Murrays had made the right decision, that the country north of the Fifty-sixth Parallel would never again return to the beaver and the Indians — as many people held it would.

By this time I was in London, assigned by the Royal Canadian Navy to SHAEF, fifty acres of gold braid and desks at the University of London, of which half, it seemed, was devoted to censorship. The point is, you figured you were doing your share to win the war for the folks back home. Until, that is, a dog-eared copy of the great family journal from Fort St. John turned up with the cigarette and food parcels, having been many weeks on the way. I unfolded it and looked it over. It was set in very compact eight point with tiny heads on stories to make more room for more stories. There was enough blood and gore in that one issue to fill a *News of the World.*

On page one, in Margaret Murray's most lurid prose, was the account of a ghastly murder in her neighbour's woodlot. "Stumbling through the slashing, her face red with her own blood, a gaping hole in her jugular, blood looping down inside her low-necked dress, her pretty hair smeared and matted, her hands outstretched, and her eyes staring in a hunted and awesome attitude, she cried, "My God, Oh my God! Help me!"

Leaving the reader dry-mouthed at the end of that front-page column, the story turned over. The girl had taken up with an American soldier and we were assured that bloodhounds had been flown in to track her slayer.

Column two reported a domestic tragedy: "She had, unknowing, used airplane gas for cleaning clothes in the kitchen. She was blown out the side of the house."

But this was still just the beginning. After an eight point cut-off, I read that a visitor from Huallen, Alberta, attending the big stampede, had driven into the rear of a big United States transport truck, and had sliced himself and companion and car in half. Two dead, one dying.

At Mile 41, same week, Dave Bodey, driving a used panel, had endeavoured to pass Don Taylor, with an RCAF transport. Bodey in some manner got his panel caught in the big truck, both doing fifty miles an hour, which swung the panel around before it, and clunked it in the ditch. Bodey's passenger had her forehead de-fleshed, the paper reported calmly, and needed silver plates to make her arms work again. Bodey was still unconscious after thirty hours, and his head bore terrible injuries.

Who was fighting this war?

Ma's Defection

George, who always painted on a broad canvas, needed no longer to be hampered by the boundaries of a district, as in South Cariboo. Here in Fort St. John his typewriter roamed all over the north. He continued to hammer away at his development policy.

"Premier John Hart is quoted as saying the Alaska Highway is of *absolutely* no use to British Columbia in its present location," he fumed editorially. Small wonder, he added, the people of Northern British Columbia, long neglected and forgotten, wished two separate provinces between Alaska and Washington state. "The dead and distant hand of officialdom very often throttles local activity and blacks out the flame of progress. Northern British Columbia has closer ties with Edmonton than with Victoria," he wrote.

A year or two later, while he was away up the Mackenzie on one of Red Powell's river barges investigating a market for Peace River Produce, Margaret went even one better. She inserted a vote coupon in the Alaska Highway *News*, asked readers to mark their X for secession to Alberta, and got two hundred and ten replies out of about eight hundred readers. All yes.

George found time to inspire and then applaud editorially the founding of an Elks Lodge in Fort St. John, the first service organization to get started throughout the British Columbia Peace. He and Hal Roche, Dave Kirkness the butcher, and one or two others did much of the foundation work and were rewarded with an incredible 209 forming members.

The Baldonnel Credit Union — 133 farmer members, eight thousand share capital and six thousand on loan — was featured in the paper by George and felt so good about the build-up that all hundred and thirty-three hustled right over with another ten dollar deposit. Twenty years later, the share capital of this credit union-minded bunch of farmers had grown to over a million dollars.

Colourful features gave zest to the columns of the weekly yet slyly punched home a never-ending crusade for more services, and for more attention to the awakening giant, the North.

An eye-stopper on medicine men still operating among the Nehannis followed a visit to Father LeCoat, Oblate missionary at Fort Liard. "A needle in her abdomen was supposed to let the evil spirits escape. And of course she died. In many ways medicine men are quite up to date along the Laird. One such forced an increase in wages for a number of Indians employed on a survey for the Department of Mines and Resources. He said the American Army paid more on the Canol pipeline for similar work and that the King George boss should come up with a dollar more a day . . ."

The rivers of the North yield up great riches to the writer who explores them. And one year, George's pen hit paydirt along the Nahanni. Frank Henderson, then a prospector (but thirty years before a band leader at the Palliser Hotel in Calgary), called in with a poke of nuggets, spilled them on the counter in the Alaska Highway *News* office, and with them a story of gold that sparked a small rush up the Highway in 1946. The city press and radio, perishing for fresh and exciting copy in that first post-war year, picked it up and played it wide. And when it was over, one young city journalist at least had got his name in lights. The name was Pierre Berton. The Vancouver Daily *Sun* hired an aircraft and a photographer, and when the Fort St. John's weekly editor could not get away for the three-week jaunt, Berton was put on the story instead.

"Break up the long honeymoon and get back to normal," George advised, referring to the union of Liberals and Conservatives who had coalesced to prosecute the war. If little had been done before on northern development in Canada's Pacific Province, less was being done now, when both the great parties of the province were bending over backwards being considerate of each other, and all incentive had been completely wiped out. The province of British Columbia had more cash in the bank than it had had since 1871, the year it joined Confederation.

"Yet all we get on the Pine Pass Highway are survey parties," said Father bitterly. "When in doubt about a highway or a railway, order a survey made, that's the way to do things. The various passes through the mountains to the Pacific slope had been surveyed countless times. Since 1930, we've known the Pine Pass has no grade heavier than one per cent. Not survey parties again, in God's name, but carry-alls and bulldozers."

The Murrays yearned to see the two parties once more facing each other in the Legislative chamber and were horrified to learn in 1945 that a movement was afoot in the province not only to continue coalition as an emergency measure but to create a merged party that would forever and altogether cancel out the Liberals and Conservatives in British Columbia.

"Over my dead body," said Margaret. "I'll fight them with every breath I've got."

"Now, my dear, they haven't done it, and they're not likely to do it, so save your strength for the move to the new building."

But neither forgot about it.

Things were going well in Fort St. John, and the Murrays had enough money to buy a lot down on the main street and move a construction building onto it for an office. The Wartime Prices and Trade Board caught up with Margaret after a few weeks, for using the Howe Sound *News* franchise to get her paper for the new publication. They forced her to continue the use of the name Howe Sound *News,* incorporated with Alaska Highway *News* on the masthead, and let the matter rest there. On this account, the British Columbia Weekly Newspaper Association for a time considered expelling the new paper, but never did.

And presently there was the Roosevelt memorial service which turned out to be the last formal gathering of allied servicemen on the Alcan.

V-E day was next. The American officers set up several carloads of Schlitz beer outside their quarters on the airport, and asked the whole countryside to a victory celebration. In August, V-J day. The children were coming home.

British Columbia was certainly riding a crest of prosperity then. In an era when money was made with a fountain pen, when war contracts abounded and provincial development was reduced to nothing, the government surplus was announced at forty-five million dollars. An election was to be called in October. And the decision to be reached before the election was called was whether to form a Coalition Party and carry on — Liberals and Conservatives together — or to break apart and resume normal operations in government.

Hurriedly, the Liberals called an August convention in Vancouver. George was in Lillooet; Margaret in Fort St. John. Both attended.

The convention was held in the ballroom of the Hotel Vancouver, where similar Liberal and Conservative conventions had been held for years. No fanfare accompanied it. The delicate-appearing gilt chairs had stood up under the weight of countless delegates in countless crowded meetings of this sort, but the 1945 meeting of the Liberals left many vacant seats. The convention was considered a nuisance. With the troops returning from the wars, and the adjustments being faced on all sides after six years of hostilities, had anyone the time to think about governments? Who cared?

Most of those who did care tended to follow the leader, Liberal Premier John Hart, and, at the same time, the line of least resistance. It seemed so easy to continue the coalition; the comfortable, easy way out, with the Socialists as a weak opposition against the combined free enterprisers; and there was the provincial treasury, bulging with money.

A stout little band of Liberals said no. They met together, lined up party stalwarts whom they believed to be with them. They planted their supporters throughout the convention, arranged their strategy so that certain M.P.s, M.L.A.s, and long-standing members would speak to the continuing of the time-honoured, two-party system on which Canadian government had been based.

The day wore on with resolutions, discussions, and the talk and hum of party business. Finally, the resolution to form a Coalition Party was moved and spoken to by Premier Hart. "The Liberal Party has decided that this is the thing to do, and we will now ask the convention to endorse it," he said.

The rebel group had lined up G.G. McGeer, K.C., M.P., to speak at this critical moment against the resolution.

McGeer, whose fine flow of words and bombastic delivery had only grown more polished and convincing over thirty-odd years, would be the rebels' hope to stampede the convention and defeat the resolution. And among this group were not only the Murrays, his old friends, but likewise other supporters who had applauded him into his first nomination in the old Gaelic Church in 1916.

Presently, Margaret, who kept looking over the assembly, spotted "G. G." coming in the door. He wore a *boutonniere* — not red for Liberalism, but yellow. Could there by any significance in the fact that yellow was the colour of the primrose, the badge of the Conservative members of the House? "I whispered to Jimmy Sinclair and George Cruickshanks that he had arrived," remembers Margaret, "and that I had a feeling he would not speak. 'He is wearing a yellow rose,' I told them."

"Are you ready for the question?" asked the Chair.

"Question, question!" demanded the convention, anxious to be done with it.

"And still McGeer did not speak. He did not move. And when I saw that he did not intend to, I did."

She sure did!

"John Hart!" She addressed the Chair but named the Premier. "Mr. Hart, you are doing something today that will end the Liberal Party in British Columbia. If you decide on this treacherous course, it will not return in my lifetime, nor in yours."

George, the modest one, anguishing from the back of the convention hall where he stood with Harry Perry, put up his hand to silence his wife, whose emotional voice had told him that she was about to make a spectacle of herself. Margaret, half turned toward the assembly, saw the hand.

"George Murray," she said to him over the crowd, "you'll not shush me this time. I will have my say."

She did. "You are selling the Liberals of this Province, John Hart, down the river and they are not here to speak for themselves. I will speak for them. Who am I?" Her voice broke and the tears started. "A foot-slogger is what I am. A blotter-carrier, a canvasser — and for a party that hardly existed before 1912 in this Province. People like me have pushed prams and worn out shoe leather to build it to what it is today."

There were mingled cries of approval, but a voice sailed across the ballroom in derision. Margaret recognized it as belonging to a woman of questionable background, nevertheless a party stalwart.

"Enough from you," she said, naming her. "In 1916, I wasn't canvassing for the same thing you were." Then she turned back to the matter at hand.

"I'll tell you what you are, John Hart. You're afraid of the Socialists. All right, let them get elected. Let them spend the forty-five million. And let them hang themselves doing it. But let us remain strong as a Party. Give us a chance to return. Because if you fail to do this, if you fail to let us stand today as a Party, we will never be elected again . . ."

Brother Dan had been back to civvy street some months before I returned to Canada. Immediately he picked up his wife and baby daughter and went to Lillooet, threw open the doors, brushed down the cobwebs, dusted out the type-cases, oiled up the linotype, and went to work printing both the Lillooet *News* and the Alaska Highway *News* at the old stand. Margaret held down the Peace River outpost, and George handled copy for both papers at Lillooet.

I stopped in Toronto on the way home. Lunching with the Eadies (he was managing editor of the Toronto *Star)* in the Royal York, the conversation was pleasant and typical of these reunions with friends — until it turned westward.

"I'll tell you one thing," said Ken Eadie, "if your mother and your father win *both* their elections, the Toronto *Star* is going to send a reporter to cover the Legislature in Victoria in February."

"Win both their elections? What do you mean?"

"I think it's just priceless," laughed Henri, Ken's wife. "Didn't you know?"

"Surely my mother isn't running?"

"Oh, but surely she is. Social Credit! In the Peace River."

"Oh, my God. I don't believe it. Social Credit is that Bible half-hour thing. What about my father?"

"Liberal Independent in his old riding of Lillooet."

Georgina left her mixed grill and went up to her room. A fine homecoming this was going to be! You expect the whole world to go crazy during a war, but somehow not your own mother and father. Mother had lost her wits, that was it. Father must have taken to drink and she'd left him.

Too long without help, too long without help, too long without help — poor Mother had gone too long without help. The wheels of the transcontinental drummed it into my head all the next day around Lake Superior, and the day after that on the prairies, and the rest of the way getting into Edmonton. I decided that I had to go straight to Fort St. John. Something dreadful must have happened.

Air Command was very decent about a flip — 8:00 A.M., R.C.A.F. Flight 19 to Whitehorse. "Warm repeat warm clothing will be worn as 'haircroft uneated.' Warrant please . . . n'kyou."

What a ghastly trip! After the first aeon, the ache in my ears told me this must be Grande Prairie. I had never been north of Edmonton. I had never been over the Rockies in British Columbia. The Peace River was, to me, just the name of an area that over the years seemed to have changed its shape from a corridor to a block. The pitch and toss of rough weather was nauseating. A civil servant in the bucket seat across the way had simply opened his six-bottle briefcase and quietly emptied his stomach into it.

I stumbled from the aircraft to get my feet moving. No feeling whatever. "Warm clothing" means overshoes, not English rubbers.

Two hundred more miles to Fort St. John? Just one more light year. *Feet, feet, feet. I'm sorry Corporal, I can't feel my feet. Could I just stand for a few minutes while we're taxi-ing up? Could you please give me a hand up?*

Wham! the aircraft door slides back. Crash! and metal hits metal as the steps connect. Hold on to your hats, everyone, there's a gale blowing. Gale, my eye, this is a gawdamned typhoon!

And presently the warmth of the Fort St. John administration building, seething with people, with a public-address system giving out instructions for lunch: officers will have their warrants ready on the right, other ranks at the left door . . .

Mother, where are you? Why don't I hear your voice?

You've got to be here! Are you sick? Finally, I asked.

"Mrs. Murray? Hell, sure I know Mrs. Murray. But I don't think she's in town. She's down in Rolla today electioneering. I could take you to her place in town if you like."

Cropland and bushland whizzed past as we travelled down the snowy road. How far to town? Halfway there and two miles to go. What are the red lights on the poles? Radio range, oh. "Uh — has my mother been ill at all?"

"There sure as hell was nothing the matter with her Monday night. She's quite a speaker for an old gal!"

Long silence.

"Up ahead is *it,* lady, Catholic Church on your right. Hospital next. And here is the great little berg of Fort St. John. That is the *News* office your ma dragged in here, oh, say a month ago. I'll go down and turn around and try to get you up close out of the mud."

Did he say mud? You might as well walk in chocolate pudding. Slurrp, slurrp, slurrp.

"Hey, watch your rubbers. Best ya get yourself some overshoes that don't come off easy. That'll be two dollars please, ma'am. Your Ma sure has it all prettied up in there."

But I was already busy reading the note on the door.

"Dearest," it said, "wonderful to have you home. I'm electioneering south of the river. You're to go over to Kirkness the butcher. It's Wednesday, so he will be free this afternoon to drive you to Dawson Creek. I will meet you there after the meeting tonight. Love, Mother. P.S. Kirkness has the key."

Well, the hell with the key! The hell with Kirkness and Mother and Social Credit and coming home!

The little office had a tentest partition which hid a kitchen and bedroom alcove. The doorway between was distinguished with a large printed sign which said SUPERINTENDENT, KEEP OUT. A big drum stove had kindling and cordwood beside it. There was the old Chinook typewriter on a table. A newly made counter topped with the usual plunder. A juice-can bristling with shears, ruler, ivory bones for folding, and that dear old bone-handled kitchen knife that mailed so many papers. Yesterday's mail in a heap. One addressed in George's bold hand was in its opened envelope. I reached for it hesitantly. What dreadful intelligence might it contain?

Lillooet, B.C., Oct. 8, 1945

My Dearest Margaret:

After the first blow, everyone seemed to settle down to the fact that you are a Social Credit candidate. Personally I would not have been more surprised if you had announced intention to take the Peace River rapids in a barrel.

If at one of your meetings, while you are in the midst of a speech, a person wearing a navy-blue uniform and a three-cornered hat rushes in and goes straight up to the platform and shouts out, 'Momma!' don't be non-plussed. It might be your daughter just home from three years overseas with the Wrens. Give her at least a chair on the rostrum and let her share some of the cold coffee which your committee will serve in a draughty hall after you have given forth on Social Credit.

I feel very much like the man who invented the atomic bomb. It was a great idea at the time but now what to do with it? It may destroy all of us. Your announcement, of course, has eclipsed me in this campaign. If I spent money like water and spread publicity all over this place, I don't think it would do me any good at all.

Quite apart from this we are all for you a hundred per cent and the trouble is you might get elected. In that event the misery you will undergo between now and October 25 will be nicely spaced out for you night and day for the next four years.

Darling, good luck and let me have any instructions at once along the lines of publicity suggestions and help from here.

As ever,

George

What a ghastly muck-up this was. But at least they were still speaking. I laid the letter down and left, locking myself out of the office of British Columbia's most northerly newspaper, and stepped out into the chill November day, and that afternoon the butcher drove me to Dawson Creek.

"Mr. Kirkness, could you fill me in on whatever madness inspired this situation where Mother runs Social Credit and Father runs Liberal in the same election?" I asked the question after we left the beautiful new bridge which spanned the Peace, and all the interesting points leading up to it.

"Aye, weel," said Davy Kirkness, "it wiz verra unfortunate. The way of it wiz nor George nor Mrs. Murray made up their minds tull they got back."

"Back? From where?"

"The convention. There wiz this convention in Vancouver where they sacked the Liberals and Tories and made the Coalition Party."

"But Dad is running Liberal."

"Aye, but your dad was as angry as your ma. He decided to go it alone."

"And she decided to kick over the traces and go it for Social Credit."

"Aye, and a grand one she is. And we'll elect her wi-oot a —"

At that point the butcher's pickup bounced onto the Pingle Creek bridge, skidded off the narrow plank tracks, swerved, and hit the rhubarb. There wasn't even time to contemplate eternity from a Peace River ditch. Davey had the machine in gear and up and away, while his passenger's neck lay back in her collar from the sheer force of the motion.

"Mr. Kirkness, just one more thing, and then we won't talk about it. Just drive. Why didn't they tell each other? Write, or telephone, or telegraph?"

"Aye, weel. Six days it takes a letter. The telephone doesna go from here ti Lillooet wi' the Yanks gummin it up. And the telegraph she sent never got there at all, at all."

"But it can't be farther away than four hundred miles from here."

"There's a coupla mountain ranges between, and ye've got ta go down by Edmonton and around. Ye'll not be forgettin' that."

At one-fifteen the next morning, Margaret embraced her daughter in Room 9, the Dawson Creek Hotel. I had heard that peculiarly carrying treble voice all the way from the street. The first snow was laying nature's acoustic covering over everything else.

The voice allowed that it had been a knockout of a meeting. Once inside the hotel door, it invited the night dozers in the lobby to another of the same tonight. "And Pete, bring your girl friend," it said to the night clerk from the stairs.

And then, there it was. Right outside the door. "Darling," it said, "you look wonderful. Are you glad to be home? We've just had the most wonderful meeting at Progress. This is Mr. Landeryou from Lethbridge. Premier Manning sent him to help me. Well, sit down, for goodness sakes. Aren't you going to say something?"

"Well, yes, but . . . well, it's all such a surprise. And Social Credit, Mother. What *is* Social Credit?"

"Yes, well that. I don't know what it is. And I don't think many other people do either. But Mr. Landeryou will answer you that one in the morning. Social Credit is good for Alberta, and it's good for that lame-brained outfit we have at Victoria."

"What about Dad?"

"At first he wasn't going to run, and then he changed his mind. But you might as well live in the Arctic circle as here as far as communications are concerned. He understands how it is. This is what breaks his heart. Not me. Look at this."

Margaret handed over a copy of the *Sun* dated September 22. "George M. Murray has offered himself as a candidate for the Liberal Party in the riding of Lillooet. This is to advise the electors of this province that there is no Liberal Party in British Columbia. *(signed)* John Hart."

Years later, I still painfully remember the reunion with the rest of the family at Lillooet. Sheer misery. Utterly awful. After being sure I was whole and complete and glad to be home, Dad just kept on splicing the main brace, for in spite of the noble words he was utterly shattered by Mother doing such a thing. What bothered Dad was, what would people think? Mother couldn't care less — never could and does not yet.

"When the women were first given the franchise, the trouble started," he said to me. "And when I subscribed to the idea and encouraged a good and loving wife to go out and air her political opinions, I was certainly there with my chin out asking for grief and lots of it. Read this," he said and handed me a letter. "It has just arrived."

It had been mailed by Mother in Fort St. John ten days before:

"Why don't you mention the things so important to

our teamwork? You force me to make my own decisions. You seem very lukewarm on this political setup. You are not ready to toss in the sponge and neither am I. I implore you to shake yourself into action. In two weeks it will be too late. Things are in a hell of a mess in this Province. Don't you think you owe it to B.C. to do what you can? You have been two terms on a back bench. You owe it to your career to have a term in opposition. We can't support Hart with you being outlawed by him. We sure as hell can't support the CCF. I want to know what you think of Social Credit and what you think of my support. I remember your conclusion when you first wrote about Aberhart in 1935 and predicted he would get elected and make it stick. What a vision you have, George. We can't please everybody so why not let's — in the name of God — try to see our own light and follow it. Go down the line and leave no shack or hovel you don't call on and talk and tell them you need them. That's all people want — to be needed. They need me up here. They need you down there. With all my love always and please let me hear from you by return on Wednesday."

"Which Wednesday?" I asked.

Added to the general upheaval at Lillooet was the fact that Dan's wife, a city girl, was being big about living in the country. And Dan, who early gave signs of concern with detail, was on an efficiency kick that somehow didn't go with the old boarding-house, print-shop atmosphere.

"How many man hours do you figure you put in on Mother's copy this week, Dad?" he asked seriously. "How many hours making editorials and news stories out of that gunk she sent down here?" The man who created this Social Credit monster at Fort St. John fixed his son with an eye and went out for another drink. And his daughter joined him.

"She must not abandon herself to this thing," Father said. "She must try to be a bit restrained, if possible. Is it possible for your mother to be a bit restrained about anything? I doubt it. What can she do? Can she perform miracles? Can she cast out devils? I know her answer: she can at least try. May she be blessed with strength to go forward."

He stood a long moment regarding his first grandchild,

Dan's Bridget, in her playpen, where hung the elegant slim gold watch and chain. The cut Masonic seal was cool and comforting to the baby's gums, so he had taken it off his waistcoat and fastened it to the pen. Then he turned on his heel and walked out.

The election was a disaster for all concerned. Premier Hart had already taken space in the Vancouver daily to denounce George and declare there was no Liberal Party in British Columbia, only Coalition. Daniel, now running the paper in Lillooet, took space on the front page to denounce his Mother and declare she had nothing to do with the Bridge River-Lillooet *News*. He said, in fact, that Margaret Murray was related to the family only by blood. And I, having fled to the seclusion of my great aunts' home in Vancouver, came out from behind the blackout curtains long enough to be photographed for one of the society pages as Western Canada's farthest north editor. But while I held down with some éclat the women's section of the weekend paper, my parents were being discussed fore and aft in the first section.

George's family held that Margaret had lost her wits. "They eat well and sleep well, but their mind's gone," said Aunt Marion with professional crispness, outlining case histories of middle-aged mental patients she had nursed. The Lally sisters in California had Masses said, and George took to the hills with a Geiger counter.

Only Margaret remained untouched by the scandal she had created. She stumped the Peace River Block, holding forth at farm gatherings from the box of a democrat or the stage of a community hall. She talked good sense, a lot of it copped from her husband's study of markets across the Pacific. She covered the Shanghai bombardment with gusto and outdid Lowell Thomas on the Straits Settlement and Indo-China. She was fantastic on a platform, quick, witty, and dramatic. Her asides on the 1937 trip to the Orient were so hilarious that listeners were apt to overlook the punch line, which was the need of the starving millions in China for the wheat that was going to waste in the Peace River because of the lack of courage of a few British Columbia politicians. People stood in the street outside the Carlsonia Theatre in Fort St. John to listen to her. Some brought blocks of cordwood and set them up for seats underneath the stage when the SRO sign went up. They clapped and stamped their feet.

But no one took her seriously. When asked a question about Social Credit, she brushed it aside with the explanation that she hadn't had time to go into it. "But it's good for Alberta," she said, "so ask headquarters." She held twenty-nine meetings in twenty days, dared her opponents to meet her in open debate, and kept the pot boiling with red-hot editorials.

George once wrote a series of articles on how to be successful in politics, years before he got around to testing the recipes himself. The first dealt with levity on the platform. "No place for other than the most banal witticims," he declared.

But this advice was lost on his wife who had not started out to be funny. It was merely the hecklers that brought out the devastatingly funny answers. It was the fast delivery, the salty speech embellishments, the disarming candour of the woman — none of it easily described in lines of type — that made her exciting to listen to. It still does.

"What would you be able to do at Victoria?" they asked her.

"I have a good right arm," she answered. "I could aim an inkwell. And when I got finished they'd know at Victoria that there was a Peace River Block — and so would everyone else in the Province."

But there was no need for the Toronto *Star* to send its own reporter to the British Columbia Legislature that year. George had the ground cut from beneath him before he got started, and Margaret fell before a young Socialist candidate, Joe Corsbie, a war hero still wearing part of his uniform, a fact that took some of the sting out of the defeat.

They could pick up the pieces now and get on with establishing a printing plant at Fort St. John.

The Right Place and the Right Time

A fellow named McLure used to truck fat cattle to the Yukon. On one of Dad's numerous trips to the territory, he travelled with McLure and talked the trucker into taking a return load south, most of which had been dredged up from the Lewes River. Among the hodge-podge, including wooden type as old as Confederation, was a Campbell flat-bed press of Gold Rush vintage, and an old Washington hand-press that had once issued the deathless prose of Jack London and the jolly verse of Robert Service. The flat-bed had been designed for hand cranking, and with a good sturdy Cantonese man it was good for four hundred or five hundred impressions an hour.

In Fort St. John, a twenty-by-thirty foot excavation awaited the end of winter for installation of the cement walls and floor of a print shop. There the salvage would join a newly acquired Number 5 Linotype from the Powell River *News,* costing $900. Most of this amazing sum was a parting gift — called a re-establishment credit — from a generous government to a Canadian Wren. As a veteran, I was entitled also to a small loan similarly sponsored and available at any Canadian bank, if its purpose was to assist rehabilitation in business.

It had long been decided by his parents that Dan would be given, after the war, the controlling interest in the Lillooet paper in which they all would be partners. And in 1943, in a Toronto hotel room, Dad and I had shaken hands on the publishing venture for the Peace River.

"You get up there and get it going, Dad, and when the war is over I'll come home and help you put in a plant," I told him the night before I left for overseas. I was to have the same arrangements with my parents in Fort St. John as Dan had in Lillooet. Lillooet was the better of the two deals, however, because its physical assets were complete.

The only thing in hand for Fort St. John in 1943 was a roll of paper and an idea.

"O Blessed Day," Margaret had intoned feelingly when George got home from the east. "This is where the children belong."

"They have the ability and the strength, certainly," said George.

It had been a long hard five-year pull at Lillooet with a twisted ending. It would take any revenue from Fort St. John to keep the printer's bill paid for both papers. Retirement was going to look awfully good to George and Margaret Murray. Let someone else carry the responsibility for a change!

As it turned out, their retirement lasted about as long as the conversation. So the morning the cattle truck left for Whitehorse, George had smiled good-bye and waved his hat to Margaret as she stood on a pile of gumbo at the rear of the Dufferin Construction Shack which served as the new *News* location. She was wringing her hands and moaning into the gaping excavation, longing for the warm weather that would allow a cement pour which would extend eight feet above the floor. Spring had come that very day. Would the frost never leave?

Three weeks later, when Dad returned with the press, the basement was poured, and the two-by-fours reached for the sky. From time to time, banker McLeod joined Margaret at the wailing wall. But they were not wringing their hands about the same thing. McLeod, who was a dandy farmer's banker, took a dim view of the whole newspaper operation. If he did not have to, he would not loan a cent for such a venture. His view was that it was just a matter of time until the beaver and the squirrels reclaimed the Alaska Highway, and anyway he was sure the town would never in the world support a weekly paper. He could envisage the overdraughts getting larger with every wheelbarrow load of cement. But this was going to be Georgina's paper, and the government was backing her loan. It amounted to $4,000.

Indeed, just about everything happened that could happen in establishing the plant. In transit from Powell River, the Number 5 had been smashed to the tune of a claim for $994 on the Northern Alberta Railway. The cam wheel was broken in four places, the mainbrace and distributor bar required welding, and countless bits and pieces required replacement — in an economy that would be at least a year returning to peacetime production. Some of the paper's less enthusiastic supporters claimed the $994 was what put the outfit in business.

In the meantime, the roof was being banged onto the living quarters above, and the Campbell was resting in a granary at the back. It had been necessary to take the side out of the granary to ease the big flatbed in, but that was considered a small matter until it was replaced, when it became evident that there was not room to walk around the press. This threw quite a curve to Bob Duncan, the Canadian Utilities man who, a couple of years before, had blessed us with the high sawhorses for an office counter. But the brains of the community zeroed in on the old granary. The steps and trays were removed from the press, the crank was torn down, and the conversion to electricity was accomplished with Duncan standing on top of the old monster and working from the inside.

You might say that the architecture of the first *News* building was a combination of early Fort St. John (unrelieved oblong) and late War Assets (barracks block). A former Dufferin Construction pay office sat at the front, and at the back the new two-story building. It remained merely to remove the mountain of earth in between, lay a floor and join the two structures with a roof. In the meantime, Margaret washed clothes under the sky between with the classic galvanized tubs and corrugated wash board. If it was possible to get the wash going, the morning visitors were expected, she didn't miss the opportunity. There seemed to be a perverse imp in Margaret that said, "If it has to be a little haywire, corn it up good!"

"Now let's see . . ." she once said to a red-tabbed Sandhurst colonel, brushing blobs of soap fuzz from her office smock, "You must be a lance corporal over here observing . . . anyway it's sure nice to have metten' up with ya."

"Mother!" I said, horrified, behind the Superintendent, Keep Out partition. "How could you possibly . . .?"

But the Sandhurst smile behind the handlebars was all for this priceless newspaper woman, and the frown was directed at the voice out back.

To this day, none of the family is quite sure whether

she does or does not recognize the various ranks and rates of the armed services. She was always safe with the Generals, anyway. She called them all 'Brig'.

Came moving day. Once again, down came the side of the granary, and out emerged the big Campbell. And standing by with his winch truck was Bert Bowes, the garageman across the street. You could tell the size and length of the moving job from Bert's cigar. He always started out with a fresh one and had it pretty well chomped down in a couple of hours, when he replaced it with a fresh stogie. That day he finished the package. And so the old iron press, with the help of many enthusiastic hands, was finally heaved into position. A little Gordon job press was already ticking over and had put out the first "extra," an eight-and-a-half-by-eleven sheet of yellow wallpaper donated by Donis and Taylor, the general store.

"It was right sporting of Rube Taylor to let us have his old wallpaper samples," wrote Margaret in the next week's paper. "In another month we'll have our own job stock." And in another month they did, indeed, have their own.

The first issue was a glorious jumble of type off its feet, wrong fonts, transpositions, upside-down hand-picked type, faded spots where the ink fonts failed. There was no editorial and no announcement that a wonderful goal had been attained. The second issue had smoothed out so that the funny old curlicue type and fancy cut-offs stood out. The third issue had a rip-roaring editorial on extending the railroad.

Three readers wrote in angrily to say various things. One said her daughter had not been poisoned with D.D.T., another said he had not sold the farm, and the third ordered the editor to stop talking about furs bringing new wealth to the country. It was a lie. Things were lousy with the trappers. Things, however, at the *News* office were getting back to normal. Only in the fourth issue did the editor take two pages of solid white space and the biggest wooden type ever made to announce: WELL, HERE WE ARE. JUST LIKE WE SAID.

With accommodations non-existent, living conditions absolutely primitive, temperatures in the extreme, and mud and dust and snow and ice marking the four seasons, it wasn't surprising that every typographical union office in Western Canada knew all about the Murrays' new venture in Fort St. John. Of the at least forty compositors and operators who worked for them over the years, not more than ten were Canadian-born. The rest comprised a sizeable league of nations — Germans, Dutch, Norwegians, Belgians, French. Some came straight off the boat, all of them were war-scarred but accepted the challenge at the little printing office and manfully wrestled with the English language. That they got out a paper at all was a miracle, but struggling with Margaret's headlong prose . . .

"Don't change a word of it!" was a command that rang down through the years, and caused other members of the family to furtively retype her copy in the dead of night. The more excitement in the oil strike, the railroad news, the water situation in town, the surer she was to pie up the letters on her typewriter, leave out verbs, and run sentences into paragraphs and then some. There was some hope for this copy with printers whose mother tongue was English, not any at all with those still thinking in another language.

Her sally into politics had given her new confidence. Her interest in the country and the people provided endless materials for her typewriter. Her years of living made her knowledgeable about all facets of the Peace River economy, and what she did not know she made it her business to learn. She was alternately the joy and the despair of anyone working with her, and she was clearly the dynamo behind the entire enterprise. She kept everything and everyone stirred up all the time. She promoted anything and everything that she thought was good for the town, often picking the idea out of her own "one cylinder," as she called her thinking apparatus.

And she thought she was pretty good. "Read that story on feed lots, and tell me if that isn't the best damned story you ever read," she would say to anyone handy.

You thereupon picked up and read the most indigestible if aromatic column of prose you had seen put together — until she wrote the next one. It progressed through "critturs belly-deep" in lush Peace River grass, to succulent legumes that had your taste buds standing at the salute. The writing smelled of pit silage and fragrant chop mixtures, and had a texture that was fork tender along with the look of a rich red slab, marbled with ivory. The words poured out like wheat through a hopper in one solid column, syntax, punctuation, paragraphing all lost in the rush. It made a townsperson want to go right out and buy a porterhouse steak and look for that peculiar Peace River "ivory" which was none other than the golden fields of grain threading their richness through the meat. And as column followed column over the years, they no doubt brsuhed off on the farmers who were being forced by encroaching civilization and all its parasites to convert from strict grain farming to feeding livestock, raising poultry, and mixing their enterprise.

"If you could harness her, what a magnificent writer she would be," George used to say, with a folio of her copy before him, pockmarked with inverted *v*'s, paragraph signs, circled periods, and other proof-reading marks.

All the weddings were "beautiful" weddings in her copy, and all brides were "radiant," no matter how uncomfortable or pregnant the candidates might be, because a wedding was a beautiful thing to Margaret. Every new baby "blessed" the home into which it was born. Every obituary asked that the deceased "rest in peace." The will of God was referred to in any announcement or commitment of future plan, outlined in the paper by the initials D.V. — meaning *Deo Volente* or "God Willing" — as in "The convention will be held D.V. at Sunset Prairie." The paper in her parlance was the G.F.J., short for "Great Family Journal," and she called herself "Ye Ed." The town was "this burg," and oldtimers were "old crocks." The editorials, important interviews, development stories from the government, and other features were George's domain. He it was who kept the press wires hot from Fort St. John, and when the exchequer got too anaemic, went off to the city to write industrial editions for the daily papers for cash money.

For the first time in almost forty years of publishing, the Murrays were at the right spot at the right time. It became evident that the idea of retirement — at least for Margaret — was receding as the weeks passed by. Three times friends and advertisers bade her good-bye as she took off for a well-earned rest. Three times I pulled the paper into more conventional paths — out of scribblers and onto filing cards, out of scribbled margins and onto dummy sheets, out of glorious clutter and onto "in" and "out" baskets. And three times, "Ye Ed" returned with scribblers, margins, and clutter more glorious than before.

It became obvious that the daughter was publisher in name only. "Anyway," said Margaret to her spouse in a stage whisper, "we have a thousand subscribers now and it won't be long before we can pay her off. And besides, how can we retire? We haven't the money to retire. And who wants to, anyway?"

We certainly had some awful rows over that paper. Mother was a do-it-yourself operator long before the words became a popular phrase. She was no executive and found it impossible to delegate authority. She rejoiced in counter accounts all over town, ran the house out of the chocolate-box till, and kept an elementary set of scribbler accounts that only she could figure out. With her thirty-year-old price list for a guide in estimating prices on printing and advertising, there was no money left over for salaries upstairs. You merely "lived" and shared in the wonderful thrill of establishing a newspaper on the frontier and watching it turn into something like the Chicago *Tribune*.

After a couple of false starts, the railroad was as far away as ever. The Hart Highway was bogged down in fifteen-foot snow drifts. Skeleton crews manned war-assets depots, and the Americans had all gone home. The Alaska Highway was now in the hands of the Canadian Army, and over it travelled supplies northward, including gasoline, coal, equipment, and food. Southward came the empty trucks. In some the Canol refinery was loaded, piece by piece, in twenty-five and thirty-five ton lots, to be set up by Imperial Oil in Alberta. Buses travelled both ways, carrying tourists. Private cars were another year venturing up the Great North Road. "When it comes," comforted Margaret editorially, referring to prosperity, "let's be ready for it."

It was during these twilight years — after the construction and before the oil development — that the Murrays' publication reached its height of accomplishment and became actually an art form rather than a newspaper.

There was no radio station north of Grande Prairie, Alberta. The farming settlements were still being served by only dry weather roads. The postwar economy was just beginning to catch up on trucks and cars and farm machinery.

Except by aircraft, the Peace River Block was still three days away from Victoria, the provincial capital, and its problems seemed the same number of centuries away from solution. Yet the frontier was rolling back. The land was being taken up. The cry for services and communications and recognition was going up from twenty different communities in the North Peace. A newspaper united them all, and turned up the volume. It became a giant public-relations enterprise to promote, advertise, inform, and entertain. Letters of inquiry about the district were printed and answered in the same column. If a specific question was asked, an answer was requested from a knowledgeable reader. Correspondents from the various wide spots in the road talked to each other through their news columns.

"Montney needn't crab about low grades (of wheat), one of my neighbors got No. 6 damp . . ." So said Mrs. Lynn, the inimitable correspondent from Cecil Lake, who often began her week's news budget like this: "As I sit here in my kitchen at 5:30 a.m. 'fast time' and see the sun chasing the moon on its way . . ."

Sawmill operators like Earl Pollon at Hudson's Hope spent the long, lonely evenings writing news into jingles: "The dancers pulled for the open air, to see the truckers fight; Said the fiddlers as they took a snort, 'We're in for a lovely night.'" Earl's efforts so encouraged one of the Babcock girls at Rose Prairie that she did her next wedding reception in rhyme. "Pass the bottle, good neighbor, was the call that night. It was passed around, believe me, till most everyone was tight." Readers were advised that at Ernie Carlson's birthday party, beer bottles had proved a good idea, strung around Ernie's cabin to hold notes leading to the hunted treasure, while up at Trutch Maintenance Camp on the Alaska Highway — population 14 people and 400 dogs — Harry Noakes entertained the folks in the land beyond the Peace with hilarious accounts of Trutch City Council meetings, discussing street lighting bylaws. Tourists actually pulled up for gas at Trutch and asked in what direction the city lay.

If brightness of copy when it affects circulation is sensationalism in publishing, and if propaganda is anything that makes the reader feel that action must be taken, the Alaska Highway *News* was certainly Canada's most lurid weekly.

"A chuckle once a week and a belly laugh once a month," Margaret assured readers on stickers attached to newspapers of overdue subscribers. But along with the chuckles, the community inched forward.

FIGURES CAN'T LIE BUT LIARS CAN FIGURE — warned George's ten-point editorials, advising farmers and others to get professional help in combating the waves of income-tax inspectors coming in to settle old scores. They arrived as wolves on the fold to many a farm and small business in the Peace. Here was a district suddenly on the map because one of the world's largest defence projects had put it there. Here was a town whose businesses were owned by those farmers who happened to be in the village the day the Americans appeared over the breaks on the Peace River hills. For two years, from 1942 to 1944, no one had time to read anything, let alone the fine print in the Income Tax Act. They were hardly aware of their new bank accounts, since there was certainly nothing to buy in those years, when suddenly the eager beavers from the inspection office of the Treasury were upon them. Legitimate or phony but acceptable, a Peace River farmer did not know one expense entry from another.

The *News* office, however, took some of the ginger out of the inspectors. They became so confused with Margaret and her endless scribblers, her shoe boxes full of receipts, her counter accounts, her barter system for subscriptions, her transportation expenses for hauling in printers and then hauling them out again, and the depressed economy that did not pay a single wage outside the print shop, that they usually withdrew with their briefcases between their legs.

As business improved, the bookkeeping situation became worse. Margaret refused to let go the scribblers. Her charities were her own business, she said. And while often in kind as well as cash, they were sizeable. She sent hundreds of free papers to prospective settlers and wrote letters to each. Her real-estate ventures were modest but always involved.

"Look dear," she said one afternoon to a toil-worn subscriber, who had just paid her account with eight frying chickens, "take this and get Alice to give you a permanent. Then we'll all feel better. It'll give that old man of yours something new to look at. Anyway, somebody paid a bill I thought I'd never collect." Ten dollars came out of smock pocket and was pressed into a mittened hand.

A newly-acquired town lot went the same way.

"Well, the poor bugger was down and out and sick besides. He wanted eight hundred dollars, but did you see that dandy little cabin on it? So I took three hundred of Uncle Jim's money, and I got two hundred for that old beat-up truck, and I'm a few dollars ahead on the current account . . ."

Receipts for food and drink took the spirit right out of entertainment, she held. Calculating travelling expenses left her equally cold.

". . . and we haven't used three dollars worth of gas in the car all week," would conclude the argument.

THE AMERICAN ENGINEERS HAVE PUSHED THE COUNTRY AHEAD FIFTY YEARS, advised another of George's efforts on the editorial page. HAVE YOU CONSIDERED A BARRACK BLOCK BUILDING TO IMPROVE YOUR COMMUNITY?

Old Fort Alcan picked up and went off in all directions — as a school a hundred and fifty miles away at Moberly Lake, as a church at Falher in Alberta in another direction, as a doctor's clinic, as six classrooms at the Fort St. John school, as stores and hotel, as church halls in a dozen different communities in the district. Half the dwellings in the Peace were sections of barracks blocks, all twenty feet wide, and you bought them by the yard — up to as long as the rig would carry.

WHAT MAKES A TOWN BIG? This was the theme of a series of pieces which paved the way for the incorporation of the village. No incorporation, no water. No water, no women. No women, no families. No population,

And water was a problem. You learned to get all the possible mileage out of it. First dry-peel the vegetables, then rinse in fresh water. Using the rinse water, wash the lettuce next. Take out the lettuce and put in the dishes. If the dishes are not too bad, rinse them, add rinse water to wash water and baptize the porch. The water is then suitable to settle the dust on the front steps or moisten the window boxes. Bath water soaked clothes, washed floors, and watered gardens, in that order.

The water wagon was something to see, with its great vat of *aqua pura* sloshing under the coat-tails of old Mac, the dispenser, who sold it at a nickel a bucket, seventy-five cents a barrel. If you lived beyond the reach of old Mac, you had a scoop-out, a man-made depression in the ground which caight the dews and damps and heavy summer rains, and held them fast. The family drank out of one end, and the livestock out of the other. Humans must have built up a tolerance to the leavings of wild and domesticated things, for no one was ever ill from the water they drank. The better-organized and more fastidious, mind you, cut ice in winter from Charlie Lake and stored this in sawdust in granary-sized ice houses. And that was quite a late winter sight. The steaming horses standing patiently on the frozen lake while their owners drilled and sawed, grappled and heaved the neat blocks into the sleighs — or wagons, depending on how early break-up was that year.

Before Christmas, 1947, the village was incorporated, the important issue of water was eventually assured, and the government could at least entertain the idea that Fort St. John was on the map to stay.

"If the American Republic handled the turnpikes as our administration handles the Alaska Highway," wrote George one time, "the Pony Express would have been held down to delivering milk in Kansas City. Buffalo Bill would have lived and died a hustler east of the Missouri River. Brigham Young would have gone into old age an irritable bachelor. Our Highway opens a land with possibilities only second in importance to those of a hundred years ago. Let the reserve be lifted and the Highway thrown open to freedom-loving people."

This blast, plus a criticism of the surface of the Highway around Charlie Lake, once brought Brigadier Geoff Walsh, with pennant flying, dashing down from Whitehorse in his staff car. The *News* office prepared for what would surely be next thing to a court martial. So lately returned from the services myself, I was stunned at the abandon with which my parents tackled colonels and up. The place was swept out, everyone shined their shoes, shovelled off the desks, and took a broom and pail of water to the front sidewalks and steps. Zero hour was 0930. The brigadier, the area superintendent, two red-tabbed colonels from England and two majors crowded into the little *News* office. The strain showed through the polite introductions.

A village is a Village and the lowest on the municipal scale.

But Peace River people did not shop'in the Village' or use the word except at tax time.

"Mr. Murray," said the Brig, when the last 'how do you do' was frostily uttered, shaking toward him the copy of the current paper, "just what is meant by this?"

At that precise moment, the situation was saved — by another arm of the postwar services. The Northwest Staging Route was often used as a rehabilitation establishment for flap-happy air personnel, a sort of decompression chamber for fliers suffering a heavy dose of the overseas "bends." Two of these lads had helped themselves to a couple of Mustangs from the airport hangar and were up in the air having an early-morning constitutional. After scaring the daylights out of a few moose and rounding up a few head of livestock, they zeroed in on the town at four hundred miles an hour, barely clearing the light poles.

The reflexes of anyone experienced with air raids are automatic. The whole distinguished company, including the editor and everyone in the building, dived for protection, knocking over the cordwood, waste baskets, chairs and other impedimenta. It was a moment to remember. When it was over, the gumbo crown on the Charlie Lake stretch was dissolved in sherry and high good humour, and a relationship was established between the Army and the paper that only grew in warmth during the next twenty years.

George Murray, M.P.

Margaret Murray was not the easiest person in the world to live with, nor for that matter was George. Their chemistries were totally different. She burnt with a nervous energy and drive that thrust her at tomorrow like a rocket — and this in spite of ulcerated legs which plagued her most of her life. Sometimes it seemed that the only mortal thing that kept her going were those legs. Because of them she was forced to go to bed a couple of times a year to heal the ulcers, and she recharged her batteries at the same time.

The blood in her husband's veins was of heavier viscosity. He required more sleep, more quiet, more food, more escape, and these in greater quantity as the years went on. He strived for but never attained the realization of a Roycrofter's type of establishment, where publishing, like a jewel, would display many brilliant facets — bookbinding, type-carving, cut-making, leather-tooling, fine engraving, artistic typecraft, and, of course, the finest writing. Margaret had never spent any time around Elbert Hubbard and she never quite caught the dream, though she tried. The battleship linoleum ruined with v-tools by eager high school children around the Alaska Highway *News* would have covered one wardroom at least. And Christmas, 1947, a thousand books were tied with red ribbon and the covers hand-coloured with school paints. "If I never see another horse's rump again, it will be too soon," Margaret was moved to say, as night after December night the afternoon's painting was laid on the counter to dry.

George would have preferred a house whose kitchen door did not open into the newspaper's bindery. He would have liked a large house, with a dining room that would properly backdrop his accomplished carving, and a den to write in and clutter, and a fireplace for conversation and contemplation. To make up, his wife carpeted the little flat in rich red plush, wall to wall, and had a hermetically sealed picture window put into the south wall. With drapes and piano, books and suitable appointments this lovely room was from another world, another era. The visitor who made it through the organized confusion of the front office, and the various useful arts in progress in the bindery, past the sauerkraut — "Well, my God, I can't waste those lovely cabbages" — and past the moose in its shroud, had to start all over again at the back of the building, and reassess his host and hostess.

"Quite a view you got out this window," said her son, Dan, on his first trip into the Peace after the shop was in operation. "I have counted seventeen privies as I was standing here."

"Ah, yes," laughed his father, "but I commend to you the valley of the Peace River beyond, the blue hills beyond the banks, the rising mists, and the golden stretches of grain fields. And have you noted also that ribbon of commerce across the centre of the picture? Two lorries and a bus. Night and day they roll northward. The Alaska Highway, my boy! We must have vision in this life to see beyond the privies."

"And what's the matter with a good privy, I want to know?" chimed in Margaret defensively from the kitchen. "In my book, a useful thing is a thing of beauty." When irritable, she was even more likely to mangle clichés.

Dan had come to Fort St. John to discuss selling the Lillooet paper. His parents were involved because they held a half interest with him in the business. Dad and I had already settled the Alaska Highway *News* years before in a Toronto hotel room. My war gratuities and savings were supposed to establish the plant at Fort St. John. My interest would be at the northern outpost. Both parents were to have retired by this time. When last entertaining the idea, Margaret could not make up her mind whether this would be on a stump ranch or in a nunnery. There was always so much unfinished business on the land, she observed at the time, but in a cloister she was sure she could write a bestseller. George would continue to guide the editorial pages for both papers and do feature writing. It was a great set-up — in the planning stage.

I was supposed to be the smart girl, with varying portions of three careers behind me — the Navy, the CBC, and the daily newspaper field. I had come north to considerable tub-thumping by my associates to get out a weekly newspaper for the Eskimos (in 1945, who knew where the Peace River was?) but it was becoming increasingly apparent that the deal was off. The Alaska Highway *News* was already top-heavy with writing talent. What *they* needed was someone to get all this bright copy into type and onto the press, not someone to write more of it.

Which is why Margaret was still irritable. Dan thought he'd like to sell out and go to California, and had said so earlier in the day.

"California?" shrieked Margaret. "Infamy! Infamy!" This word, and a choice Anglo-Saxon one of four letters, were the strongest in her repertoire. "That indolent, artificial, stultifying California! Where old people go to die! Where the flowers do not smell, only the movie stars! Where you live in a little house on a street with a hundred other little houses on a hundred other little streets, and carry your lunch in a briefcase, and . . . and . . ." She was so furious she stuttered, then found her way back. "And all this God-given opportunity right at your feet, this glorious north, this wonderful Peace River country, these splendid people . . ."

"I got it figured I could make more money in California," said Dan.

It was that word 'money' that did it.

"Censored, censored, censored!" said Margaret, shooting the works with that four-letter word. "Censored to money. What good is money?"

"You pay your bills with it and buy milk for the kids with it," said Dan, baiting her. "And my wife wants to go."

Margaret choked with anger, but forced back further comment. George had walked in.

"Either lock the front door and pull the blind, or you two – you, Margaret, with this bar-room invective — kindly remove your argument to the privacy of the house."

There was no mistaking when Dad had had enough. He was so cold and formal about it.

Voices got back to normal and the afternoon wore on, with only one flare-up. A farmer had come in to pay his subscription.

"Keep your money, Bill," said Margaret, "and Saturday bring me a couple of sacks of spuds. That was tough luck last week."

"What tough luck did that bird have that you haven't got more of?" asked Dan when the door had slammed shut.

"Ah, the poor devil lost a load of grain on the Peace River hill."

"How can you run a paper that way, Mom? Can you pay those guys downstairs in potatoes? How can you get to be Audit Bureau with that kind of bookkeeping?"

"Oh, we manage to pay them somehow," said Margaret. "And we'll get Audit Bureau too, you just watch."

But Dan was not interested in watching. He wanted no part of his parents' brand of journalism. Anyway, he wanted to make it on his own. He had tidied up the Bridge River-Lillooet *News* into a thing of neat black and white. There wasn't a transposition or a wrong font in the whole six pages. Anyone who liked a good printing job, order and neatness, and just the facts, ma'am, were well pleased with the new order at Lillooet. But it did not produce a paper that was required reading on any city editorial desk, and it therefore did not attract the public notice to its publisher or to their great hinterland that his parents revelled in.

But Dan was dedicated to the proposition that a weekly newspaper should pay off in more than laughs and the joy of playing to an enthusiastic audience. He wanted coin of the realm for all the hard work. And when he had made sure that Lillooet did not sit exactly over a publishing motherlode, he prepared to pull camp. He got the books in order, the subscriptions on a cash basis, the shop refurbished, and the machinery ticking over smoothly.

The Little Log Cabin Theatre went first. This was the old horse barn, converted by George during the early years of the war to a theatre. The Saturday afternoon that two miraculous medals showed up in the matinee cash was the day Dan decided he had had it as a theatre proprietor. The show house was sold to the Canadian Legion at Lillooet, and the proceeds turned over to George and Margaret. Next, he had a large-sized conflagration on the lot next door into which he dumped everything that would burn and did not have a cash value. He had made up his mind.

But so had his mother. She would wage two major campaigns. One to get the daughter as far away as possible, and the second to bring the son and heir into his rightful inheritance.

"This newspaper holds no future for you, Georgie. The only proper career for a woman, after all," said Margaret to me, "is marriage. Just fill my arms with grandchildren is all I ask." But to Dan she wrote variations on a theme that with his production know-how there was no limit to the prosperity and success of the publishing business in the North Peace.

Fate, with an unsubtle assist from Margaret, brought campaign number one to a successful close. On a cold November afternoon, a mountain of khaki and sheepskin brushed through the little *News* office door, plunked a bottle of overproof rum on the counter, and announced in a gravelly voice, "Major Lovatt-Fraser's respects, ma'am. This bottle of rum is for the editor of the paper, guy named Georgie Murray. I would like to see for myself a fella'd have a name like that and drink this stuff . . ."

"Oh," laughed Margaret, "that's not a man at all. That's my daughter, but she's out right now." She lingered on the words, making note for future reference of the height, breadth, and looks of the messenger. "Ah . . . uh . . . that is, why don't you come back at five o'clock and meet her? We'll pour you a drink, maybe."

"Say, how about that?" said the mountain, having just received his best news that day.

"By the way, what are you, under all that overburden — a wing commander?"

"Sajamajah Keddell, Royal Canadian Engineers, ma'am," He boinged into a parade salute that riffled the papers all over the counter, and turned to leave.

"I'll tell my daughter," said Margaret, guile in her heart and honey on her lips.

And so it was that by letter number ten to Dan at Lillooet — at two a week that would be five weeks later — Mother was moved to write as follows:

"Don't look now, but if you could have seen this great big sergeant-major pick up all 140 protesting pounds of your sister and plunk her in his pick-up, you would know that things are working out beautifully. My novenas are being answered. Ha. Do you have some old English wedding script down there?"

The wedding was ten weeks from the day the overproof rum arrived and got coast-to-coast coverage, since Wren Murray's branch of the service seemed to have provided more than its quota of wire editors strung across the continent.

"Her friends in Vancouver give it six months," mourned George, who came hurrying home from the coast after the announcement was made.

"We'll have the reception on our wedding anniversary, February 5th," said Margaret. "Now where in the world have I put that white chiffon dinner dress we got in Shanghai?"

Wailed Father Otterbach: "I don't see how it can last. This young man tells me, one more instruction and he will make a good Protestant out of me."

The prospective groom waved an Edmonton *Journal* in a threatening gesture: "Christ Almighty, I was born in Three Hills, Alberta, not Three Rivers, Quebec! Who gave them this?"

"Well, I knew it was three something," said Margaret.

"Yes," I said, walking in from the office and hearing just the last words, "and I have three something else. Three thousand tickets for Whimp's Dairy — only by a small oversight, they turn out to be Whimp's Diary — and the very best of luck to you, too! Mother, really — you read the proofs."

"Well, damn it all, wouldn't you think those krauts downstairs would know better! Never mind, darling. A week from today it will be all over but the shouting. Hearts and flowers, you know . . . tra la." She wasn't going to have any of the glow of this wedding removed by three thousand dairy or diary tickets. "Jim Keddell, you have six days to change your mind, but I hope you won't," said mother-in-law to be.

"Oh, Mother, shut up," said her daughter.

"By Jeez, after today I don't know. Three Rivers, Quebec, for Chrissake! My mother will be smoking . . ."

But he didn't and they didn't and seven days later, with the fire truck screaming towards the airport and Bert Bowe's winch truck hoisting the baggage at the rear, I flew off to 'the greatest career of all' and left stouter egos and hotter tempers to fight it out in Fort St. John.

And fight it out they did for the next ten years.

It is doubtful if Margaret would ever have sweet-talked her son into coming north if it had not been for George. The tags had finally been readdressed "California" on the Dan Murrays' freight when George got himself elected as the federal member for Cariboo.

The trick was no doubt turned in Prince George where the name of Murray had for years been associated with progressive thinking and writing and boosting, and where prior to 1950 the Liberal Party was honourably entrenched, with roots and trunk and fruitful years. Over on the other side of the mountains, in the Peace, the new communities were not sure yet whether they were part of British Columbia or Alberta. Private enterprisers escaping Saskatchewan mingled with Social Creditors from Alberta, Democrats and Republicans from south of the border — and to add to the confusion the war brides were only settling in, and the first wave of European immigrants arriving.

George's campaign was such a whirlwind affair that Margaret barely had time to get out of town. "They say I've fouled his nest with Social Credit," said Margaret, calling down bad cess on "them." "I'll have to think of something. I just can't stand here." Her only role to date had been to forge a name to a wired reply to National Liberal Headquarters asking of George's Fort St. John agent a statement of his chances "in view of his wife's recent defection."

"Well," she offered later as defence for this decision, "in the first place, there was no agent in Fort St. John. And in the second place, it was the least I could do since I really felt badly that any action of mine would ever hurt him. And in the third place, I knew I was right."

She wrote: "Hock the family plate and put every cent you have on Murray. He can't lose."

"I forget whose name I signed to it," she said.

That out of the way, Margaret hopped the first plane for Whitehorse and proceeded to cover the creeks and gulches in support of Aubrey Simmons, Liberal candidate in the Yukon and Northwest Territories. She paused long enough at Cemesto Number Thirteen to raise a few eyebrows in the army's married quarters and admire her new grandson, Master Brooks Keddell.

"Up here," she said in explanation, "they don't know I'm tainted. Besides Aubrey can't speak for sour apples and he needs me."

There followed two weeks of campaigning in a frail little single-engined aircraft that would reduce a strong man to the snivelling shakes. After the first couple of days, she travelled light with only a brown paper bag for her "unmentionables." It had become necessary to lighten the plane, and the decision had to be made whether to dump the campaign literature or Margaret's travelling case.

"As long as it isn't the candidate we have to dump," she said blithely, "who cares about clothes?" She thereupon took a black chiffon nightie, a spare hair net, toothbrush, extra pair of bloomers and rubber stockings, and stuffed them into a sack. The next day, to plug a puncture in one pontoon, she lightened the load a little further. She tore the skirt off her slip and wadded it into a stopper.

Sixty-two years of age, bespectacled, her complexion glowing under a thatch of white hair, Mother hit the creeks in a one hundred and fifty dollar black coat-dress ensemble and small felt hat that she thought she might as well wear since she did not like it anyway. "Makes me look old," she said. She harangued the miners whenever she found them – at church, in the movies, in the dining halls, and at work. She talked to men unloading machinery on the river, turned show night into a double-featured bill, bought a round in the beer parlour, and once, for a dollar tip, persuaded the manager to lock everyone in while she spoke.

At a camp dining hall near Mayo, she got some interference from two drunks who insisted on conversing while she spoke. After asking for quiet, she backed up to the reversed crockery on the ever-set dining table and picked up a cup. "Damn you fellas," she yelled with exaggerated quavers in her voice, "you shut up and listen to me or I'll let you have this right between the eyes!"

They listened. When the meeting was over she called over to them. "I'm sorry to have to get rough with you fellas, but I didn't have much time. Come on over here and shake hands. Let's kiss and make up."

"Kiss you? Why I wouldn't kiss you for all the gold in the Yukon," said one.

"Come here. I want to whisper something to you," said his companion. When he got her ear, he bit it.

"I slammed him a good one with my purse," said Margaret. "It was a rough trip."

"I remember her on one of those junkets as something out of a Charles Addams cartoon," says Margaret Fielder of the CBC who was in Dawson City with her. "She made an eerie picture in that trailing chiffon nightie on the slanting boards of the first floor of the Royal Alexandra Hotel in Dawson. The ornate hallway to the bathroom heaved like the deck of a ship. No rooms with bath, of course. And then her sitting in this outfit, glass in hand, recounting the day's experiences on the campaign trail."

On the way back to Whitehorse, the pilot could not read the map because he had got into the oh-be-joyful. They made a forced landing at Stewart River and heard later that the RCAF were about to organize a search for them. The plane had no radio, of course. "All right," yelled Margaret, "now everybody shut up and let me concentrate on my rosary. You fellows pray your own prayers and we'll talk our way out that way." And they did.

At Fort St. John, however, it was the palest election campaign ever waged by a Murray newspaper. George mailed in his own press, a couple of times written by a coal-oil lamp and taken by horseback or river boat to the Highway for onward passage to Fort St. John. The Cariboo riding from north to south was eight hundred and fifty miles, extending one hundred miles on either side of the Alaska Highway, and west through the Rocky Mountains to take in Prince George and the Cariboo Highway down to Marguerite, and all the settlements in between — Vanderhoof, McBride, Fort St. James, the Finlay-Parsnip country. In this vast land, thirteen thousand voters spoke for a total population of thirty-one thousand people.

It took George three days to get from the Yukon border to Quesnel, and the Finlay-Parsnip trip took another of the same. It was an area bigger than all the Maritime provinces combined, with Newfoundland thrown in. It was larger than all of Ontario from Sault Ste. Marie eastward to the Ottawa River. The Highway alone was the distance between Ottawa and Chicago, or between Ottawa and Richmond, Virginia. All of New York State, all the New England states and most of Pennsylvania would fit within it. The British Isles could be dropped between Fort St. John and Fort Nelson, and Ireland would be flat on the ground, well inside the Rockies.

"The riding I wish to represent," wrote George to the outside press, "is of interest today because of its vast raw land area, rich in natural wealth, where homes could be provided for the homeless; work and wages for all who come — providing they are of sound mind and body and come like other settlers of other days — with a good heart. Cariboo surpasses in natural resources any other similar area in North America. Let us fill the vacant land."

He won the election handily. I was in Vancouver and shortly after the polls closed voting day in June, 1949, I had a wire from Mother: GOT BOTH MY MEN IN. BULLY FOR US.

Dan had cancelled the bookings to California and came to the Peace River country instead. "I figured it's Dad's big chance," he told me, "and Mother should be with him. I will look after the paper while they're away and see how things go."

George ordered a sixty-five-dollar hat from Calhoun's

in New York and a new pair of Church's oxfords. He was then ready for Ottawa. "This particular model," the salesman had said, "is favoured by Mr. Frank Lloyd Wright. You have the build for it." And when that hat was held high, waving at Margaret in the crowded Ottawa Union Station as she arrived for the opening of Parliament, it put a lump in her throat and mist in her eyes.

"I could see the darling man sixteen cars away," she wrote me. "Your father is never more compelling than in that courtly way he has of lifting his hat and waving it. Shades of Vancouver 1912."

"As for me," wrote Margaret for the paper, "while other country women donned the latest in flares, gaudets, berthas, etc., with lots of red in it, I was gorgeously draped in six of the handsomest mink ever taken by Charlie Brandt." She hastened to add that she also wore a modest but voguish black wool crepe made by Georgia Ramine in Fort St. John. "The mink kept slipping down my back and I'd look behind to see if anyone was going to swipe them from me."

The home folks got their lessons in democracy, wrapped up in some racy reporting.

"Seems scarcely possible so many bombastic candidates of such recent vintage could all be deflated into such small spaces," she continued, referring to the crammed chamber full of dignitaries. "And I'm telling you about all this colourful ceremony because the ritual, after all, is significant. Without it we might be wearing iron collars instead of furs around our necks."

She complained bitterly about the prices. "A hunk of jerk (dried wild meat) would sure help keep the expenses down in Ottawa. Filet mignon, no better than Cuthill's tenderized, is a dollar seventy-five. Sixty-five-cent eggs, Nellie's kind, are eighty-five cents a pair. Doug Mah's sixty-five cent lunch costs a dollar twenty-five. Alice's dollar twenty-five shampoo and set is double here with a tip extra. And that's all for this week, folks. In my next, I'll describe a Gatineau Hills luncheon and what they thought of my description of a squaw wrestle. Never mind, it perked up a pretty dull party in a hurry — MLM."

"Save your mother's letters," George used to instruct them at home whenever she was away. "Mark my words, they will be literature, some of them. All they need is a firm blue pencil." He now wrote the same old advice on the margin of her weekly "budget" from Ottawa. But Margaret wrote letters daily, or twice daily, and no ordinary household could contain them. The letters which carried her column, however, were safe for posterity.

"Daniel Murray, don't you leave out one single line of this. And don't change one word!" The typed command would fairly leap out of the page at him. Margaret would have been overset on the New York *Times*, let alone the little old Alaska Highway *News*.

But Dan did not enjoy being told what to do. He would not indulge his mother as his sister and his father did. Fifteen years later, it still rankled.

"Coming to the Peace River to accept my heritage, as Mother calls it, sounded pretty good after we had sold the paper at Lillooet. However, it didn't take long to see that it was only my heritage as long as I conformed to her iron will. This I couldn't do."

He vividly remembers arriving in the muddy little berg in 1949. The print shop was in the basement and in bad need of good management. The man running the linotype had his chair so arranged that he could jump clear in a hurry should the machine splash hot metal all over the place. He came in when he pleased, and Mother quite often had to send someone down to his shack to wake him up after a hard night on the town.

"Nobody knew which way he was going in that shop," Dan said, "and my family never learned the mysteries of type--setting or casting a mat. The result was that they were beholden to kookie printers ever since I could remember. These birds had to be coaxed out of beer parlours and dried out, buttered up with little gum drops all the time, put to bed, loaned money, given marital advice, and you name it. The same slaphappy approach applied to the business end of running a weekly newspaper."

The Sunday before Mother left for Ottawa, Dan was going over the subscription list. Hundreds of people had not paid. He was knocking them off right and left. "And what was Mother doing? She was weeping tears. This one had milk-leg after the last baby. That fellow had erysipelas in the hogs. This one had rust in the wheat. I had no charity. No heart. Suddenly the front door rattled. It was George Broadhurst, one of the departed whom I had axed a few days before. He saw us working and came in to pay up. 'Golly,' he said, 'I didn't know you had to pay for the paper.'

"Boy, was I popular around there! But I was aiming at Audit Bureau of Circulation, which takes the boast out of boost for a weekly, and they wouldn't tolerate any such hit-and-miss accounting system as Mother enjoyed.

"You see, Mother was a nonconformist. She hated regimentation, routine or anything approximating it, and it was always good for a big hassle when the unemployment men or the income-tax man paid a visit to our office. I just couldn't go for this.

"My father was a brilliant writer, but he wouldn't perform on cue as he grew older. He should have been the head of a history department at some great university. He should have had a classical education. He had an awareness of the future that was uncanny, but it was responsible for spells of introverted dreaming and an almost constant agony of remorse that he wasn't accomplishing more. Although he wished his wife might be a little less rambunctious, her management of the business was fine with Dad. He had bigger things on his mind."

And so they had hard words. Mother would make fists, tighten up her mouth and to get the point across would add a few four-letter Kansas invectives. Dan kept insisting he wanted to build up a neat tidy organization with no overdrafts, and then go out after the reputation of a top quality weekly. He wanted no off beat journalism, no drunken printers, but copy that was properly typed and clearly written, to cut down on type setting time. "Our printers used to waste more time running up and down to the office checking on lousy copy . . ."

But Mother was Mother. She would clasp anyone to her busom and worry about their love life, their bowels, their spiritual being. She'd feed them big meals as only she could cook them, have a drink in the cupboard for their hangovers. "There was no officer-other rank status around our place."

Dan worked very hard in those early days at Fort St. John. Seven days a week and often late into the night. His wife, he says, naturally wanted to know what he was getting out of it, and as he looks back, it was not very profitable financially, "but I sure as hell got a lot of experience."

"I assumed I was taking over the paper, my heritage. But Mother was not seeing it this way. She wasn't signing over anything — yet. To use her words, I wasn't dry behind the ears."

Hard words, long hours, and a lot of frustration finally had their effect. He packed up and left.

This was one crisis in the lives of the Murrays which was not met with a special edition to lift sagging spirits. Instead, back in the Peace, someone left the heating stove in the "red" room with its damper open. Poplar pitch and a brisk wind completed the job, and a first-class fire not only warmed up their living quarters for George and Margaret's first trip home from Ottawa but completely gutted the entire flat. Water congealed in the forty-below temperature, and shrouded the print shop below in sheets of white. The unforgettable acrid odour of burnt wood and varnish nauseated them as, just home the next night, they stepped in the old *News* office door.

"And tomorrow is New Year's Day," said Margaret, in a stricken voice. She opened the door to the bindery out back. "Well," she murmured after a moment of straining through the light from the open doorway, "I see the sauerkraut is still there!" She slammed the door shut and turned. "There's no sense, my dear, in going further. We're not dressed for it. There's no light. We'll leave it all to God tonight and go down to the hotel."

They elbowed through a lobby filled with boisterous fringed jackets, jumping tassled mukluks, dripping shuffling overshoes, and muddy floors fast turning to dust as a hot blast from the stairwell indicated that while it was certainly a trifle noisy, all was snug and warm in the bedrooms above.

"Hey, whaddya know! Here's old San Lorant himself — and Mrs. Murray. Here, Mizz Murray, how about a snort. Hey?"

"One side please, one side! Look, you son of a bitch, I said one side *please*. The voice belonged to the hotel manager, not a patient man. "Make way and let them register." Doc was turning the hotel's log book around for a signature. "Jeez, folks," he said almost inaudibly, "Thassa gawdamned mess down there and I wanta tell ya, it is. And I'm sorry. Your son left a message here he's at the officers mess."

"We saw him" said Margaret, her eyes swimming. Sympathy usually fractured her anyway.

"I'm sure sorry but all I got left is right next to the woman's can. This is a bad night for it too." The hotel manager was a dead ringer for W.C. Fields and had a heart as big as the forty six shirt that covered it. "And you Christers," he admonished the lobby in general, "Let them up the stairs! They've had a bad home-coming."

"You boys come and see us tomorrow. We'll be at the old stand," said Margaret from the first landing. "I got lots to tell you . . ."

Last night the Chateau Laurier. Tonight Fort St. John, with the contributions crashing in next door like Niagra Falls on the empty galvanized bucket, and you worried only when the falls stopped crashing for then you knew that the elderly night man, unsteadier than usual on New Years Eve, would be around to replace the container and carry his burden down the stairs. "My God, do you remember the first night we stayed here and old Harry fell down the stairs with it? asked Margaret. But George, whose sixty one years were leaning heavily, did not laugh. The beer parlour thumped and banged underneath them.

"You're a wonderful woman, Margaret, and I love you more every day that we live. On the other hand, I don't know why I should have a night like this wished on me. But anyway, Happy New Year!"

"You, too, dearest man," she answered, and flicked off the light.

A world of whites and greys, quiet as the tomb, confronted George when he stepped out of the Condill Hotel the next morning. New Year's Day is morning until darkness falls in Fort St. John. Not a soul. Not a single idling motor. Not a sleigh nor a jingle bell. No a snow buggy. And the smoke from a dozen chimneys along the main street going straight up.

He stepped out briskly onto the board walk, past the theatre, the Elk's Hall, and the bowling alley. Then up a couple of feet and over the dark grey glacier that extended in front of two vacant lots. And down again where festive boarders at the Police Barracks had recently swept and shovelled yesterday's snow to the corner. Across the street and along the second block you were on your own. Indian style. Margaret had negotiated it two hours earlier, going to Mass. Her slender, bandaged legs were no match for her husband's and she had often taken the problem up editorially. "Ye Ed's old gams have a full-time job to stay on the perpendicular even when the walking is smooth. Won't you please shovel your sidewalks and remove these booby traps?" But the snow whirled down, the wind blew drifts, and the Chinooks reinforced the lot with blue ribbons of ice, and most walking remained Indian style in the village throughout the winter.

She was waiting for George now "at the old stand," the big oil drum throwing out a mighty heat in waves that lifted the spirit and warmed the heart. The door to the bindery was shut fast against the sickening odours of yesterday's fire. Snow water bubbled in the blackened coffee pot, however, and out back in the ravaged suite, the kitchen cupboard, festooned in icicles and frozen ceiling paper, had yielded up a pound can of Nabob coffee, none the worse for smoke and water.

"You're just in time for coffee, dear," she sang out cheerily as George held open the door and stamped his boots on the step outside. "I've been reading the mail. Uncle Dudley's copy says that this storm has been general all over. He calls himself 'Your scribe, well furred and prime, comes out of his den to say . . .' Here's the mail. Read it."

They sipped their steaming coffee as they sorted, read, and scanned headlines. "There are two things we must do now," said Margaret after a few moments. "Get a hoopin' big fire going in the shop and dry the place out. A lot of that ice can be knocked down and carried out in washtubs beforehand. And the second is to make some decisions about 1950. This is going to be *your* most important year. Get your coat on. We may as well go out back and see how bad it really is. Put your overshoes on — the kitchen floor is solid ice.

Presently they were standing in the midst of it. Their breath smoked in the windowless livingroom. "What do you say to this?" asked George.

"I say at least five thousand dollars," said his wife. "All we had was building and contents in the insurance, and that was mainly thinking about the shop. Oh, it'll be a fight. Everything has gone up since we built this — material, wages, everything."

"And five thousand dollars is almost my Ottawa stipend for the whole year." His voice was wistful, and so was Margaret's.

"Going back to Ottawa for me is out of the question, I guess," she mused. "Even if Dan were staying, it would be out of the question. Maybe, now, it's a good thing he isn't staying.

You can lead a horse, as the old saying goes."

"You will have to admit, my dear," said George, looking out over fifty white-plumed Yukon chimneys, "that from this vantage point at two-thirty in the afternoon with the mercury standing at minus sixty-three, California under some circumstances could look rather attractive."

"Never!" said Margaret flatly. "Grab that wash tub and let's go down to the shop."

Fourteen Million Dollars

George went to Ottawa on a declared policy of an extended railroad and increased immigration for the Cariboo, but his next love was an old one too — trade across the Pacific. He did not merely want these things to come to pass. He anguished for a lifetime that he could not convince those about him that they must happen if Canada were ever to grow up and take an honourable place at the council table of nations.

He saw the House of Commons as an amplifier for his arguments, and in his heart he was naive enough to think he could, if not accomplish his dreams for Western Canada, at least bring them closer.

He had waited fifty years for this, exactly that since he had carved his name on the barn door in Zorra — George Murray, M.P. But even as the old Prince George Hotel bounced with victory on election night, he dulled his wife's shining eyes for an instant when he said, "It's wonderful, Margie, but a man's too old at sixty, too old. We have our time on stage, but then must soon depart the scene. And I, do you realize it, am an old man."

"Gie me your hond!" ordered Margaret, laughing at their worn but comfortable joke. "Now get you on your feet and downstairs. This is no night for feeling old. And they're waiting for you in the lobby."

Thus he pushed any misgivings to the back of his mind and went off to the Twenty-first Canadian Parliament, full of determination and hope.

He carried with him a railway brief which respectfully asked "This Royal Commission upon Transportation to recommend to the Parliament of Canada such railway extensions in the Peace River country . . . as will link the settled areas of that region with Northern Alberta Railways at Hines Creek, Alberta; and Dawson Creek, British Columbia; and with the CNR at Prince George; and that the undertaking be carried out by the Canadian Pacific and the Canadian National Railways jointly." It created a fine impression and made fascinating reading, besides giving valuable information on a region which post-war magazines and periodicals had not yet discovered. It was a new look at a problem before the public of Canada for fity years. Interviews in the press and speaking engagements in Toronto and Montreal quickly followed its presentation, and his days in Ottawa were filled to the brim from the very start.

He found the capitol of forty years before, blending easily into it's 1950 situation. The old landmarks were as they were — Bowles lunch, the Armories, Elgin Street, the Russell Hotel, St. Andrews Presbyterian Church, even the dark little alley into which the sun shone only a half hour a day through the brick and mortar. Though Benny, the philosophizing restauranteur had long since gone, it was a delight to George to recall the little beannery proprietor and to discover some of the old customers — reporters of forty years ago — around as well, though nowadays they were apt to lunch at the Club or the Chateau Laurier.

Another thing which hadn't changed in forty years were the officers of the ministers. The hansome cab era was long gone and the present day hazards might be any of twenty seven bicycle messengers, nimbly whipping around pedestrians on the wide causeway leading to the main block of the House of Commons, running files to and from the same number of office buildings. George's steps were slower and more measured ascending the worn marble to the great front doors. A brief case replaced a wad of copy paper in a jacket pocket, and mature girth now blurred the hard clean lines of youth. But the offices were the same and he swore the chairs in the waiting rooms were the originals. Certainly the time spent waiting in them had only for him increased.

"I've been cooling my heels in the Transport offices all morning," he wrote to Margaret. "We're getting five thousand telephones for Cariboo. Two hundred and fifty thousand dollars. This ought to improve the stomach ulcers around Fort St. James where they have thirty phones on one line, and other places the same."

He won a public building for Quesnel, another for Vanderhoof, a government building for Dawson Creek. He made repeated calls and more calls to the Post Office Department, Public Works, Finance, Mines and Resources, Indian Affairs and Northern Affairs. He asked for better postal services, improvements to airfields, attention to agricultural problems and those regarding mining — especially coal mining. "If you see any of the Pouce Coupe people, tell them to hurry through their official endorsement for federal aid at Victoria. Their hospital grant is passed, but they don't act down here unless Victoria gives them an official request." A good member needed a strong right arm to write letters, as well as stout legs to cover the pavement and the marble corridors from office to office.

"I haven't got into debate yet," he wrote home, "but will do so when I think the time is fitting. Meantime, there are a hundred and one things to keep me going from early to late, and if you would hear some of the newcomers here repeating themselves in long, dreary speeches, you would realize the golden advantage of silence."

But suddenly he was on his feet in the Commons, and sooner than he expected. "This fellow Fulford has about seventy members away with him on a cruise and we were short Saturday in committee when the Tories moved a resolution to cut down forty thousand dollars for air radio for the Northwest Staging Route. In a case like this you don't ring the division bells! I was able to hold down the floor for about twenty minutes until they rustled in the members. I got some good licks in for Cariboo on both sides of the mountains and was quite a figure for about fifteen minutes after I sat down. Chevrier (the Minister of Transport) was delighted."

Well he might be. On a drowsy Saturday afternoon, what luck to find a backbencher not only carefully following proceedings, but equipped to deliver off-the-cuff a twenty-minute address, right on target, and allow the whips time to search out washrooms, coffee bars, and offices for enough Liberal M.P.'s to defeat the resolution and save the government.

Lionel Chevrier may have been pleased to have the day saved on this occasion, but he was somewhat less than delighted with George Murray's other enthusiasms. When George was hounding Transport for telephones, Chevrier pleaded that there were non available. Taking him at his word, Dad went off to find some. He stumbled over 35,000 of Alexander Graham Bell's 1920 model in a dusty basement of the Northern Electric Corporation in Montreal, got them to mock up an invoice for him, and highly pleased with himself took it back to the minister. Right here he learned Lesson Number One. Never go over the head of a minister. Especially not the Minister of a Portfolio as important to your constituency as Transport was at that time important to Cariboo.

Margaret wrote: "I see where you made the *Province* and the Chicago *Tribune*. Good for you. Don't forget the weeklies. It may be corn but it's filling, so send them something at least twice a month." Thus Margaret, three thousand miles away, held a watching brief on Room 644, the House of Commons, and supplied almost daily *communiques.*

Fort St. John, B.C.
"A weekly is like a street car," she wrote. "There'll be another along shortly. But this week we had bad luck, knocked the hell out of the Whitlock (press) and didn't get off until Thursday afternoon. Harrison forget to lock in the form. The Front page dropped. I didn't bawl him out. I just poured him a good drink of rum. He needed it. It took us all afternoon to sort. As always the good little people were with me. If I'd been a minute sooner, down to check the proof, I'd have been cut in two."

Ottawa Ont.

"Saw many of our newspaper friends covering the Princess's visit. They all asked for you. The guest of honour, while a nice little thing, has hardly all the grace and glamour advertised, I thought. Charlotte Whitton is a small package of impudence and energy. To Senator Turgeon she said, "I have not seen you since you attained Old Age Security.' There were many MPs and Senators around and they all caught it."

Fort St. John, B.C.

"I am dull and tired and it is raining and there is no good in us today. Varnishing the suite. It has taken a lot of doing to get it straightened out after the fire. Our man here is underpaid according to the Indian Agents. He has a large, hungry family. See what you can do. Got a youngster a job with Moore at mile 81 today. No day goes by without some incident to lift it out of the mire. But darn you, one letter from you in two weeks shows a lukewarm attitude towards the likes of me, slugging it out here alone . . ."

Ottawa, Ont.

It's lambing time in Oxford county. I was down to spend the weekend with Mother. The stately elms along the concession roads are coming into leaf. A million birds burst their throats in song. The grass is suddenly green and the numerous streams hunt their way out with the spring thaw to find the river Thames."

Fort St. John, B.C.

". . . the town is bristling with Texaco, BA, McColl Frontenac, Imperial geologists and Rene Dhenin and Knox McCusker, as well as everyone else who owns a nag, is getting the pack saddles on them and away for four months prospecting. Wish you were here to enjoy the atmosphere. Get up to Mass every morning and makes a long day. Do you think you could get the library to loan me a handbook that would wise me up on oil patch lingo? My adjectives are getting pretty worn out . . ."

Ottawa, Ont.

". . . I hear bad news down here about the B.C. Liberal. Harry Perry says the public feeling has cooled both provincially and federally in the past year and that the dillydallying, the filibustering, the lack of firm action is creating an impression of weakness. Probably a period in opposition where repentance, penance and meditation might resurrect great visions, would be the cure in B.C. . . ."

Fort St. John, B.C.

"We had four hundred dollars biz this week and it cost three hundred and thirty to produce. This latest printer you sent is the biggest blank of all the blanks I have met yet and that's a few. He eats bread, butter, and honey with his potatoes and meat. You might as well feed a calf. He is what we used to call a blue belly Yank. He might have done a fine job of brushing you off in the men's room. The point is, how do I do a fine job of brushing him off here? You should never drink anything stronger than coffee."

Ottawa, Ont.

"I have been very busy in the library researching some Asiatic material which I will require in a day or two for presentation to the External Affairs committee. I long to see Canada make some attempt to encourage the friendship of the Chinese people. We are a young country and our hands are clean in China. Why not endow a chair for Asiatic studies at some of our universities? Restore the White Empress service, or an alternative? Study the possibilities of taking over the tropical Islands of Fiji as a base for air services in the Pacific?"

Fort St. John, B.C.

"God has returned our bread on the waters with cinnamon, nuts, and raisin on it for good measure. Revenue is better. Just the same I get low in spirits. There is so much to do and to think of. You would sink right down in the sump if you had to put up with the chore you wish on me. What point is there working like a fool, seeing mats all jimmied up with squirts, hearing screeching gears because some one isn't thinking what he's doing? I have been a long time at this job of being married to an idealist. It isn't too long, mind you, but the territory the idealist reaches out for gets a little too big for my one cylinder. What are you doing about a post office, gaol, court room, police office, telephone office, V.L.A.

and Indian office for Fort St. John? Answer me that. Love from your Martha wife. M.L.M."

George had it in mind to put his theories concerning immigration into practice. Get the new citizens — not for the cities — but for the wide open spaces of Cariboo.

Margaret certainly hoped it would work but wasn't putting any money on it. So many printers had come and gone, she couldn't keep track of them all. There was Chris. Chris liked chicks, slick ones, but not just several, a whole roost full. "Though", he added generously, "The quality is good around here," Chris left.

Then there was the fellow at the Veterans' Tech school at Red Deer. He ruined $137 in lino mats in 2 days. Margaret went down one morning to see what the commotion was and he was standing on the chair kicking the key board and swearing hysterically. He left to go back into analysis.

Some were good craftsmen but couldn't see the country. Others could see the country, but like the men's attendant at the Chateau Laurier, had misrepresented themselves. One man was queer for door knobs and small boys. "He'd sure have to go some to teach the little devils around here anything," wrote Margaret to her husband. Another was sixty nine years of age and couldn't stand the youngsters he worked with. Another took down with mumps. Still another was the great grandson of a prime minister and brooded about it. Life was raw in the early fifties, water scarce, and quarters close. Fastidious persons would rather quit than put up with mouldy feet working on the other side of the roaring stove. It took a heap of love for the frontier to retire at night to a one-room granary, light the air-tight heater and the dangling electric bulb, lie on your cot and digest Mark Wah's liver and onions, and dream of the prosperity and development as presented in the editorials you'd been setting all afternoon. To the less timid who voiced any complaints, Ye Ed had a pat answer. "Hell," she'd say, "you haven't got the vision that God gave a mouse, If you don't think it's a privilege to just BE here, this is no place for you."

And here presently were two more for the bunkhouse.

When John Quelle learned from the Canadian Embassy in Amsterdam that a Canadian MP wanted two printers, his application to immigrate to the land of the Maple Leaf — then nine months standing — was cleared in three days and he was on his way. "Mr. Murray is a fine journalist and a personal friend of mine," said the Consul, who was from Edmonton, "And you are a lucky young man."

"But this is Saturday. The Immigration Offices will be closed," ventured John.

"Not for you, they won't. This is a special case."

John hung up his apron at the big offset plant in Amsterdam where he operated colour presses, waved goodbye to his fellow workers who numbered about a hundred and twenty five, kissed his parents farewell and caught the next boat across the Atlantic.

Here was opportunity, he thought. The fabulous Alaska Highway! A publisher successful enough to also become a member of parliament must have a prosperous daily, indeed. He had learned that Fort St. John was not a large city, but Northern Canada was opening up. Though not exactly at home in English, he could speak and understand if he put his mind to it, and was just a little surprised that as the rocks and Christmas trees and miles of wheatland streamed past his coach window and he tried conversing with fellow passengers, no one seemed ever to have heard of Fort St. John. But then, of course, the country went on forever. Canada was a big place. He had now been three days and three nights travelling.

He was in Edmonton before he found anyone who knew anything about Fort St. John. "Oh, thass a lil berg up the line, here," said the Northern Alberta Railway baggage clerk, jerking his head backwards. "If they have the washout fixed, you'll be there tomorrow night about now."

"Where could I buy a newspaper of this town?" asked John.

"Ya got me . . . D'ja mean they got one?" The man laughed, and John, wondering, took his questions into the one pullman which stood at the end of a fourteen car train.

"I don't know if that's it's name or not, but Fort St. John does have a newspaper, because I've read it," said the salesman across the aisle, when the train got underway. "John, is a cowtown, you know — cafe, a few houses, a couple stores, like that. The paper isn't very big, I know that. And as for what kind, let's say when you get there you'll get your name on the front page, How'm I doin'?"

John came from a land in which there were daily newspapers and magazines and nothing in between. But he began to get an idea that perhaps he shouldn't expect too much.

I thought the well dressed man who came up to me as I stepped from the train at Dawson Creek might be George Murray. But instead it was Harry Noakes," recalls John of the former correspondent from Trutch. "I had changed my clothes out of Grande Prairie, and shined my shoes, and now wondered what for. The dust was flying but in the ruts the water was deep and the ridges all soft mud. I saw the Mile Zero pass through the haze. I thought it was a hitching post. Noakes took me to the New Palace Cafe for a sandwich, and explained they'd just had a three day rain.

"Ya feel better, buddy?" he asked when we finished the sandwich. "Let's go. Got five minutes to make the bus."

"The bus?" asked John.

"Sure. To Fort St. John. It's fifty miles north."

The BYN for British Yukon Navigation, — bus, a high riding, boxy affair to negotiate the ultimate in any kind of road situation, hurtled off along the gravel into the northern evening, past crops and homesteads and, further along, a smoking peat field; down to the Kiskatinaw River bridge which joined the Alaska Highway dangerously on each side at an oblique angle, and up onto a higher level after a long climb on the other side. Presently, the banks of the Peace River, and the feeling that if you got out and lay down on the roadside, you could see all the way to Siberia. Down a long way again to the big suspension bridge, then Taylor Flats — a patchwork in May of loam brown and sprout green — and finally, Fort St. John.

The bus parked in the middle of the biggest puddle on the main street. It was seven o'clock. John Quelle scraped the soles of his shoes on the mud iron on the wooden step of the one--roomed bud office. "Where is the newspaper?" he asked.

"Up the street, Mac, painted white with green letters N-E-W-S."

John looked around at what he later described as a 'high noon town'. The evening sun made everything too bright — the shiny, wet sidewalks, the surface of the puddles, the gleaming wet gravel, the multi squared windows of the old co-op, and the new white paint on the older Pomeroy Hotel, against which loungers in makinawa and rubber boots were anticipating the after dinner opening of the beer parlour.

When John set his bag down outside the little white frame newspaper office, he was sure that this could be only a depot for news boys, or a bureau office for a plant which no doubt was located along the great Highway. No one was in, so he walked around the building and knocked on a door which opened on the red room.

"My God," said Margaret, opening to him, and slinging the tea towel over her shoulder, "you must be the boy from Holland. We didn't expect you till Saturday. But come in, come in. Have you had supper? How long since you left home? Where are your bags? What about a cup of coffee? Where's your partner?"

"He comes on another boat," said John.

"I've got a place at the Titus rooms," said Margaret, so we will take your bags over there, and then you would probably like to see the plant?"

"Oh, yes," he answered, brightening, "the plant." The appearance of the little flat indicated that things got better as you went along. Twenty five yards of mud, six introductions and thirty stairs later, John set his bags down in number 8, the Titus rooms. It was clean and sparely furnished, an electric light fell from a long wire in the centre of the room. He was assured that he could have a second pitcher of water for nothing, and the dry toilet was just down the hall.

"Now," he turned to Mrs. Murray, " we go to the plant."

They retraced their steps to the office across the street. "Is it many miles?" asked John.

"Is what many miles? Margaret was busy with the key in the latch, and now was inside and moving purposefully beyond the 'Superintendent, Keep Out', across the bindery and home arts division of the establishment, to the door of a sort of ship's gangway that led down. "You go first," she ordered.

"What is down? asked John incredulously. For him the light was just clicking on.

"Why this is the plant. The dandiest little plant you ever saw," said Margaret. "Just watch those pipes there. The bathroom is right above, and I lose one hairnet a week on that S--strap."

Years later, John said that if he had had one hundred dollars, he would have left the same night for Vancouver. But he hadn't a cent. This basement room, with eight big war assets windows in it, measured twenty by thirty feet. The floor hadn't been swept because a large patch of it was wet in the spring run-off and rain, and a pump churned and gurgled busily in the floor beyond the linotype. "I looked in the type cases, and there was more dust than type in them. I had never seen such ancient equipment as the old flatbed. The heavy iron chases stood on the floor against the comp table which was home-made, and a little wooden trough ran down it's centre with divisions for slugs and spacing, and border. Over-run pages of the current edition haphazardly covered it, where the folding hands had tossed down the bones and left clean-up for tomorrow.

"Oh, no", said John.

"Oh, yes," said Margaret. "Isn't it wonderful?"

The really wonderful thing was that John stayed. Publisher George arrived three days later from Ottawa, and Quelle has said that he looked and talked exactly as he expected. George arose early the next morning and invited John to Mark Wah's for breakfast. Mark made up in friendliness what he lacked in fanciness, and over ham and eggs John Quelle was sold the Peace River country, lock stock, irrigation projects, industrial plants, steel mills and oil barrels! "He was terrific to talk to." recalls John. "He could make you see it, actually see it. I remember so well this plan he had for irrigation. You were like mesmerized. It was a dream of his, and yet not a dream, but as if it were ahead of himself many years . . ."

The long waits in the creaking reception furniture of the minister's offices at Ottawa, and the "golden silence" for almost a year, paid off at this time for Cariboo.

"The saints preserve us," said Margaret, fervently, as she laid down the long embossed and franked envelope from the capital on top of the morning mail, the day the immigration scheme materialized. "Fourteen million dollars for north of Fifty-two thirty. That's us, kids! That's Cariboo! That's the kind of a member to have! Yell down to Harvey we'll have to remake the front page."

Then she went back to the letter: "Ten million, eight hundred thousand for airport extensions; two and a half million for Alaska Highway improvements; a hundred thousand for telephone and telegraph lines; four hundred thousand, Fort Nelson barracks; two hundred thousand, Fort St. John water line from Charlie Lake; a hundred thousand, Prince George federal building; fifty thousand for the same at Quesnel; twenty-five thousand, Quesnel airport improvement; two hundred thousand, Indian schools; twenty thousand, seaplane landing at Prince George."

She scanned the list looking for a federal building for Fort St. John, for a post office, for something in Dawson Creek, that would be nearer her readers than a paved runway, or a six-inch water line.

But another year was coming.

"When a Good Woman..."

The Ottawa years grew troubled for George about half-way through his term, when he began to realize how little real influence a backbencher could bring to bear on any situation. Despite such issues as the Korean War, hoof-and-mouth disease in Saskatchewan, and horses on the payroll at Petewawa Army Camp, the Twenty-first Parliament was a dull affair. Canada sat on a knife edge between two great powers, almost, but not quite, at war, and the Conservatives gloomed that their country had become a one-party nation. The liberals' political strength, even after an unpopular wheat subsidy, new taxation, unhappy trade unions, and other headaches, was the highest on record.

In these years, Parliament looked less able than it really was. There was probably more human ability in the Twenty-first Parliament than in any other since Confederation. But there were no issues to seize the imagination of the electorate. And while the members' ability could work in the administration of government, it could not come to life in a

Parliament which had nothing to enliven it.

One of my father's great disappointments at this time was his failure to promote a trade mission of Canadian M.P.s to China. He worked for almost a year on this Parliamentary delegation and had carefully earmarked for it men of skill and varied backgrounds, including another backbencher from the prairies, a lawyer named Diefenbaker. There were three weekly editors in his corner of the House whom he intended to have represented. "Find, solid, mostly young men," he wrote Margaret, "who if they are to be our future leaders, must get to know the Orient, must be ready to feed and perhaps in that way make friendly this dragon which is China."

But General MacArthur flatly overruled the Canadian plan, and George was left to put his hopes and fears into speeches which did little more than make good copy for the press gallery. But he offered no apology for taking part in the debate. "Those of us who come from the northwest corner of this Dominion are likely to be more concerned than honourable members who feel the security of the Atlantic Pact," he said. "The Alaska Highway is the great international highway of this continent and I live on that Highway not far from the bridgehead at Peace River. I therefore see by day and night, by land and air, the great rush of the western world to make Alaska secure against invasion."

George's argument was that the Pacific was Canada's lifeline, and across its wide expanse lay Canada's market. Troubled Asia, he held, was merely continuing an industrial revolution which had been sweeping the continent since the Russo-Japanese War of 1900; China the sleeping dragon was awakening, and as Li Hung Chang, China's great statesman in the days of the Empire, had predicted, the world was being shaken.

"We Canadians have an opportunity of establishing ourselves for all time in the hearts of the countries of Asia. We are a young country and our hands are clean. We have done nothing in China other than to help the Chinese people. The effort of our Christian Missions in Asia and our part in the conference in 1898 at Shanghai to cut the trade in narcotics make the brightest chapter in the history of that ancient continet. Is it too late to think of ways and means of making peace with these people?

"I suggest to men who are more wealthy than I to consider the proposition of endowing each university in Canada with a chair for the pursuit of Asiatic studies. Set aside funds to make possible sending our young Canadian people to study, at first hand the language, the customs and the culture of these people."

Hansard had columns and columns of George Murray of Cariboo on the Asiatic problems of that time. It made good reading and good listening, for it was gathered from wide study, from two trips to the Far East, and from a lifetime of newspaper interviewing in the port of Vancouver, where for a couple of generations the glistening Canadian Pacific Empresses embarked and disembarked the great and important travellers of the world. It was entirely possible for an alert journalist to sit at the feet of a Tagore, a Sun Yat-sen, a Li Hung Chang, a Kipling, a Churchill, and to drink deeply at the fountain of philosophy, wit, knowledge. George had never missed an opportunity. And watching him, one was apt to forget that this was a backbencher from the bushland. Intellectual, aesthetic, and religious — prime characteristics of thoughtful Canadian Parliamentarians whom he had studied — these words also described him. Besides, he had a certain amplitude of utterance, a great knowledge of literature and history and contemporary affairs, and withal, a dignity of mind and character to match the worth of what he wrote and spoke. For political and social wisdom is drawn not from the passing hour and day, but from the ages. Men will not look forward to posterity who never look back to their ancestors, and George's sense of history marked everything he wrote or spoke during his lifetime.

Margaret, at home in Fort St. John, read speeches and wept for him. Men are noblest when, realizing the futility of their efforts, they still struggle against frustration. But was he remembering to send out monthly news budgets to the weeklies and radio stations? Why did he not answer more diligently her letters? And how was he coming with a post office for Fort St. John?

The mail situation in Fort St. John was something to behold, but the district's M.P. was caught in an age-old squeeze between the property owner who wanted all the traffic would bear on the site of the new building, and the government which refused to pay that kind of money.

"This is the second time this little town has been knocked

into God's right-hand breast pocket," was how Margaret described for readers the boomed-up situation in Fort St. John in 1952, at the same time begging them to "shove over and make room for an oilman." In tiny blackface type, six points in the centre of a sea of white, it said, "The copy for this quarter-page is deep in the deluge at the post office. But ask for Stirling's anyway, folks. It's darned good drinkin' liquor." And Stirling's, the makers of gin figured they got good measure for their space and paid the shot.

For the first time since the American "occupation," bored troops in khaki enjoyed the indoor sport of twisting spoon handles while they waited for food in cafes—only these troops wore hard hats and safety boots with the Great West Garment uniforms, and there wasn't a trouser crease in sight. Juke boxes moaned into the night in half a dozen such eateries. Roughnecks had nowhere else to go. The police barracks moved off to the airport to await the construction of a federal building and there handled traffic and liquor-act offenders as the little North Peace town did its best to make ends meet. It appeared to strangers as starting in one long block at the cemetery and ending at the liquor store. Offenders often landed square in the middle — in the hospital — where they lay in the halls, or on the treatment tables. If not too badly off, they took turns on the x-ray table, or a rocking chair beside it. Two hours on, two hours rocking.

Oil trucks sped back and forth. Oil planes were in and out daily. Tycoons were a dime a dozen giving the drilling sites the once over. Skilled operators in a dozen places pierced the heart of the petroleum-rich giant while other specialists were opening up arteries and veins with a network of seismic roads and test holes so that the wilderness fluttered with their bright plastic ribbons. Remote trappers and ranchers allowed that they never did see the like. The Upper Halfway folks, who used to take three days to get to town by horseback, piggy-back, stone boat, foot, and wagon, now made it in three hours by truck — if their nerves were good.

Duncan Cran, dean of provincial land surveyors in the near north, was given all the type he wanted to plead for attention to surveyors' posts or monuments, ever in danger of being knocked out by tractors and bulldozers taking off over the wide blue horizon. The destruction of these markers could cost the province hundreds of thousands of dollars in new survey lines, and Duncan felt justified in backing his warnings up with a Biblical paraphrase, "The wrath of God is upon him who digs up his neighbours' landmark."

To add to the confusion, just after break-up in April, Father was able to get the town a contract with the Department of Transport for all the water it could use at thirty cents a thousand gallons, using the government's water line. No sooner was the ink dry than back hoes and shovels were clawing into streets and lifting out thousands of yards of gumbo for water and sewer mains, which only needed the ever-present spring rains to turn streets into a greasy adhesive sea of slurp in which no one on foot was safe.

"Who is it down there?" asked Grandma Foster, hurrying out of her house at a cry for help. "Oh, it's you, Mrs. Shepherd. I'll get Mr. Melville next door to bring you a plank. Don't move!" It was Melville who shouldn't have moved, for he and the plank both were presently in the hole with Mrs. Shepherd, and might have been there yet had not a Central Department Store delivery truck happened by. The driver had a dry hand and his tool box yielded up a dry rope. The water and sewer excavation continued for years, whenever money was available for its extension, and the main streets were a hazard for all the exploration years. Cars all but disappeared, light poles fell, and foundations ruptured. And when the worst seemed to be almost over, it all started again for gas mains.

Faraway readers were just as much interested as the locals in following the fight for water. Particularly they enjoyed the editorial which started out "In God's Name, Mr. Bracewell, get a little ink into that pen . . ." Mr. B. was Inspector of Municipalities at the time, bound hands and feet in red tape, according to the paper. "And if the town is ever going to get the go-sign before the snow flies, someone is going to have to raise a little hell. And," concluded Margaret, "I seem to be good at it."

Week by week the paper reported on wells numbered one to eleven in the Fort St. John field. The little handbook George sent her served his wife well. In no time at all she had the oil-patch lingo down pat.

"Number Four is tough going in shale and hard formation, drilling cut thirty-five feet a day. Tool-push Leper thinks it will be mid-May before the Perma Pen is encountered. Rumours are without foundation that Bouffioux farm is for sale for seventy-five thousand dollars, and they don't budge old Mother Earth who holds her secrets deep and resents too fast bit work in trying to find out what she is hiding."

As far off as Bartlesville, Oklahome, the Fort St. John "rag" was required reading on the desks of many an important oil man, investor, banker, lawyer, or editor. They enjoyed learning that Farmer Bouffioux was back from his winter holiday at Excelsior Springs where he had been boiled, massaged, purged and rested, and looked fit to wade into the fray. And fray it was, with farmers digging into old trunks for deeds to unravel their surface and mineral rights on land suddenly very interesting to George and Frank McMahon's Pacific Petroleums, laying adjacent, as it did, to Number Four which, they were assured, was Fort St. John's "hottest" gas well to date.

Margaret, who used to kick the door of the *News* office to gain entry with arms loaded with fruit of field and garden, in 1952 changed the load over to drill cores, discarded bits, jugs of naphtha, and other evil-smelling petroleum juices. Once she spotted oil on the roughnecks tumbling out of a taxi as they came off tower, and picking up the tip without a word being spoken, was off to report on such an embarrassing occurrence as oil in a gas well.

It was not, however, until she went to the hospital for surgery some time later that Bartlesville paid her its highest compliment by ordering fifty extra copies of her paper. In an effort to help her legs, she was having some long overdue repair work done. Thirty odd years before, following the birth of Dan, they had left her like an old Mack truck with the gate down, she said. Wrote Margaret from St. Mary's Hospital, New Westminster:

"I remember last winter at Fort Nelson, listening to Gadbury in the Gulf Oil office, trying to tell Houston on the phone the trouble at No. 3. 'In trying to regain,' he said, 'the heat of the hole baked the mud and nothing could go ahead or back out.' Well folks, No. 3 was just a patch on the fishin' they did on me down here. Frames suspended bottles of liquid, tubes and clamps clanked around me, the casing blew, then needles — not tracing but punching — put holes in me until a self-respecting season's ticket would be ashamed to associate with me. I tell you, like No. 3, I damned near terminated progress altogether. With liquid pouring into the veins and out the catheters, no water jack had a busier time than me trying to regain circulation. A small hole rig, working over a tight bottom hole — that describes this poor old scribe. In fact, we can't say yet whether we're drilling ahead for sure. As there was no choke on the escape, it's anyone's guess."

The Murrays were now in their mid-sixties. Sometimes George looked his years, but Margaret never did. Her day started at 6:30 a.m. at Mass at the hospital, after which she never failed to swap banter with the patients, admire the babies, and compare notes with Sister Philomena Mary on their combined leg ulcers and fallen arches. This ritual strengthened her, one day at a time, for whatever might come along.

What came along one day was the May issue of *Chatelaine* magazine with an article about — M.L.M. The old *News* office rocked over this one. And so did Room 644, the House of Commons. For the first time, the family — and Margaret — saw themselves as others saw them.

It was something of a shock.

Earl Beattie, all agreed, had written a rattling fine story. "The Queen of the North," he had titled it. But was this their Margaret? Was this the woman who wrote the pleading, tearful letters to them, who moaned in her sleep with the pain in her legs, who wept all the way through Mass, and who never really drank whisky because she never had to? He did not say she drank whisky, but you got that idea.

Was this the wife whose whole aim in life seemed to be appreciation, who never knew discontent because she hung firmly onto that ancient conception of humility and the thanks of the unworthy? Was this madcap of the creeks and the oil rigs the woman with the "M" in her hand? "Look you," she would say to the children when they were small, "that's an M and it stands for mors which is Latin for death, and remember you carry it in your hand all the time." Indeed, was this the wife who saw the divine hand in everything, good or bad, that ever happened and who said out loud "Thanks be to God" so many times a day that it stopped being a prayer to everyone else, and was instead just Margaret standing still for a moment?

Apparently it was. But she was not Margaret any more. She was "Ma." From that moment a star was born, aged sixty-two years. Margaret joined a rather distinguished company of

"Ma's" in their Canadian Northwest. All were known for their courage, their plain speaking, and their colourful personalities. It was reasonable that a weekly editor should join them.

But it affected her husband deeply. George Murray — neither humble nor proud, but a third thing, terribly aware of the image of those he loved, and of the opinion of others — was utterly shattered. An election was coming up, and the timing of Margaret turning into "Ma" could not have been worse. Here was the old Social Credit skeleton rattling like mad, coast to coast, from the depths of the past. Here was some highly amusing dinner-table conversation in print for all to see:

On marrying George instead of an Okotoks cowboy: "Well, we got an effervescent start, God knows. His friend, Bob Edwards of the Calgary *Eye-opener,* bought the wedding champagne."

On her rug-making adventure of the thirties and her success as a Toronto Exhibition spieler. "You may be sure the Ontario yokels got an earful when they came around the B.C. booth."

On future plans: "Now I'd like a year in a cloister. And I would not *either,* Jim Keddell, need a crock and all the latest magazines. A person has to have peace to gather their wits. I want to leave something after me when I die. Not a book, maybe, but a brochure, an imprint. A person ought to leave something."

And here was this polished, soft-spoken, dignified Parliamentarian from the Peace River in the East — addressing the dairyment at Chatham; the subject of an Arthur Ford feature in the *Free Press* at London; reminiscing in the *Evening Journal* on Ottawa forty years ago; representing Canada at the launching of the *Nautilus* in Boston; dining with India's foreign minister.

What kind of a nut was the guy married to?

There was simply no answers.

You could hardly blame Margaret for being too distracted to think. On top of producing a twelve-page newspaper on machinery that was pushed to produce six pages, acres of six-point oil leases which required experienced machine setting, breakdowns that required mechanics to fly in eight hundred miles to assess the trouble, keeping on top of the petroleum story, and taking an editorial hand in every fight that affected the community, all of a sudden there was Victoria to think about.

"The shotgun marriage using CCF ammunition has broken up," wrote Margaret. "The Coalition government has come apart. It lasted six years and knocked colder'n a mackerel both Liberals and Conservatives except federally. There isn't a grassroots organization for either one of them left. Membership has been stifled. And now we must pick up the pieces. The miracle is that it didn't get to be a den of thieves long ago. But it didn't. And we have had good government, withal."

And they had. Coalition had given the Peace River the Hart Highway. In the interval between de-coalescing and the election which resulted, Premier Byron Johnson took thirteen million dollars out of the treasury to lay tracks between Quesnel and Prince George and get the PGE Railway on its way — at last — to the Peace River. Assets of the Province exceeded liabilities by over a hundred million dollars, and the provincial debt was down to $164 a head.

But it was too little and too late as far as the railroad was concerned, and in spite of the full treasury in the election which followed, the people repudiated both old-line parties, exactly as Margaret had predicted it. They installed a rather shaky Social Credit crew under the leadership of a man who had got the message a little ahead of the rest, and months before had deserted his place among the Conservative coalitionists to cross the floor of the House. He was a hardware merchant from the Okanagan named W.A.C. Bennett.

The new party was rude and noisy in its victory but probably as surprised as the voters to find itself so well supported. In the Peace Block, so close to the green fields — and folding money — of Alberta, the electors paid that province its supreme compliment and elected as its M.L.A. a man as close to the image of Premier Ernest Manning as they could find — a broadcasting Nazarene minister.

"A nice man," said Margaret editorially, "but knows as much about politics as a hog does about Sunday." The Liberal representative for several terms they turned down flatly.

"Who knows about public works?" You could imagine the hardware merchant from the Okanagan searching around the room, sizing up his surprised candidates.

"Well, I used to skin a cat before I went in for church work."

"Okay, you're on. You take Public Works."

"Now, education. How about you? No, you've had experience in the woods, you say. You take Forestry."

"Education any one? Did you say a high-school principal? Wonderful. That settles Education."

Old pros at the game were aghast at the prospect of such a Cabinet. But British Columbia badly needed new blood in its government, and the very youth and inexperience of the legislators gave them confidence and courage to meet the challenge. A year later when the hardware merchant went again to the people to bolster his position and add to his numbers, he received a clear and solid mandate to govern.

At this point, Margaret was again in the public eye.

"My dear, we're not going to Prince George for the welcoming ceremony unless we're invited," said her husband. The PGE was to be completed that far by late summer, but was running a couple of months behind.

"You'll be invited. You're the M.P., she said. "Boss Johnson would see to that."

"Don't count on it. Johnson has no say. Anyway, much as I'd like to, I don't see how I could afford it from Ottawa."

"But George, we've waited forty years to see this." There were tears in her eyes.

It had been a disheartening interval for both. Prime Minister Louis St. Laurent himself had consented to visit the historic old riding of Cariboo that summer, and everyone in the Peace country was too busy to be interested. His reception in Prince George was not exactly riotous either. Everyone was too busy. The hum and roar of the lumber industry from the newly opened Hart Highway was getting louder. "*That* for St. Laurent," they said, and snapped their fingers.

"But my dear people," said George in radio talks designed to stimulate interest in the visit. "this is our Prime Minister. This is the head of our country. *His* people, *my* people were the displaced persons of their day."

Yeah, they said, guess you are right, and stirred up a batch of instant Brownies, Guides, and Scouts for the guard of honour. The whole Cariboo seemed to have turned into a frontier branch office of Dallas or International Falls, Minnesota, in which Dutch, German, Italian, Texan, and British accents were commoner than Canadian, and the First of July was just another day.

Here was a Liberal being embarrassed by the very things that made him a Liberal. The free market. The invitation to American capital. An immigration policy to fill the vast emptiness of Canada.

When the Prime Minister's visit was over, George swallowed his hurt at the chill he felt everywhere and chasing it with some Scotch whisky climbed into Dick Corless's little river boat and disappeared for a month. From this safari into the Rocky Mountain Trench, he produced six valuable articles to support his claim that the railroad should follow the Peace Pass route through the Rockies. "How Canada manages to seal off this significant wilderness is one of the mysteries of the day," he wrote.

The articles were timely, for daily the British Columbia north-south railway inched closer to the hub city of Prince George, where the decision would have to be made for its extension. But it's doubtful in all the hoohoora of development that anyone ever read them.

Eventually the day arrived, even if the invitation to be present did not. Margaret took care of *that* with a phone call to the Mayor of Prince George.

"No matter what your father says," she told Dan and me, both now back at the paper, "someone needs to get over there and remind those bigwigs that Prince George, after all, is going to be just another station on the PGE. And the PGE isn't going anywhere until it comes over here to the Peace."

"I'm going over to drive the spike," she wrote for her readers, "or spike the drive, or something. When Mr. Bennett gets to Prince George — he's never been there before — he might just get the idea, seeing those CNR tracks to Edmonton, that he's got her made. All the Cariboo people care a hoot for anyway is grain from the prairies. B.C. politicians have always been loafers. We can't afford to take any chances. Garv Dezeh is inviting me and told me to bring my six-bottle briefcase," she concluded. Certainly any image of Margaret Murray was aided and abetted at all times by herself.

The briefcase, in fact, held besides leg bandages and ointment, a revamped edition of that week's Alaska Highway

News — two hundred copies of corn and laughs and reminiscences designed to be handed out at Williams Lake to the first train passengers boarding all along the line from Squamish up. The passengers were in the right mood for it. Big cotton signs on the three Williams Lake coaches declared that their town had "The Biggest Bull Shippers in Western Canada" — until the rival Quesnel folks worked the slogans over.

Mother wrangled herself a spot on the banquet program which concluded Prince George's big day. She would reply to the toast to the ladies. She tossed off the fact that she had wiggled her way in, in a manner of speaking. This was no time for tiresome modesty or protocol. The whole Peace River was at stake. "It was an honour to be on the same program with the Premier and five Cabinet Ministers and all the other tycoons," she reported later.

If there is anything that a radio actuality man likes, it's genuine, honest-to-God noise from a crowd, sustained cheers or sustained clapping or sustained laughter. With Mother at Prince George, the CBC got all three. But the speech was so "salty" it never was rebroadcast outside British Columbia.

"You young fellows maybe don't know that this track was all built before, graded, rails laid, and left to rust in the sloth and idleness of an apathetic electorate for twenty-five years. The bridge over the Cottonwood was never connected and the rails pulled up and sold for junk. The promoters were put in jail and the consulting engineers should have joined them. This railroad has been the glaring example of two generations of political bungling. Byron Johnson will be remembered for carrying out a promise . . ."

By the way, where *was* Byron Johnson, the former Premier whose short regime had been responsible for this much of the new line? They forgot to ask him, they said.

Margaret's speech wasn't long getting to the point. She told the story of Henry Steige of Hudson's Hope who waited forty years for the day. One morning he heard a whistle down the canyon. "She's coming!" he yelled to the neighbours. "By God, hear the whistle? She's coming at last!" But all that came for Henry were the men in the white coats, and there must be no more of that sort of disappointment. She had the "tycoons," as she called them, rocking with laughter when she delivered her punch line.

"The fact is, you fellows know that we in the Peace River

have been sucking the hind teat too long."

The volume needle on the tap recorder jumped the dial and the listening audience was treated to laughter that echoed and re-echoed, to table thumps, loud guffaws, and the sort of choked noises that people make when they've laughed too much. Then Aunt Fanny took over, having just spied the recording equipment: "What have I said? My God, it's a blessing my husband isn't here. George would never forgive me. Anyway," she said a couple of times, trying to make herself heard, "anyway, it's no laughing matter to our people over the mountains."

If personality and a thorough knowledge of your subject ensure success on the platform, Margaret Murray was well endowed to talk about her Land Beyond the Peace. Advancing years gave her poise and confidence. Thus relaxed, she could not only think easily on her feet, but turn a *faux pas* into a triumph. She had learned this trick only lately.

On a spring evening in 1951, in Irvington, West Virginia, a hundred or so distinguished guests, delegates at the Joint International Committee of Chambers of Commerce of the United States and Canada, called to discuss the proposed St. Lawrence Seaway project, were dozing around a beautifully appointed banquet table in the Tides Inn Hotel. The seafood dinner had been delicious, the speeches were long.

As the last speaker quoted the last seven-digit cost figure, folded his notebook, and sat down, Francis Winspear, Secretary of the Canadian Chamber of Commerce, got to his feet. "Now," said Mr. Winspear, "we will give three minutes to our farthest away delegate, Margaret Murray, editor of the Alaska Highway *News,* wife of George M. Murray, M.P. for Cariboo, Canada's largest electoral district. Mrs. Murray's home is in Fort St. John on the Alaska Highway."

Yes, but Margaret borrowed it for the occasion.

"It certainly is," said Mother. "I come from a point considerably nearer Russian Siberia than you people live. Do you, down here in the United States, realize what you've done to these Canadians by building that Alaska Highway? Have you — any of you — been to China or Japan or Russia? Do you know about those teeming millions of people who look yearningly to our wide-open spaces in Canada? Do you realize that unless you help us to do something about developing our country, the Orientals will come across that tiny Bering Sea and take this northern land of ours?"

Margaret was away on her favorite subject, the North, the crops, the weather, the big game, the scenery, the people.

'I am a Kansan. I was given my chance to live and be part of our glorious Canadian north by my husband George, a newspaperman who hired me right off the Seattle boat one day in May 1912 to be his bookkeeper." She looked over at my father, who was studiously regarding his water goblet, waiting for the bombshell that always fell somewhere in his wife's speeches.

"The chairman's stop watch buzzed. Three minutes.

"Shall I go on?" asked Margaret.

The guests were all awake by this time. "Go on," they said.

"George Murray was working for northern developemnt then, in 1912. He is still working for it. And as you ladies here know — when a good woman gets under a man — he moves!"

Whump. The shocker had fallen right on target.

She wasn't finished, far from it. Into the howls of laughter, she said, "We grow everything big in the Peace," and straightening her shoulders and throwing out her chest, popped the top button on her two-piece faille tailleur, bouncing off her forty-four-inch bosom, and pinging loudly on a water pitcher in front of her on the table.

Again the tables rocked with laughter.

"Well," she said, not waiting for quiet, "it's just like I told you — everything is big where I come from. As a matter of fact, I shouldn't have worn this dress. It's Helen Moore's. But I came in a hurry. And I thought it looked kinda smart. Helen got it in Edmonton." And she bumbled on about the dress while the Lords of Commerce on this continent literally howled in merriment.

When the speech was finished, the Chairman called on the M.P. for Cariboo. "I think," he said, "that the assembled company deserves a word from the man who gave this woman her chance, and who taught her so well."

My Father rose to his feet, a big man, greying, handsome, polished in delivery, good to look at, every inch a statesman even from a back bench. He was given a standing ovation.

"Ladies and gentlemen," he said, as the applause died down, "President Roosevelt is said to have included in his nightly prayers this one: 'Please God, make Eleanor more tired tomorrow.' But like Eleanor, my wonderful wife is never more tired tomorrow. If anything she is more enthusiastic, fresher for the task, and more dedicated than ever as the days go by. She is fond of saying that I rolled back the map and she stood on it. But she couldn't just stand here — she had to *do* something. Well, for fifty years she certainly has!"

All Three Votes

Margaret came back from Prince George very aware of a climate warming to Social Credit. In her heart she must have had mixed feelings about what she saw and felt. But whatever her feelings provincially, they did not apply federally. Anyway, there was no question as to where her real loyalty lay.

"This election is going to be pure blood, sweat, and tears for you, George," she said to her husband. "There are no real issues. Everyone is too well off. You will have to fight for your government and convince the electors that Social Credit M.P.'s in Ottawa are a waste of time."

Harry Perry, George's wise old friend of the thirties, put it another way. "Public moods go like the pendulum of the clock, swinging one way, then the other, until the clock stops or better still is effectively wound up. That's it — we need winding up!"

How to wind the clock up for their father was now the probelm confronting the Murrays. George was home for twenty-four hours, *en route* to the coast to a convention. It was late November, 1952, and the family gathered together in the "red" room for a council of war.

"Dad, ya gotta have a gimmick. Now take the price of drugs." Dan was all wised up on drugs, what with three little girls and a lately mis-carried wife and the population explosion in California. "Something should be done about the shameful way of these cartels, and up here in the north, where we are forced to pay sometimes six hundred per cent profit on drugs, we need to just . . ."

"Yes, but Dad, what about income tax?" This was my contribution. "You don't need any expensive research to know that a reduction in income tax for us north of fifty-four is only fair. Every government employee, all the armed services, all the telegraph, telephone, post office, and bank employees get a cost-of-living bonus — *just to live here!* A hundred dollars a month northern allowance for putting up with outside toilets, water in a barrel, and no sidewalks. Why not some relief for us *bona fide* residents and investors who have to scratch to create our own salaries?"

Margaret slammed the oven door on the hot biscuits for dinner, picked up a sheaf of galleys in her floury hand, and paused at the doorway before going down to the shop with corrections. "The Angel Gabriel couldn't get elected on a Liberal ticket around here this week — not that this week is election week — but while you're all discussing this, remember to consider the possibility of your father resigning and coming back to B.C. to lead the Liberals in opposition. One of the great pities is that you, George, have never been in opposition, never on the offensive. John Oliver was older than you when he had a whack at it. Think of the fun. Go out in a shower of shrapnel!"

There is something about the fundamentals of politics that instills into its ethical victim a quality of vagueness. He reacts as if he is being heckled and at the point of asking for notice of question. The more wisdom he acquires and the more responsible he feels, the hazier he becomes. Only the young and unknown have decisive doctrines and strongly declared convictions. And so George gave the family his best statesman's inscrutable smile, ended the discussion with thanks, and flew off into the night.

It had been a killer of a day. The Gething-Baseley coal mine at Hudson's Hope needed contracts, a Dawson Creek restaurant proprietor wanted relatives brought into the country from China, a civil servant sought promotion, an oil executive wanted telephones up the highway, and a board of trade delegation was difficult about a post office — but no more so than the landowners who sought an increase in the price of expropriated property.

As a matter of fact, the post office itself was a *fait accompli,* being merely buried in some civil servant's in--basket. The money had been voted and the architect had completed the plans. But elections are sometimes won or lost for want of a signature. The building, before it ever got started, was already too small, and George was pressing for adjacent land for the future. No parliamentary representative ever heard so many gripes in twenty-four hours, nor turned aside more forthrightly the wheeler-dealers with votes to sell for personal services rendered. (A few years later the family opened his safety-deposit box seeking his will and found a blank cheque of this date signed by a constituent who was worth a half million dollars.) Two days later, on the back of a Canadian Pacific Airlines menu, his frustrated family at home read some lines of verse he wrote to "My Granddaughter Margaret."

Yes Margaret dear, it seems to be
While grownups seek security
And shout and argue over things
That commonsense must oft take wings
Your gran'pere almost meant to weep
O'er problems difficult and deep,
But pausing at your cradleside
Restored his dignity and pride,
And sent him back into the night
His torch held high and gleaming bright.

The new and somewhat shaky government at Victoria celebrated the new year, 1953, by putting out feelers as to which route the PGE would choose across the Rocky Mountains from Prince George. The Premier of British Columbia sought the advice of his Social Credit kinfolk in Alberta, was careful to invite the press along, and almost at once threw the whole Peace River Block into a tizz by suggesting that the Monkman Pass on the Alberta side would be the cheapest way.

"Infamy! Infamy!" wept the Alaska Highway *News.* "This would leave us right where we've been for thirty years."

The announcement jolted both Fort St. John and Dawson Creek into action. The situation was viewed with loud alarm, petitions were handed around, the papers of the two towns were swamped with letters to the editor. Dawson Creek held out for the Pine Pass route which was the shortest by sixty miles. It would follow the Hart Highway, cut through no more than a half a dozen sections of good farm land, and be forever confined as a local provincial north-south railroad. No timber to mention, no hydro or mineral possibilities, and a gradient of eleven per cent.

Fort St. John was for the Peace Pass, lowest on two continents. It was not even really a mountain pass, but a corridor so much more level than the alternate route that engineers had typed it heavy prairie construction. Where a given power unit would push twenty-two grain cars through the Pine, the same power unit would push seventy through the Peace. Where snow removal would be a severe problem in the Pine, it would be scarcely any in the Peace, and maintenance likewise. Where the railroad would follow two hundred miles of unproductive land in the Pine, it would pass through the Peace billions of tons of coal, untold millions of board feet of merchantable lumber, countless acres of rich, frost-free trench land, at least one mountain of mineral and hydro power in three stages.

But the voters could be heard louder and clearer through the Pine. An existing highway would expedite the building of the track, they said, and it was, after all, a railroad at last. It would give a second rail outlet to Dawson Creek, already grown fat and prosperous and populous on the great bread--basket and petroleum empire north of the river. Northsiders, who actually sat right in the bread-basket, did not really have time to care how the railroad got there, as long as it eventually did arrive.

So desperate was the situation that George at this time was doing his utmost to have established in Fort St. John a storage elevator, which would accept and pay for grain right on the spot, avoiding the long haul to Dawson Creek, and keeping some of the grain cheques at home to pay for water, sewer, and gas improvements. Meanwhile, "the battle of the passes" raged on for months, and the time came at last for the M.P. to declare himself on which he favoured.

From Ottawa, he wrote, "In God's name, by any route at all. But the Peace Pass strategically and fundamentally is the only route by which northern resources can be tapped. Finlay Forks is the keystone of northern areas where development can be looked for. North and west of this point, further railroads will be built. From Finlay Forks lies the shortest route to Alaska. One thousand miles."

"Now George, don't get too far above the people's heads," warned Margaret, looking over his shoulder.

"You ask me and I tell you. What is sixty more miles when you've waited forty years, spent millions in surveys to find out which route will provide tonnage for the future?"

"Well all right, but get a par in there about the four cents reduction in cigarettes. Can you say something about when they'll turn the sod for the post office? Give them something they understand, for God's sake. Half of the people up there never heard of the Rocky Mountain trench, or even Finlay Forks for that matter. And when you're finished with the typewriter I'll write them about yesterday."

"Yesterday" had been their fortieth wedding anniversary. The Prime Minister and Madame St. Laurent had come to lunch. "Do come," George had written. "There will no press and no photographs. After all, we Scotch have played a part in building up Canada. But the Irish were always there as a sort of spark plug. And as to the French, well, there had to be poetry." Senator King and Senator Turgeon of British Columbia, their wives, the Donald MacKays, the Rupert Broadfoots, and even, by a great stroke of luck, Father Connelly, who had married them so many years before.

"What we missed on that wintry day in 1913, we made up for," Margaret told her readers. "Anyone who could weather out forty years with me is entitled to a celebration. Red roses, red tapers, red wine, and red-blooded friends."

Also red ears for George, because Margaret, naturally, got into an argument with the P.M. "Trust your mother," he told the children later, with a sigh.

The fact was that George's stock across the Dominion was very high in the spring of 1953. His defence of his government at the time of the Currie Report, which dealt with waste and pilfering during the construction of the Alaska Highway, made headlines on every front page from Atlantic to Pacific.

G. Walter Miller, president of a large Toronto company, was typical of many a tycoon who subscribed to the Fort St. John paper "to relax, smile, and get some mighty good reading". He wrote, "I just wanted your readers to know that every now and again I read in our eastern press articles about Mr. Murray, and I just wonder sometimes if people up in his country realize what a good job he does for them, and for Canada as well."

Mr. Miller was correct in his wondering. Few Edmonton *Journals* were sold in Fort St. John each day. But the same material, briefed down for a weekly, and run in the Murray paper, was apt to be considered propaganda.

"It's nice," said Margaret, back now from Ottawa, "to know that the people outside think he's such great shakes. Because right here in Fort St. John, his stock isn't any higher than that miserable twenty-by-forty shack of a post office."

The incredible thing was that two solid years had passed since the money had been voted for this public building, six months had passed since it was dug out of somebody's basket and confirmed, and tenders had still not been called to build it. Quesnel, Prince George, Vanderhoof, and Dawson Creek all had their public buildings or were about to have them.

"This little postal department chap we had to lunch in Ottawa," Margaret wrote her spouse, "was in this morning. He says he never had the plans for Fort St. John. Everyone is in such a lather about this. Can't you do something? Anything?"

But the rain continued to drop in on two hundred mail sacks in the back stoop of the existing facility. Sorting continued two or three days behind schedule. Queues formed down the street for the wicket. And mud inside and out dried into dust which tore at the remaining lung of the first World War vet postmaster, and eventually felled his young assistant, who took to her bed for a year.

"Have you tried to buy a stamp lately," said a letter to the editor. "First you get ready for a days outing. Sandwiches, coffee thermos and folding camp chair. Cancel all engagements for the day. Usually you don't get in the door the first try, but keep pushing against that milling mass of humanity inside and eventually you're in. Whip out your camp stool, unpack the sandwiches — you won't have much left if you offer them around to the starving mob — gulp your coffee and enjoy a rather comfortable day. Along about evening you get to the one wicket and one clerk. If you're not lucky, she will say, 'Oops, 5:30' and slam the door down in your face. But if you win, you say 'one four cent stamp please,' and oh, the thrill of it as you stagger out the door clutching your trophy!"

The Alaska Highway *News* in these years was a racy ten pages, well produced, well edited, bursting with controversy over dozens of community issues, thoughtfully presented. Margaret felt it was only adequate, however, because it did not have her personal supervision. But she could not do much about it and still help her husband on the hustings. Also she had very decided views about the Sisters of Providence getting a new hospital to replace the old frame one in which the first floor x-ray maching threatened to fall down on top of the basement washers at any moment.

"If Mother asks how the collection is coming for the hospital's new boiler room, just say everything is jake. Otherwise she might write an editorial," said Dan. Margaret was coming in on the noon plane to swap her Ottawa accessories (mink and sixteen-button gloves) for something more in keeping (Dr. Locke shoes and an old Dobbs felt) with the terrain on the canvass for George that she planned along the CN line out of Prince George. Dan and I were anxious that she reserve any of her biting commentary on the hospital fight, or any other fight for that matter, so as not to embarrass Father at this vital time in his career.

The town and district were splitting down the middle on the hospital issue. Should the hospital be run by nuns, or should it be a secular operation? In mother's vocal view, whether they were Buddhist or Catholic, the sisters had nursed the citizens from the early days, and they deserved the opportunity to carry on. Religious liberty might be supposed to mean that everybody is free to discuss religion. In practice, it means that hardly anybody is allowed to even mention it. But that message never did get through to Margaret.

She was not alone. The Social Credits in the Peace opened their meetings with hymns and sacred songs. And George, at once bewildered and indignant at an impertinent letter asking him why he did not also open his meetings with hymns, cried, "I refuse to be listed among the unredeemable and the unforgiven simply because some political opponent says so."

"Skip it," said Dan. "Don't get into it."

"Skip it! Great God, man, it has been more than three hundred years since we abolished the doctrine of the divine right of kings, and a hundred years in Upper Canada since —

"And a hundred years, I repeat, in Upper Canada since we settled the clergy reserves question. I am not prepared, out of loyalty to my forebears, who stained the heather with their blood . . ."

"I know, Dad, I know."

"You know nothing. Are you condoning the return today to revival of the divine right of party leaders?"

"Get it off your chest, Dad. Just don't print it, is all I ask."

But George printed it anyway. And his speeches were no more helpful to his cause.

"A railroad in the north should be one of our Canadian systems. A local railroad has no place in planning a region which includes interprovincial, territorial, and eventually — if not already — international questions. A route through the Peace Pass would draw to it tonnage from half a dozen lesser northern river valleys, and help us build up our Pacific and coastal trade, and with it all other coastal cities. There is a law of life that men and nations grow in proportion to their contribution to the new life of the world. We have these unfortunate flood victims from Holland and Belgium and the East Coast of England coming to us right this summer. Let us build for the future! Communities which give their spirit and energy to the new task of building the North Pacific area will be rewarded manyfold. Those who refuse the task will be swept aside."

"What the hell is he talkin' about?" asked a Baldonnel farmer out on the sidewalk in front of the community hall.

"Well, I don't know, but it sounds like it'll take another thirty years to get her here," said his chum. "It ain't even on the map."

And it wasn't. The Victoria government had blanketed the country with maps handed out to everybody, and they did not even show the Peace Pass.

But the same speech in Prince George, where PGE diesels were already switching in the yards, spurred the daily *Citizen* to say, "Only the biased, the uninformed, and the ungrateful voter will deny Mr. Murray a chance to continue.

This modest but capable and conscientious parliamentarian is the best representative Cariboo has ever sent to Ottawa."

The electorate, during the campaign cacophony, was a confused group through the summer of 1953, voting in a provincial election in June and a federal election in August. Many of them did not know the difference between the two. Fifteen years later they still do not.

"Godamitey," said Mabel, the Murrays' cleaning lady, screwing up an eye against the smoke from her dangling cigarette, "ain't I just vote? Didn't Mr. Murray get us the railroad areddy?" Mabel, who didn't read or write, was a voter who had the returning officer mark her ballot — and there were plenty like her.

George, by this time, had grown into a regular Edward Arnold of a man. Newspapermen used to write that he looked every inch the politician, his white hair carefully kept and affecting a long style.

He was clean-shaven, except for the summer on the Mackenzie River when he returned with a Van Dyke beard, grown to protect his face in the fly country. It was stark white against a bronzed skin and went well with the old Washington hand-press that attracted tourists' cameras outside the *News* office in Fort St. John.

"Give me a reading, Daddy," would command plump American matrons, camera to eye. "And ask Mr. Mark Twain to come stand by his press."

But all his family could see in George now was the misery of an old bear being attacked by bees, being stung front, left, and center by the apathy of his followers, and flailing away at an enemy he could not see but could surely feel. However well taken his position on hymns and prayers at political meetings, in the Peace River country, with several congregations each of at least half a dozen "literalist" church groups (some people call them fundamentalist but orthodox groups object that they too are fundamentalist), his stand was something like being against motherhood.

But he fought on at poorly attended meetings, on the radio, and in the columns of the paper which, because it was really his paper, even if in his wife's name, was of doubtful value to him. He had never acquired the touch which would enable him to mingle and talk with the farmers at the Co-op unless he knew them, or to sit for a half hour to meet people in a local pub.

Dawson Creek is one of the most progressive communities in British Columbia. Its business fraternity were eager young imports from Edmonton and other points in Alberta and Saskatchewan, with dollar signs in their eyes which lit up every time a train whistled. Everything came from Social Credit Alberta. Wholesalers were located there, car dealers, taxation offices, banks, telegraph and telephone, postal services, petroleum head offices. And all these agencies supplied the portion of British Columbia which lay east of the Rockies.

George Murray made his last stand at Dawson Creek where he had gotten a five-hundred-thousand-dollar federal building in the works. It was a night or two before the forty-eight-hour political cease-fire which Canadian law requires before election day.

And the night of George's meeting, Alberta exported one other commodity. Thirty-eight Social Credit M.L.A.s chose this particular time for a social call on their Dawson Creek friends and business associates. When no one came out to hear Mr. Murray, he packed it up early, went to the telegraph office and, over the magic byline, franked a couple of hundred words to Canadian Press on the Socreds, and provided the necessary excuse to the South Peace community for flatly rejecting its author at the polls later that week.

The irony of George's defeat was the fact that he was run over by the railroad, by the Pacific Great Eastern Railway, the very thing he had spent a lifetime urging through the Rocky Mountains to the great fertile empire of the Peace.

"For forty years," he said bitterly to Alwin Holland, his old friend, as the returns came in election day, "I have talked and argued and written and excused and defended this project. For what? So that men of small minds may walk in and take the fruits of other men's dreams?"

"It were ever thus," replied the old dominie. "Some day it will be their bitter portion, as it is yours today."

The people waiting at the railroad's Peace River terminal in the foothills of the Rockies could not know this. They were not British Columbian's but Albertans, or free enterprisers from Saskatchewan, or Americans, or Europeans.

But mostly they were Albertans who wanted the government they admired in their native province for their adopted one. They reasoned if the one Socred they had just elected for Victoria was good, then the same for Ottawa would be doubly good. And they campaigned with a zeal that was unmatched by the most sophisticated senior party.

In the settled, solid old British Columbia part of Cariboo, it had been different. They turned down the Socred in his own hometown of Prince George by four hundred votes. "The salesman with the fat order book — five million dollars in four years — is a desirable member of any man's staff. Let's keep Mr. Murray at our Ottawa office," was how the *Observer* at Quesnel had put it.

But Dawson Creek, with the train whistling in its ears, with its fear of the Peace Pass route in place of their own Pine Pass, embraced Social Credit with a majority of three hundred.

The real heartbreak was Fort St. John. Four hundred people did not bother to come out to the polls at all. In the midst of the most frantic prosperity, largely government-inspired — airport extensions, new waterline, heavy defence budget because the world was still breathing hard after the Korean war — the government candidate was given a bare majority of twenty-three.

He lost by less than four hundred votes. The final count took weeks because of the inaccessibility of trading posts and other isolated communities. He left untouched eleven thousand dollars in campaign funds in a Prince George bank, an unheard-of situation with the Murrays who, in less plushy times in the Cariboo, had dug down months after an election to take the hall rental or whatever from their own pockets.

"How's Dad this morning?" I asked, coming in the next day to work. I spoke in a low voice outside the closed bedroom door in the "red" room.

Mother shook her head. "Pretty low. Go in and see him."

"Hello, honey," I said, opening the door on the cool, breeze-freshened room. There was no answer. I could not see the bed for the clutter around it, but a groaning sound reassured me, and somewhere a watch ticked loudly.

Here was a room. Here was a scene that caught the

characters of these parents of mine, and photographed them for all time.

Here were three rough boxes of bound books, sessional papers, correspondence files, briefs, and assorted stationery piled where the trucker had left them, and beside these the big black trunk. Here was his beautiful morocco Bible, the first thing out and the last thing in when he unpacked or packed his travel-weary club bag. The bag was open but untouched save for the Bible. Here were crumpled trousers over a chair-back with the pockets so, and the galluses dragging the floor, the dusty brogues of the campaign trail, side by side. The sweat-stained, broad-brimmed Stetson was placed carefully on the top packing box.

This heap on the left looked like someone had been frantically searching through it for something moments before. The six mink rakishly festooned over the open top of the case, the Washington hat, a copy of the *Confessions* of St. Augustine, the Helen Moore two-piece — all her clothes were identified by the occasions which originally required them. Her "Sunday" corsets, a rubber stocking into which were stuffed perfume and mentholatum. A bit of veiling, never unfolded, some Dr. Scholl's, the Liberal Platform mimeographed for 1953, the Crown Royal bags which embraced Arden and Colgate, on the one corner; and scissors, collar buttons and corn plasters, needles and hair pins, a screwdriver and paring knife, on the other. (One of the better things about Crown Royal, she often said, was the useful little bag the booze came in.)

"You would think," I said out loud as I waited for some response from the bed, "that Mother had just up-ended a gunny sack in this room."

"Unnnnh," said the mound under the bedclothes, sighing heavily.

"Hey, Dad!" Dan's voice sailed through the bindery kitchen door. "We're waiting for that statement. And there's a long distance call out here for you."

"Tell them I'm not accepting any calls today," said the bed.

"I'll say to call back." The voice left, and returned. "Whattaya know, Dad, ya gotta landslide at Chinaman's Bar — all three votes!"

But the laughter did not quite ring true. And it died

right out altogether when, three days too late, tenders were finally let and announced on the Fort St. John post office.

For people who rode so high on hopes, the lows of the Murrays were indescribable. The old Celtic failing of George's, that agony of spirit that was especially his, all but destroyed him for the next year. Any physical agony that may have accompanied it he took great pains to hide.

The rest of us took various means to put the election out of our minds. Margaret declared she was a Leo woman — she bruised easily but healed quickly. Against family advice, she ran and was elected that fall to the town council of Fort St. John. "You can do more for the community writing editorials. If you're one of the council, you can hardly criticize yourself," said Dan.

"But I can't just stand here," she answered and immediately launched the council on two of its stormiest years on record.

Dan decided to beat the post-election depression with colour. Behind his thinking was a zeal toward efficiency, and anyway he had just finished reading a book on colour engineering. "They have found in California that if you paint a bar blue, nobody buys any booze. But if you paint it rose and have warm bronzy lights, you double your sales," he said. "Colour wakens you up."

He therefore proceeded with a four-alarm treatment on the front office and editorial staff in glorious technicolor. Magenta and chartreuse, to be exact. Buckets of it. Customers made entrances in the manner of melodrama with their forearms shielding their eyes. Government inspectors and others who spent any time in the office became more than usually jumpy.

"This will not only get our heads up off our desks, but we'll all have a nervous twitch by spring," I said.

But Win, the bookkeeper, made peace all around and observed that, after all, it was nice to have it all cleaned up. This did not, however, apply to the new battleship linoleum which was to remain lumpy with gumbo for the next three years while the main street got water, gas, sewer, water, sewer, water, gas. Wherever the yells were the loudest, the village started either digging or covering up.

Dan and John Quelle never smiled around the shop

until Thursday when the paper was off. John, however, relaxed a little when the first automatic machine was installed — a Heidelburg press which cost four thousand dollars and fed itself, counted itself, stacked and jogged itself, even cleaned itself. But Dan worked the clock around, timed motion, checked hours of work, deplored the off-beat journalism his family delighted in, sent curt notes to old subscribers, and gave a daily lecture to his mother on management.

They fought about the editorial content of the paper. "Christ Almighty who cares?" he fumed. "Or anyway who cares twenty galleys worth?" Mother and son were going to it in the back office. "Yards of this crap, but no fillers. Get me twenty galleys of one- and two-line fillers, and I won't say a word."

"Get your own damned fillers. I'm not letting Bennett-Gunderson & Company away with it," shouted Margaret. "In office twelve months and the gall to tell us they've saved us thirty-eight million dollars. Us! The people of B.C. Liars! They've just jimmied up the books. That's what they've done. Censored to them!"

"Yes, but Mother, who cares? And anyway, look at this tabulation work. It will cost sixty dollars just to put it into type."

Margaret was determined to publish a series of articles by former Premier Byron Johnson, defending British Columbia's financial position when the Socreds assumed office. "Put it into type then," she gravelled through clenched teeth. "Who's paying the shot around here, tell me that!"

And George, who was examining asbestos rock through a glass, got up from his easy chair beside the big window which looked over the valley of the Peace and shut the door on the row.

The Silence Eddied around Her

It was just a matter of time — and type — until Dan headed out. Years later, he put the circumstances into perspective:

"I had been happy in California. I was making good money pounding a linotype and selling vacuum cleaners. Don't laugh like that. At least, it was my own show. My kiddies were healthy and growing. And then the letters started coming from Fort St. John. I suppose I should have known better, but I thought it would be different. It had been about four years.

Sure I should have had my head examined, but I sold out and bought a Mack truck and moved back to Canada, back to Fort St. John. It was *going* to be different this time! I was positive. Only it wasn't. Mother was the same as ever. She was right and the world was wrong. She bought a farm when she should have bought a new linotype — still enthralled with the romance of the Kansas City stockyards. She sold the Lillooet property and slapped the dough into a packing house when she should have bought pipeline stock or town lots.

"It had cost me about five thousand hard cash to settle my family in Vancouver, and I got to thinking that this 'heritage' jazz wasn't worth the effort. All I wanted was a neat little profitable operation. Like Audit Bureau. And no overdrafts. And no overtime. But Mother was going to live forever and had it planned that way. I still hadn't dried up behind the ears, she said. I was a slave driver. I had no charity. My family were poor sports for staying in the city. She would criticize me in front of the staff. 'Why you little turd!' she'd say when I'd fire somebody or enact some sensible change in company policy.

"So I left again."

Dan went off to Vancouver to punch a linotype once more

and dabble in the importing business, and good old Georgina, who said "yes" to everybody, was around to pinch-hit at the newspaper when necessary. "That one," observed Margaret, referring to me, "has the heart of a bondswoman."

But there has to be one in every high-powered family to keep the members speaking to each other. Daniel she dismissed as the natural sequence to the union of two people who did not really think that money was important. "The swing of the pendulum. Cut off my hand at the wrist if I know who in the world he takes after." But possibly behind all that she was just a tiny bit glad that he could and did stand up to her.

George wrote editorials, but he seemed to have lost his zest. He turned out brilliant copy only when he felt up to it and wanted to, or when some local happening stirred memories of colourful history forty years before. Not only had he the facts, but also the physical attributes of his characters — the moustaches, the watch chains, the voice inflection — so that when he painted these vignettes, they lived. Margaret could not figure out why he did not do them more often.

George's editorials were geared to a more glorious British Columbia and a nobler Canada, but his wife took care of the local scene. As a scene, literally, the town itself had not changed in appearance until paved streets came along in 1957. They rode in on a giant hassle in which the paper, naturally, was out front slugging. Should the telephone poles sit there in their original position and just have hard surface poured around them to the curbing? Or should the whole thing not be done properly? The paper lost that round because the public Works Department was using strictly an election mix. "The poles sure could sit there," was the government's decision. In the newly converted ridings of the Province they were spreading the works appropriation — and the asphalt — mighty thin in those days.

The telephone system, according to the paper, had bugs in it. The service was awful. B.C. Telephone hurried in to investigate the complaint, and was forced to reveal that some of Alexander Graham Bell's ea·liest model switchboards were installed for use in Fort St. John. When anyone banged the door shut on the office, all the little buttons fell down so that the operator could not tell how many were real signals and had to proceed to answer them all, slowing the service considerably. On one occasion a bottle of spilled coke stuck the buttons firmly in place and achieved the same effect. Meanwhile the hospital fight continued for ten solid years, good for a column of type any time, and several columns between lulls.

The income-tax people used to fix a very skeptical eye on Margaret Murray, but it is doubtful if they were ever around to note the countless Mark Wah meals doled out to journallists, the small libations poured for newspapermen, magazine writers, television and radio people, the oil and gas which fueled a car about to take cheerfully off to Hudson's Hope, or Pink Mountain, or down the gravel roads to East Pine to see how the railroad was coming. For although the sheer size of the paper forced her out of a chocolate box and scribbler-type of newspaper management, she was as abandoned as a bird about the petty cash. At the same time she wholly lacked the cunning to win an argument with the tax men when it came to a new-fangled, expense-account system. All she ever had was an impressive bundle of cancelled airline tickets. Was the trip without cost because the railways gave the Murrays press passes? "What's the odd taxi, and a dollar for the porter? I didn't have time to eat. And the Gregorys had me for overnight," she'd say. The turnover in bookkeepers became, as government regulations grew more rigid, as bad as that of linotype operators in years gone by.

George in these years, handled the PR extension of the newspaper, and convoyed the VIP'S, the *Satevepost* writers, the Wall Street *Journal* people, and assorted big-name journalists and publicists. This he loved, for he could talk and be understood. The locals were apt to consider him a slightly dotty elderly man, reaching always further out with dreams for development that no one else could see. Personality stories for the outside were always written about his wife who lent instant colour to any copy in which she ever featured. Stephen Franklin, the Canadian journalist, once remarked to Dan and me, "I should really be doing this piece on your father, but it wouldn't sell."

As for Margaret, half the town loved her and half hated her. But the balance was tipped on the love side, for she made them laugh. "Who is the wickedest woman in town?" A young evangelist passing through once took a quarter-page ad to pose this question. The copy read that the townsfolk would have an answer at the Elk's Hall on Monday night. Mother, whose conscience must have been bothering her that week, hastened into type to make a general confession of her life.

"Good grief, Mother, what brought this on?" I asked. "What does that young sprout know about you?"

"Well, never mind that," she answered. "I'm not taking any chances."

Early in 1958, an acute water shortage in town raised her dander and, in the lead editorial, she wrote, "There has been a terrible waste of water in this small town. We get our water the hard way, via a pipeline. We sure as hell need to use less if we are going to have this modern convenience. To head off this catastrophe, only flush for No. 2, curtail bathing to the Saturday night tub, go back to the old washrag, which could always move a lot of B.O. if applied often enough."

People laughed, yes, but Mother's embattled words also reduced the pull on the local reservoir a hundred gallons in a single night. The noise in the pipes which ensued gurgled right into *Time* magazine's Calgary office so that during that particular week all Canada was brought up-to-date on the water emergency in the Northwest's newest boom town.

"How else can you get your point across unless you do some plain speaking?" asked Margaret in defence of her blunt editorial. "Lots of these trailer people who run their taps all night to keep the pipes thawed are so recently here they don't even read the paper. But make it plain enough and they'll hear about it all right."

When Princess Margaret came to Fort St. John, the Alaska Highway *News* did that week's issue just for her.

It was a great day, the day of the visit. It was Thursday, and the paper had been put out a day early so the shop and office could be shined up. The village spread fifty thousand gallons of water on the streets to lay the dust so the Princess could see the people, and closed all the bars for two hours before touchdown so that all the people could see the Princess.

Fifty copies of the Alaska Highway *News* were cheerfully bootlegged aboard both the Royal Plane by Mother's friends at CPA and the press flight which accompanied it the night before take-off in Vancouver. "Are you the local press?" asked Lady Elizabeth Cavendish, H.R.H.'s Lady-in-Waiting during the tour of the Taylor refinery.

"I am."

"Jolly little rag," laughed Lady Elizabeth. "We read every word on the way up this morning."

With such animation on the editorial side of the paper, it grew in pages and circulation. But the best paper in the world is only as good as its production staff, and here was an operation growing too much for the publishers "one cylinder" and for the worn-out machinery of the plant.

Too much, too, for the poor old bandaged legs. For Margaret was the pilot, and George the ship, and as the great engines faltered and missed, it was obvious that quieter waters and balmier climes must be sought. Here was Margaret with one leg bent to kneel on a wheeled cart that Dan and John had built for her. This replaced a peg-leg rest which she held by a strap in an effort to keep the old ulcerated ankle that had plagued her all her life off the floor. In spite of a racy sign which read, "This vehicle not to be driven more than ten miles an hour," it was still a sight to evoke sympathy from even the most case-hardened hospital feuder.

Perhaps the greatest legacy parents can leave their children is the circumstances of a child's birth. Dan was conceived in poverty. "What I wouldn't have done for the taste of a strip of bacon," Margaret said the day her young husband brought home the silverware and eiderdown, purchased with Mr. Welch's twenty-dollar gold piece. But the boy was brought up never to hear the word "rich" as applied to wealth. Nor had he ever heard the word "failure" applied to his own family. Failures — and there were plenty of them with the Murrays — were always on the grand scale: the general who lost the great battle, or the industrialist whose schemes put him into temporary bankruptcy. There was no snivelling, no personal feeling of failure, no loss of heart — just as there was no acknowledgment of riches.

Chris McRae, whose kids were brought up with the Murrays, was merely a clever man who knew lumber. Mr.

Fillion, whose wife drove the sedan with the merry little edging of dancing balls at the top of the windows and the rose on the dashboard, was possibly a smart merchandiser, like Charlie Woodward. Bob Cromie, with whose children Dan attended school, was a man of vision and application whose father-in-law happened to know a deal in grain when he saw one. The fact that the Cromies, the McRaes, the Woodwards, and other contemporaries lived in Shaughnessy Heights with *porte cocheres* and gardeners, was incidental.

And so, nowadays, merging out of Marpole into Kerrisdale, on the way into the city of Vancouver from the airport, it was strange to George to query the name of the boulevard they were traversing, and to hear his grandchildren say, "O Grandpa, this is where the rich people live."

"The who?" asked Grandpa, startled.

"The rich people, Grandpa, with Cadillacs and swimming pools."

Financial security was of prime importance to the Murray's son. And if he ever again came to Fort St. John it would be on his terms — and in writing.

When steel started inching it's way through the Pine Pass, the question of railroad station and yards came up. The profits of three months operation on the *News* went into a highly colourful controversy in which the paper accused the government of playing politics and purchasing land so far away from the village that the community, for revenue purposes, would be twenty-five years growing to embrace it. Cuts, pages of type, art work — nothing was too much expense or trouble to preserve the pros and cons 'for the record'.

But badly as they disagreed over the various facets of the publishing business, it remained the fondest wish of George and Margaret that Dan indeed, would come to Fort St. John and stay, and inherit the business they had built. Blood had very tender ties for George Murray, and in this respect his blood was Margaret's.

"Fond as are my sincerest thoughts for your welfare," wrote Margaret upon receipt of Dan's "terms," "I could not do such a right face to those who are close by. Georgie is entitled to a slice of this heritage whether she works or not. I could not eliminate John, who has been so faithful to carry on during your two retreats from here, and still live with my own mind. You have your good points and your ability, but you are not super, and as limited beyond your depth as anyone else. You need John, and you'd need me, and we'd both need the freshness of Georgie, at least until we'd be making enough money to hire a lot more people to do the same job. You could not expect John to deliver a hundred per cent if he was cut out of the deal, and you need him. You need the editorial ability of your Dad — but you couldn't expect it or get it if you suddenly came in here throwing your weight around in the way you write your letters."

"It seems to me the paper has been a means to an end," wrote back the son. "The real star of the show is the Murrays rather than the development of a closely knit, well-organized printing and publishing business. I will tolerate no more of that. Man management and organization is everything these days. I will offer, of course, a benevolent dictatorship."

Harsh words flew back and forth via Her Majesty's mails.

"There is no need for the new building until you have three shifts and a hundred per cent efficiency utilizing the present accommodation," said Dan. But the old news building was extended to the lane, just the same.

"Don't get a new car. Take taxis. Put the money into a new linotype," he urged. "Have you got the intercom hooked up? Answer 'yes' or 'no.' No tears, please. Or are you — as I suspect — running around that barn of a place on your legs, instead of with your voice?"

Margaret set her lips, bought the Mercedes, smothered the intercom station in papers and third-class advertising material, and continued to scoot around the premises on one foot and four wheels. Her irritability, that scourge of the Irish, went up and down with the sting in her ankle.

There was fault on both sides. Margaret wanted her son to have what she felt was rightfully his, but she feared being "run off" as she put it. "My heart is crying inside me at the injustice of it," she told George. "What can you do with someone as arrogant as that boy?"

But Dan had his own ideas on running a newspaper, and they had nothing to do with being quoted in *Time* magazine. He wanted to make it on his own, and not stand in the shadow of his parents. He wanted his mother and father to retire to a quiet house and be the sort of grandparents other people had. Full cookie jars. A little golf. The winter in California. "I have been kicked from pillar to post in this family," he charged.

"Your belligerent attitude," replied his mother, "indicates that you have built up a straw man of faults toward everything about your father and me. The time is long overdue for you to take over, and you are trained to do so, but not at the price you ask and the frame of mind with which you approach it."

When it appeared that this was one fight that would never finish, George and Georgina, the family's two appeasers, sat down in the living room.

"Dad, look, why not offer him fifty per cent? John and I will split the remainder. He'll make us all rich." It was agreed, but when I returned to the living room with Mother and John a few minutes later to further discuss it, Dad was sound asleep.

"The next time I came back," says Dan now, "we had the little chit signed. The price we paid for the paper was fair but not a giveaway, as she let others think. The machinery was just about junk. A whole new organization had to be built up from scratch. We still had our words, but we at least knew which way we were going and have since then built up a 'very tidy, neat organization' with never an overdraft from that time, and commanding some prestige among the other British Columbia weeklies.

"It would be different if I had it all to do over again. I'd have nothing to do with my family in a business way. I'd read about the doings of the Murrays like everyone else, as I operated my little peanut-stand in Santa Rosa, California.

"It reminds me of the man who continually hit himself over the head. 'Why do you do that?' his friend asked. 'It feels so good when I stop,' he says."

In the years between, whenever they thought of golden days and balmy nights, of lawn sprinklers and drowsy afternoons, the Murrays returned in spirit to Lillooet, on the banks of the Fraser a couple of hundred miles from Vancouver. They even heard that the little newspaper they had started so long ago might be repurchased. But there were one or two things to accomplish first. They had to leave the

Peace with torches flaming.

In the spring of 1959, to meet the retirement crisis, they put out the biggest and best special edition of their careers. Because it was such a large and elaborate issue — and also to avoid any controversy about copy or wasted man hours — they had this printed in North Vancouver. It was a magnificent edition.

"But did you make any money on it?" asked Dan.

Well no, they didn't, they said. But was money everything? And while they were at it, could they inquire what he was doing about the Fort Nelson page? Surely he wasn't dropping it?

He was, he said, because it was not paying for itself.

"Infamy, infamy! Make it pay, then!" snapped Margaret through clenched teeth. She was so furious she hopped a bus for Fort Nelson, gathered ads and news, and mailed them down to George for the first four-page issue of the Fort Nelson *News* — her paper, not the Alaska Highway *News*. She gave them five memorable months at Fort Nelson and bowed out on a stretcher bound for hospital.

One evening in the summer during her convalescence, she and George walked again up the tree-shaded main street of Lillooet to the old stand. Grey and forlorn, the old building stood there, uglier than ever with the porch lopped off for the new cement sidewalk outside, and empty and lonesome because the machines had not turned in years. The paper was produced in Vancouver.

As the door creaked open on its rusty hinges, the ghosts of all the years rose to meet them. Physically nothing had changed in the shop. The stove was there, even the iron bucket on top. The old linotype was in its original position, and on the floor underneath it, in fine filigree, lay the metal from a squirt, no doubt molten and shiny when the last operator grabbed his hat and left the place forever. Now, like a panel of tarnished silver lace, it rested in George's hands as he leaned heavily against the composing table.

Seeing his tiredness, Margaret ventured, "Now if we'd just give this place a good sweeping out, wash the windows, take down the cobwebs . . ."

She bustled more than usual to hide her misgivings. Did they really have the strength to start all over again?

Was there a printer alive who would stay a single day in such premises — type cases upended, rollers flattened, gears rusted, dust whitening everything?

She waited for him to say something. To project something about their plan. You had to have a plan, a goal. It did not matter in all the world whether you attained it or you did not. But without the dream, without the star, if you were a Murray you couldn't live a day. *Where was his old arrogance, his old conceit?*

Conceit is like the natural unguent of the sea bird's plumage, enabling him to shed the rain, and the wave into which he dips. When all conceit is gone and all illusions lost, his feathers soon soak through, and he will fly no more.

So now she said it for him. "Where are we going to put those linotypes if we *do* get them?" This time the plan was to have a trade school in Lillooet, buy up some old linotypes, and teach the machine to eager youngsters who were dying, surely, to launch themselves in the weekly field.

"In the morning, dear heart," he said, "in the morning. I'm too tired tonight to think."

Later that week, driving north to Fort St. John to complete the move, George went off the road at Hat Creek, hurtling down the bank a hundred feet in the Mercedes-Benz.

"Mother, the doctor thinks you should be there a couple of days before his operation." I had driven to Lillooet to get her.

"If I know your father, he would want me right here seeing to things for him and not sitting around a hospital room making conversation. He hates hospitals."

"I know, Mother, but the doctor insists. He had a great week last week. He was in New Westminster, out Main Street to see the old *Chinook* office, out to Marpole and the foot of Fraser to see where Uncle Ken lost all the money. He was telling me the story of that chronic hospital and how Jake Grauer built it. He took a cruise up the harbour, up by Moody and Ioco and Indian Arm. But he had a bad turn up at Sunnyside. I told him not to attempt to walk to the back of the land, but he did anyway."

"Well, you should know your father by now. He just loves that place."

"Everybody has been in to the hospital to see him that

he wants to see. The McGeer girls brought down a big picture of Gerry. His room is full of flowers. But he was pretty low yesterday and told me what a failure he'd been."

"Failure? Your father? Well, that's different. I'll soon fix that. Get down my bag!"

But George was beyond fixing. The shock of the auto accident had unleashed a malignancy which he had cunningly, even furtively, hidden from his family for years.

He died August 19, 1961, in St. Paul's Hospital, Vancouver. They buried him in Fort St. John, under a sheaf of fifty-two red roses, one for every year since he rode the Ottawa streetcar with Laurier, in the little cemetery next to a waving grain field.

"Who're they planting today?" The blond youth climbed down from the combine, and walked over to the waiting pickup.

"Dunno. The wife says the stores are shut for two hours. Some relation to the newspaper owner in town. Useta be a member of parliament or sumthin'."

"Ha. One of them, hey?"

Margaret went through the funeral as though it were another election defeat, after which you set your jaw, got down your best hat, and admitted nothing.

She never looked more striking. "I've worn this before and George liked it," she said referring to her daughter's hat, "and I'll wear my mink today too and do him proud." She had left one travelling bag in a hotel lobby somewhere on the way north to Fort St. John and was wearing borrowed clothes.

"And don't argue. Get a half-case of Johnny Walker's Black Label. Your Dad liked that, and this is for his friends. Some of them will come a thousand miles. Don't look at me like that, either. Fine Catholics you kids are. Pat Lally would be ashamed of you. The gates of heaven swung wide for your father on Friday and there will be no tears around here today."

On the way to the cemetery, she broke the mourners' file here and there with an embrace for an old friend, a thank-you-for-coming to an old subscriber. For Margaret, to whom tears were an emotional cure-all, there could only, on this day, be dry eyes. She left the next evening for Lillooet, making her usual exit from the Fort St. John air terminal.

Regulars among the air passengers did not have to be told. Who else but Margaret would descend on a Northern terminal building in such a fashion, pausing inside the door to clarion "Well, here we are!" while aides and grandchildren were pinned inside the swinging doors behind her, lugging briefcase, travelling bag, typewriter, and a sheaf of this week's edition of the *News*! "Best damned reading in the North," she'd say as she handed out copies on her way to the passenger desk. Or, "Margie, take your hair out of your eyes and come over here and meet your grandmother's friend, the Minister of Northern Affairs. I read yesterday's *Journal*, Hammy, and you're dead wrong, but shake hands with Mr. Hamilton anyway, Margie!"

But this time, as the flight was being called, she whispered to her son and daughter, "Don't look so worried. I'll be all right when I get to Lillooet and gather my wits."

At Lillooet, she had them hold the paper for a day so she could write her husband's obituary herself. "Fill it up with these, Dave," she instructed the operator, and pushed the most newsworthy condolence letters and wires over the stone to him. "The Governor-General's comes first, then the Prime Minister's, and on down. And now don't anybody say anything to me for twenty minutes and I'll get this written."

The gnarled old fingers found their place on the typewriter keys. She looked across fifty years into the Bank of Montreal's thirty-six red roses, drooping in the late August heat, and wrote, "He was our light and life and inspiration. We will never have the depth or the girth of his lovely heart and fine mind, and our flapdoodle vernacular or daring courage only came from the inward security he gave us."

But still the tears didn't come. *When I get upstairs, alone tonight,* she thought.

Feverishly she threw herself into a flying trip to Ontario. *When I see the Gladstone Murrays, or that barn door at Woodstock,* she comforted herself on the plane. *When I hear the clock chiming from Parliament Hill,* she thought on the Ottawa train, and later, pulling into Chicago, it was *When I see Maxwell at the Trib in the morning.* But on this whirlwind trip she felt nothing, except perhaps the mood of the audiences who listened to her at a luncheon address, or in a television interview.

It was the end of October, and the Northwestern Chamber of Commerce convention at Missoula, Montana, had been a real triumph. "Bob Angus was with me, and he clocked the standing ovation, and it went on for fifty seconds. Was that *long?* Try it sometime. I talked about the Alaska Highway."

Thus she checked in by telephone to the family at Fort St. John on her way from Calgary back to the Cariboo.

All the way to Lytton on the CPR she thought about what she must remember to tell them about the trip. And on the stage run through the silvery sagebrush to Lillooet, she talked about it to Ritchie, the driver. And presently they were crossing the old Fraser River, and here was the dear, ugly old news office, in its white siding with rocking chairs on the side porch. How wonderful to be home where people loved you and you loved people and there was blessed work to be done.

She set on the floor her typewriter and bag. Gloves and purse she tossed on the counter. Hat and coat on the folder. And attacking the stairs purposefully for all her seventy-three years, she burst into the yellowed french door at the top, almost toppling the hall-tree where his hat and coat had hung since the trip home from the hospital.

"George, wait till I tell you what hap—"

She stood there, dismayed at what she'd done. The silence eddied around her, pressing in on her temples, so that the maple bug which flew crazily into the floor made a sound of smashing.

Suddenly she knew there would never again be an answer. She reached down for the dear man's hat. And hugging it to her, she attained the bedroom before, at last, the tears started.

Epilogue

Margaret Murray is a legend in her lifetime. No one is quite sure how this happened, least of all Mother, but there it is. She continues to live her life one day at a time, convinced that in some inexplicable way each day is a bonus from her Creator and that she must wring the last ounce of accomplishment out of it, for there may never be another. So now in her eightieth year, she prepares for a day's activity that wears out her staff by wakening early, sitting up in bed to say, "Thanks be to God, here I am again," and switching on the CBC news.

The first winter without George had been rough. "I thought it was all over for me but the shouting," she wrote to the family early the next spring. But the box-elder tree in a friend's garden was coming into bud, and spring was crowding right behind. And as the warming new year stirred her and revived her spirits, she brightened, and so did her paper.

Soon she was grabbing a wad of copy paper, sticking a pencil in her hair, backing out the little old Mercedes and, at seventy-four, toddling once more up the wide main street of Lillooet to collect the news. "I think of George and emotion smothers me like a melody that unfolds the years. Then I think of this gift of life the good Lord has given me, and I know I mustn't waste it."

If anything, the paper grew sassier, even the obituaries: "Agnes Campbell has gone to her reward. She used to be a beautiful singer. I remember her around Vancouver forty years ago. She would inflate those bellows of hers and almost knock the steeple off Mount Pleasant Methodist . . ."

Today's youth caught it under the editorial heading. "Read and Weep." You could almost see the typewriter smoke as she wrote, "Is this the nothing society? They are unable to speak coherently. Is it because there is nothing coherent in the vegetable condition of their minds, or is it because there is no banner of dreams to excite or intrigue, no burning visions or creative ideas sold to youth by parents to make these sad, dead, young people break out of the shell of their boredom?"

George, in his wisdom, well aware of his wife's need for an objective for the days ahead, had, during that summer of his fatal illness, laid on the speaking engagement at the meeting of the combined Northwest Chambers of Commerce at Missoula, Montana. "They want to hear about the Alaska Highway," he told her, "and who knows more about it than you and I? You will, of course, accept."

She was at her free-wheeling and impassioned best. She was only in mid-speech when, with time running out and the men anxious to get to a football game by kick-off, they flicked the ballroom lights to gently remind her that, in America, games are serious business. The maverick in Margaret promptly took over and thrusting her awesome bosom at them she declared, "Where I come from they only do that in saloons to get rid of the drunks. Now this ain't no saloon and I ain't one of your drunks and you will, but the Lord Harry, listen!"

They listened. Not until she covered the last fifty miles on the Alaska Highway did she let them go. And they told her afterward that they would not have missed a mile.

And then suddenly she was all over the newspapers and magazines, blasting Premier Bennett with joyful abandon, appearing on national television with absolutely no concession to the accepted amenities, no trace of inhibition when she had something salty — and meaningful — to say. When the television program "Front Page Challenge" cut her short during a panel discussion, they got so many letters of protest that they rescheduled her at the first opportunity. In 1965, when she was invited to speak at Bennett's testimonial dinner, she told the press, "Everybody in B.C. knows I don't give a damn for him, his government or his policies. I'll be delighted to speak at the party — but they're crowding their luck."

And somewhere along the line, "they" realized it. The invitation was withdrawn in a whirl of coast-to-coast publicity and good fun. Only Mr. Bennett was not laughing.

There are Wednesday nights when she is apt to observe wearily that "life is just one damned Thursday after another." But, as of old, publishing day finds her totally immersed in the worry and work of getting the paper in the mail. The only difference these days is that her Thursdays are invariably noticed.

She may be part ham and part crusader, but her love of Canada remains pure and unadulterated. Her contribution to the sixties is a valiant effort to help her country find an identify of its own. And in her inimitable style, she is feverishly at work trying to brighten the blurred tapestry of nationhood. And no one who recognizes this really minds that she has worked a few Kansas cornflowers into the tracery, nor that the embroiderer herself was an American export fifty-four years ago.

In spite of her all-out style, Margaret Murray brooks no nonsense about faith and morals. Her husband's Sermon on the Mount is as sustaining to her as her own Act of Contrition. "I have no credit coming because I was blessed with parents who aroused a conscience in me. I could not live with myself if I didn't follow it," she says. "I never honestly realized my own ignorance. For everything I had to know, I had George. From both sources has sprung any courage that I have."

At Fort St. John, where Dan has made a tremendous success of the Alaska Highway *News* — *his* way, mind you, concedes his mother — Margaret's family and friends read about Ma Murray and love her, and occasionally blast her, like everyone else. When the phone rings at two o'clock in the morning, I personally wonder whether she is in a heap in the back of a Vancouver taxi, or whether she has just got the word that Premier Bennett is slapping her with a libel suit and she will end her days in jail.

For the answers, like all the rest, I consult next week's Bridge River-Lillooet *News,* "Printed in the sage brush country of the Lillooet every Thursday, God Willing. Guarantees a chuckle every week and a belly laugh once a month, or your money back. Subscription: $5 in Canada. Furriners: $6. This week's circulation 1769, and every bloody one of them paid for."

END

Dual Allegiance by Ben Dunkelman
A hard-drinking, hard-fighting soldier tells his true-life adventure story.

"A fascinating story. I couldn't put it down." —*Quill and Quire* / 326 pages / 50 photos / $5.95

E. P. Taylor by Richard Rohmer
The best-selling biography of one of the most successful Canadian tycoons of all time.

"A marvellously comprehensive picture." — *Montreal Star* / 352 pages / $5.95

The Fighting Fisherman: Yvon Durelle
by Raymond Fraser
A moving, honest account of the life of a great boxer from the Maritimes — his triumphs and his tragedies.

"An authentic Canadian tragic hero—superb!" —*Montreal Star* / 282 pages / 17 photos / $5.95

Halfbreed by Maria Campbell
The powerfully told life story of an unforgettable young Métis woman.

"The daring account of a strong-willed woman who defeated poverty, racism, alcohol and drug addiction by the age of thirty-three." — *Saturday Night* / 184 pages / $4.95

Her Own Woman by Myrna Kostash et al
Profiles of ten contemporary Canadian women, famous and not-so-famous, including Barbara Frum, Margaret Atwood, and sports hero Abby Hoffman.

"Insightful, well-written, wonderful to read." — Doris Anderson / 212 pages / 9 photos / $4.95

Hockey Is a Battle by Punch Imlach with Scott Young
One of the game's great coaches offers a lively, revealing account of his first thirty years in the game. More than 100,000 copies sold, this is an all-time Canadian bestseller. / 203 pages / 27 photos / $4.95

Hugh MacLennan: A Writer's Life by Elspeth Cameron
The prize-winning biography of one of Canada's greatest novelists.

"Deeply understanding of its subject, this impressive biography does justice to the man and his work." — Margaret Laurence / 420 pages / 23 photos / $5.95

The Indomitable Lady Doctors by Carlotta Hacker
Stories of courage, heroism and dedication — the experiences of Canada's pioneering women doctors.

"Admirable, enjoyable." — *Edmonton Journal* / 223 pages / 20 photos / $5.95

Letters from a Lady Rancher by Monica Hopkins
The lively, delightfully written adventures of a young woman who married a homesteader and started a new life in the West.

"Highly readable...an irrespressible personality." — James Gray / 171 pages / $4.95

Louis 'David' Riel: Prophet of the New World
by Thomas Flanagan
A sympathetic portrayal of a great Métis leader — a man too often dismissed by historians as mad.

"Absorbing." — Hamilton *Spectator*. "A most sensitive job, neither obscuring the reality of madness nor dismissing the basic truths of the visionary." — *Calgary Albertan* / 215 pages / $4.95

Ma Murray by Georgina Keddell
The outspoken newspaperwoman who became a legend in her own time. / 301 pages / 12 photos / $5.95

The Making of a Secret Agent
by Frank Pickersgill; edited by G. H. Ford
The story of a young Canadian who abandons pacifism to become a spy — and whose courage and idealism cost him his life.

"A marvellous book, a Canadian classic." — Ramsay Cook, *Canadian Reader* / 274 pages / 10 photos / $5.95

Morgentaler by Eleánor Wright Pelrine
The surprising life story of the controversial Montreal doctor.

"Fascinating reading." — *Toronto Star* / 222 pages / $4.95

My Uncle, Stephen Leacock by Elizabeth Kimball
A young girl's memories of wonderful summers at the lake and of the Leacock clan at play.

"Draws you in to the Leacock family like a magnet. You hate to leave." — *Kitchener-Waterloo Record* / 174 pages / 13 photos / $4.95

Nathan Cohen: The Making of a Critic
by Wayne Edmonstone
A book which captures in print a man who made an indelible impression on Canadian arts and entertainment.

"How did we ever produce such a giant?" — *Toronto Star* / 286 pages / 9 photos / $5.95

The Patricks: Hockey's Royal Family by Eric Whitehead
The story of a four-generation family that has been right at the centre of hockey history for seventy years.

"A finely-crafted book by a good storyteller . . . with fascinating anecdotes aplenty." — *Quill and Quire* / 280 pages / 19 photos / $5.95

Radical Tories by Charles Taylor
A personal journey of discovery, and portraits of Canadians with a unique perspective on our country.

"An immensely readable book." — Dalton Camp / 215 pages / $4.95

Shaking It Rough: A Prison Memoir
by Andreas Schroeder
The story of life inside, by a young writer who could understand the prison world because he bore no grudges.

"Crisp and telling." — *Maclean's.* "Fresh and interesting." — *New York Times* / 214 pages / $4.95

Something Hidden: A Biography of Wilder Penfield
by Jefferson Lewis
The life of the world-famous Canadian surgeon and scientist who explored the hidden mysteries of the brain — and the mind.

"One of the most valuable and fascinating biographies I have read in many years." — Hugh MacLennan / 311 pages / 22 photos / $5.95

Ticket to Hell by A. Robert Prouse
A young Canadian's story of three years in a German prisoner-of-war camp — told with warmth, humour and honesty.

"A fascinating, yet terrible, memoir of what it was like behind barbed wire." — *Kingston Whig-Standard* / 161 pages / 50 photos / $4.95

Tommy Douglas by Doris French Shackleton
A warm, lively account of one of Canada's most loved — and most successful — political leaders.

"Vivid, compelling, and authentic." — *Calgary Albertan* / 329 pages / 20 photos / $5.95

Tomorrow Is School by Don Sawyer
The adventures of two young teachers in an isolated Newfoundland outport.

"Honest and love-filled." — Canadian Press / 12 photos / 205 pages / $4.95

Troublemaker! by James Gray
One of western Canada's favourite historians relives his days as an irreverent newspaperman witnessing the golden age of western Canada, 1939-1955.

"Vividly portrays a span of western Canadian history." — Saskatoon *Star-Phoenix* / 315 pages / 22 photos / $5.95

Walter Gordon: A Political Memoir by Walter Gordon
The memoirs of an establishment businessman turned politician who fought for his vision of an independent Canada in the Pearson years. / 395 pages / 9 photos / $5.95

The Wheel of Things: A Biography of L. M. Montgomery by Mollie Gillen
The remarkable and tragic life story of the woman who created Canada's best-loved heroine, Anne of Green Gables.

"A perceptive and sympathetic portrait of a complex personality." — Ottawa *Journal* / 200 pages / 32 photos / $4.95

When I Was Young by Raymond Massey
The vivid account of growing up in the richest, most establishment family of the day in Toronto by a man with an actor's gift of recall and a refreshingly irreverent attitude. / 269 pages / 42 photos / $5.95

Within the Barbed Wire Fence by Takeo Nakano
The moving story of a young Japanese-Canadian man, torn from his family by the events of the Second World War.

"Sensitive and moving . . . this book holds the bloom of a beautiful parable." — *United Church Observer* / 126 pages / 8 photos / $3.95

CANADIAN LIVES . . . ON FILM
Documentary films of the lives of many of the Canadians featured in the Goodread Biography series have been produced by the CBC and the National Film Board, and are available to borrow from NFB distribution offices. Among those available are a film on Dr. Wilder Penfield written by Jefferson Lewis and based on his book, a film on E.P. Taylor, a film on Lucy Maud Montgomery, and one on Hugh MacLennan. A new film by Harry Rasky on Raymond Massey is scheduled for NFB release in 1984. Check with your local NFB office for details.